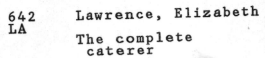

THE COMPLETE CATERER

The Complete Caterer

A Practical Guide to the Craft and Business of Catering

ELIZABETH LAWRENCE

DOUBLEDAY
NEW YORK LONDON TORONTO SYDNEY AUCKLAND

Published by DOUBLEDAY, a division of
Bantam Doubleday Dell Publishing Group, Inc.,
666 Fifth Avenue, New York, New York 10103.

DOUBLEDAY and the portrayal of an anchor with a dolphin
are trademarks of Doubleday, a division of
Bantam Doubleday Dell Publishing Group, Inc.

Library of Congress Cataloging in Publication Data

Lawrence, Elizabeth.
The complete caterer.

Includes index.
1. Caterers and catering.   2. Self-employed.
3. Quantity cookery.   I. Title.
TX911.2.L376   1987   642'.4
ISBN: 0-385-23479-1
Library of Congress Catalog Card Number: 87–5377
Copyright © 1987 by Betsy Lawrence
All Rights Reserved
Printed in the United States of America
2   4   6   8   9   7   5   3

BG

Contents

PART THREE

THE CATERING EVENT

PART FOUR

A SAMPLING OF PARTIES: MENUS AND RECIPES

181

Foreword

Moments ago, catered parties were a way of life only for the rich and famous, but all that has changed now. Caterers are finding themselves among the most popular people on the block and their telephones never stop ringing. Increasingly, those who enjoy entertaining their friends at home find themselves too busy to undertake all the myriad details of giving a party and are calling for help so that they, too, can have the pleasure of being a guest in their own home. The host need do nothing more than plan the menu with the "cook" and leave everything to other skilled hands, to do all the planning and preparation and even to wash the dishes. What could be better!

Elizabeth Lawrence has written *the* book for the beginning caterer—the book that everyone already in the business will be wanting to have at their fingertips and wishing they had had in hand when they catered their first party. I have worked with Elizabeth for several years and admired her many abilities. She has the enormous skill of being able to take a look at a huge mass of information and distill it so that it makes rational sense, and this is precisely what she has done with this book. She has interviewed several experts, all working in different areas of catering, and made them into "expert witnesses." Between them, they have faced just about every problem and emergency that can crop up. Their experiences and ways of snatching triumph from the jaws of disaster will be invaluable to the reader.

In this book Elizabeth has skillfully covered the field. She offers the novice in the business a very informative and helpful guide to all the hidden pitfalls, and simultaneously manages to make the profession so attractive that I venture to predict that anyone who is looking for an entrepreneurial outlet will be enticed and intrigued into exploring this most satisfying area of the food world.

Anyone with a love of cooking, an affection for a people-oriented profession, and modest ability to count can be a caterer—whether it is on the simplest scale of providing boxed lunches to take on a boat or staging a spectacular party for feeding five thousand. This book shows you how to get started, how to make your business grow, and, best of all, how to have a good time while giving other people good times.

IRENA CHALMERS

Introduction

CATERING PROFILES

We will be hearing from and about a diversity of people throughout this book, so let's look at how a few of them got into the business.

• Dounia Rathbone and Donald Beckwith, founders of Remember Basil, Ltd., in Brooklyn, New York, met when each was between jobs. Donald had just left a career in broadcasting and Dounia, trained as a dancer, had most recently worked as a private chef. They both went to work for the late Donald Bruce White, dean of New York caterers. Dounia was an assistant chef and Donald a part-time bartender, waiter, and kitchen helper. They soon decided to hang out their own shingle and name it after Dounia's grandfather, actor Basil Rathbone. Today, they average forty to fifty parties a month in the busy season and have a full-time staff of nine.

• Ray Bonifer of Bonifer's Catering Service in Ferdinand, Indiana, was working as the director of personnel for a large manufacturing company when he saw a newspaper ad that described a "lucrative catering service" for sale. It was the word lucrative that interested him: "I thought I could probably learn to cook," he says. Today, his business, based on good simple food, caters within a 70-mile radius of his rural home kitchen.

• Paul Neuman of Neuman and Bogdonoff in New York grew up in his family's fish business, but started his cooking career as a result of working with a caterer for a few months. Stacy Bogdonoff, who trained at the prestigious Culinary Institute of America, joined him several years later, and together they built Neuman and Bogdonoff into a thriving catering business and take-out store.

• David Ziff and Alan Bell of David Ziff Cooking got their start as a result of David Ziff's restlessness with his careers as a lawyer and then as an importer—his real interest was always food. Alan was fresh out of school and interested in "entrepreneurial stuff." Even though they are among Manhattan's most innovative (anybody who is asked, for a first party, to bake a cake in the shape of a tooth has to be) and sought-after companies, David still refers to the business, which they run out of a Manhattan brownstone, as a "Pa and Pa" operation.

• Ann Vivian and David Hart met while attending the Boston Conservatory of Music. Ann was studying to be a concert organist and David was studying voice. They started out as itinerant cooks to supplement their earnings as professional musicians, but their food and service were so good that word spread fast and they were soon featured in *Boston Magazine.* Their popularity forced them to expand. Today, six years later, they have a professional management staff and do up to four parties a day for as many as 500 people.

• Fanny Farkas started her business, Panhandlers Catering Service in New York, in response to the requests from the students at her cooking school. Today, she and her partner, Arlene Cotler, cater hundreds of parties a year from a converted loft space. Fanny still teaches, though now her instruction is in seminars on catering offered at Peter Kump's New York Cooking School.

• Sally Godfrey of Gallimaufrey in Providence, Rhode Island, saw a real need for good catered food that coincided with her love of cooking. When she began, there were only four or five caterers in the state. She has seen it grow into a thriving business—for her (Gallimaufrey now includes a take-out store, too) and, she estimates, well over fifty other caterers.

• Sara Foster of Greenwich, Connecticut, planned her career in food. She worked for two years for Martha Stewart, the well-known caterer and writer, Ronnie Davis of Washington Street Caterers in New York, and several restaurants. Then she opened her own successful business, working first out of her home, but soon taking over the lease of a candy-making store.

• Pamela Mitchell earned a degree in theater, but found work in a bakery. She was soon joined by her friend Andrea Israel. Needing a change of locale, they picked a random spot on the map of California and settled near Monterey. Faced with the need for jobs, they turned to the one thing they loved, baking, and opened Sweet Satisfaction, a muffin and afternoon-tea catering company.

• The partnership of Gary Goldberg and Martin Johner of Culinary Center of New York was born of a series of parties that Martin, fresh out of the Culinary Institute of America, had agreed to do. Martin, who had been catering on a very small scale, had let himself get talked into cooking dinners for the bedridden spouse of a catering client. He spent all day cooking for the one customer—and he lost money. Business-minded Gary fortuitously arrived on the scene, stepped in, and became Martin's partner, freeing him to concentrate on the food. Today, Gary and Martin not only cater, working out of a Manhattan townhouse, but increasingly consult for restaurants, give seminars, and arrange cooking classes and demonstrations.

• Sean Driscoll of the famed Glorious Food never intended to open a catering business. It was just something to pay the bills while he decided which ad agency to join and partner Christopher Idone raised money to open a restaurant. Today, Sean and chef Jean-Claude Nedelec run Glorious Food out of a converted carriage house, from which they sometimes prepare five parties a night. They are considered by many the preeminent caterer in New York. Christopher Idone runs Glorious Food 2, a food consulting company.

As you can see, there is no one route to the catering "Hall of Fame," nor are there prerequisites for success. The one thing all these pros share, besides an interest in food, is that they started out small. Almost everyone began from their own kitchens, and built their businesses from scratch, learning as they went, expanding as the demand for their services grew.

This is all well and good, but how do I start, you ask? What will I cook, who will buy it, how long will it take? Be patient, and we'll help you answer those questions, one at a time.

PART ONE
The Business of Catering

1

Choosing to Cater

You are a great cook. All your friends look forward to coming to your house for memorable parties. Acquaintances and family alike have been telling you for years that you should sell your lemon chicken or your cheesecake.

Perhaps you've spent time working for a caterer and that helped you develop organizational skills. Every time you go to a party, you find yourself critiquing the food and the service. Often you feel frustrated, knowing you would do things differently if you were in charge.

Nothing you do at your regular job ever seems as satisfying as your work in the kitchen. Maybe your kids are a little older, and you've got some time to put to use what you've practiced in the kitchen. Perhaps the cooking classes you've taken have helped make you confident as well as competent and you need an outlet for your skills.

You've been to parties where the food never has the imagination and flair that yours does, and you know the hosts paid a bundle for it. You know of people who have started catering who have both made money and enjoyed the freedom it has given them to create their own schedules. You know you could do it, too.

If any of this sounds like an echo of your own thoughts, you've probably considered catering yourself. And why not? People enter the profession from many different backgrounds and with varying levels of experience. There are no dictates regarding sex, age, or level of training. Some people come to catering through a hobby of food, others train professionally at cooking schools or by apprenticing. Many people arrive from other careers, spurred by an interest in food and an entrepreneurial spirit.

However, before you buy supplies and take out advertising, consider carefully what you want and need from a business in food. Ask yourself the following basic questions.

Why Do You Want to Cater? If your answer is because it's an easy way to make a lot of money, consider another field. If it's because you think it will be a glamorous way to make famous friends, look elsewhere. If it's that you love good food, be it through cooking or eating and you want to make people happy with it, consider yourself on the road to a rewarding career. If, along the way, you get rich and famous, that'll be an unexpected bonus.

What Do You Want out of a Catering Business? Do you want full-time or part-time employment? Your answer will dictate, to a large degree, the scope of the catering you do. Whatever your long-term goals, keep in mind that in the beginning your business almost certainly will be part-time while you attract clients. Be prepared for lean times at first and busy times once you've become established.

Do You Want to Build a Business Empire? Or are you going to cook primarily for your own satisfaction? Since you will be your own boss, you have the choice. However, before you settle on an answer, you should know that unless you have the luxury to accept only the rare plum jobs available to a new caterer, you will have to devote a good deal of time and effort to building your business. The rewards can be great, but the work is hard.

What Kind of Food Do You Enjoy Preparing? Do you enjoy dinner parties most? Do you love baking above all else? Are desserts all you really care about? Do you prefer to make hors d'oeuvre platters rather than full meals? Are ethnic foods your specialty? Do you like to experiment with new dishes or do you prefer traditional favorites? There is room for almost any kind of food in the catering world, as long as you can find your way to the audience looking for what you are selling. But don't commit yourself to specializing in an area you don't love just because it is there. Take the jobs as you need to, but keep in mind what you want to do, too.

How Do You Prefer to Work? Are you organized and methodical or instinctual and free-form when cooking? Do you like talking with people on the phone and in person, or do you prefer being in the kitchen while someone else handles the public? Do you enjoy creating menus and organizing tasks or do you prefer following a preset plan? Do you like to work alone or with other people? None of these is a trick question, and there are no right answers.

You may decide to do anything from preparing full-scale formal dinners to picnic lunches. You may specialize in Southern soul food or French haute cuisine. Perhaps you are an assembly-line chef, or maybe you are a painstaking taste-method cook. You may want—or need—a staff of fifty or prefer to work alone. You may be shy or gregarious. But you must understand yourself and how you work in order to plan your business. That way, you won't find yourself with a setup that doesn't suit the way you work.

THE KINDS OF CATERING

At its most basic, catering is the act of providing food. So every time you take a dish to a potluck supper you are helping to cater the meal.

In today's world, however, catering most often refers to the business of providing meals to groups of people—it's a food service, for which the caterer is paid an agreed-upon fee. The groups and meals vary, and the money, not surprisingly, varies too, depending on whether it is a full-service, no-service, or partial-service party for social clients, corporate clients, or cultural clients (a cross between social and corporate clients).

How Much Service Should You Offer?

Full-Service Catering. Full-service catering is the backbone of the business and the kind that most people associate with the term catering. A full-service business offers meals, usually a full range from afternoon tea to seated dinners, and the staff to serve the food. Full-service caterers are usually capable of arranging for most other aspects of a party as well, everything from glassware to napkins, flowers, music, decorations, and even the party site. Since it covers so many aspects of a party, full-service catering is often the most challenging, particularly in organizational and logistical terms, as well as the most lucrative form of catering.

Rookie caterers sometimes start out doing less demanding forms and work their way toward full service, but once there, will continue to do other forms of catering. As Sean Driscoll says, "We'll do just as much as you want."

No-Service Catering. In so-called "no-service" catering, you provide only the food, either delivered to the client's door or picked up at yours, and nothing else. People who start with one or two products often find this route the best one to take. If you bake muffins, as Pamela Mitchell did, then all you have to do is deliver them to your clients. You don't have to worry about preparing food on site and arranging for help, rentals, or any other services. No-service catering is, for practical purposes, a retail operation.

Partial-Service Catering. Partial-service catering is the kind of catering many people starting out find themselves doing, and it is a good way to begin if your goal is to become a full-service business. In partial-service catering, you can, if you want, be what's called a service accommodator and act as an itinerant cook, preparing a meal entirely on the party site, and even serving it sometimes. This is often the most legal way when starting very small, but we'll talk more about that in chapter 2.

Who Are the Potential Clients?

Just as there are several broad kinds of service, there are several broad categories of clients: social, corporate, and cultural.

Social Catering. Social catering is the kind that people are apt to think of when talk turns to "hiring the caterer." Until recently this kind of catering was almost exclusively for very special events such as weddings, bar mitzvahs, and anniversaries, but increasingly people are using caterers for smaller and more informal parties. Caterers these days are called upon to prepare breakfast, lunch, or supper as well as cocktail parties and buffet dinners for just about any occasion.

Social catering calls heavily on a person's interpersonal skills, since it is the most intimate form. Clients are entertaining their friends, often in their homes. Frequently the events are important family events, and the client is interested in planning the party with the caterer. Many people find this aspect very rewarding because when the party is successful it means a great deal to the client. Keep in mind, however, that it can be a lot of work dealing with the concerns of the demanding customer.

Social catering is also the area that most often calls upon

a caterer to exercise his or her creativity. For Glorious Food, food for the social clients "has to be very new yesterday," says Sean Driscoll. His clients are aware of current trends, and want to be at their crest.

Many caterers find the challenge of preparing their best and most innovative dishes for clients exciting. Others, however, prefer the relative safety that is expected in the second area of catering, the corporate.

Corporate Catering. Today, corporate catering is booming. Businesses large and small are increasingly hiring caterers to provide the food for events ranging from board meetings to corporate conventions. Traditionally, corporate catering was largely limited to office Christmas parties, but in recent years attitudes have changed and the market is growing rapidly. Sean Driscoll notes this move to entertaining "in-house," and observes that by keeping a business lunch in the office the flow of a meeting may be maintained and less valuable time wasted. Caterers are also able to provide services that businesses can't, such as valet parking, decorations, flowers, bar service, cleanup, and equipment rental.

Corporate catering and social catering alike can be done to fit most budgets, inexpensive, moderate, and lavish. Common corporate events for caterers include breakfasts, mid-morning breaks of coffee and fresh pastries, in-house working lunches, and more elaborate gala banquets and company picnics. They can also include ground-breaking and ribbon-cutting ceremonies, product introductions, grand openings, VIP receptions, open houses, and political events.

Corporate catering tends to be less personal than social catering. Since corporate parties rarely involve serving a client's emotional needs (as at a wedding or family celebration), corporate dates usually offer the caterer more latitude and require less creativity. Often the contact is made with a public relations director, or administrator, or in small businesses with the office manager, boss's assistant, or owner. The tendency is to leave more of the details of the party to the caterer, as planning of special events is often in addition to other duties.

There is generally less interest in innovative dishes than in well-prepared, basic popular foods. One primary difference between social and corporate catering is that corporate parties are usually larger and the logistics are more difficult. That difficulty is often counterbalanced by the fact that corporate clients are generally less concerned with price than private clients, and more concerned with having the party done nicely.

Cultural Catering. The third distinctive area is cultural catering, and it is a mix of social and corporate. Cultural catering involves museums, orchestras, ballet companies, artistic and cultural foundations, and charities.

We all read about the fund-raising dinner dances for the local orchestra and cocktail parties at art show openings, but cultural catering also includes catering the lunch room for volunteers working at a charity book sale, or providing the refreshments for working meetings. This is a natural area for caterers, especially since it provides high visibility. Many of the events are written up in newspapers which can offer valuable publicity.

Cultural parties are not personal like social parties, yet they aren't strictly business either. The organizers of the events are often volunteers who themselves entertain, so there is about a fifty-fifty chance you'll meet up with a client who will understand your job and leave you to do it or a semipro who elects to interfere at every opportunity. Cultural groups often have limited budgets, like many social clients, yet like corporate clients, they are often less concerned with the truly imaginative meal than that the overall look be correct and appealing.

Each of these three main categories has its desirable aspects and its irritations. But most important, each has a need for good caterers. You may want to develop your business focusing on one group more than another, or you may find in your area the need among one is greater than the others; a mix of clients is probably best, at least starting out. But in the beginning, you will probably be happy to have any client, no matter what kind.

THE QUALITIES OF A GOOD CATERER

What makes a good caterer? Talk to ten different caterers, and you will get ten different profiles. Since the business is made up of so many different elements—dealing with customers, pricing the party, planning and preparing the food, serving or delivering it—it's hard to say what is the most important quality you need to possess. It is safe to say, however, that you must be able to provide a good product and sell it well.

To do that, there are several qualities that are useful, no matter what kind of food you prepare. The stated assumption of this book is that you like food and either cook well or will hire a cook; it's also a given that you are a person who likes planning and organizing, or are willing to learn how to become one.

The fact is that catering is a business dependent on thorough planning and sound organization. Every caterer I've spoken with has said that you can't ever plan too much for a party. So if you are an inveterate list maker, so much the better; you will be one step ahead when starting out. "We quickly learned that organization is the basis for a well-run catering service," says Ray Bonifer. "A lot of time is spent planning, but it pays off later with fewer mistakes."

If you don't like the planning and organizing, can you do it if you have to? Lots of people who take no joy from planning are perfectly capable of doing it. If you are one of those people, you may be able to get the business started and then hire someone to take over that aspect, leaving you to tend the kitchen. If you just can't stand planning and details, you might consider taking on a partner who does, either from the start or as soon as you can get yourself established. Alan Bell, of David Ziff Cooking, feels that the best thing a caterer can do is have a good business partner, one who likes dealing with the public and the business aspects of scheduling, pricing, and marketing.

If you are concerned about your organizational skills, you might consider starting out catering a specific food, such as breads, cakes, or sandwiches, that requires a little less organizational ability. If you offer only a limited selection of food and no service capabilities, you can also establish a standard price list that frees you from the necessity of making and remaking quotations and adjusting to budgets. You will still need to meet schedules, of course, but the logistics will be vastly less complex.

Another helpful attribute is a good head for numbers. Fanny Farkas feels that her love of numbers has been important to her success. Having come from a career as a cooking school teacher, she hadn't expected to take great interest in making quotations and creating menus to match budgets. She was surprised to find that she enjoys crunching the numbers, and finds it a stimulating part of the business.

Since catering is a service industry, another helpful trait is an interest in dealing with the public. "You have to like to talk to people," concludes Alan Bell. This doesn't mean you have to be the most gregarious person, but it does help to feel comfortable with people, to be able to listen to their needs and desires, and to be relaxed enough with them to think on your feet and offer suggestions of how you can best serve them. Donald Beckwith of Remember Basil puts it another way. He feels that an important quality of a good caterer is an interest in the success of a client's party. "You have to keep the customer's interests in mind, but that's just good business sense."

"You have to have good legs and nerves of steel," Sally Godfrey told me. For most caterers, particularly at first when they are doing almost everything themselves, the hours are long. Cooking is primarily a standing operation, as is setting up, serving, and cleaning up, so one is vertical for hours at a time. Things are also bound to go wrong at some point, and that's where the steel nerves come in. You have to be able to put a good face on things and not let anyone know just how rattled you are.

Fanny Farkas puts it this way: "You have to be able to think on your feet. You have to be very flexible and never panic and never short-circuit, because there are always emergencies."

She tells a story about an electrical problem at a party her company, Panhandlers Catering Service, was doing at the World Trade Center in New York City. The circuits they were using overloaded, and they had to figure a way to continue. Fanny and crew quickly spread out their equipment—into six different offices. The change in setup meant that they had to finish cooking the meal sitting on the floor, but they went about their business as if everything were normal, and the party was a great success.

Fine, you say, I'm a good cook, I like to talk to people, but I'm scared to death of figuring prices. I don't always get the meal on the table on time, and I have weak ankles. Does this mean I can't be a good caterer?

Of course, no one is a perfect combination of desirable qualities, and besides, many of these things are a matter of learning and practice. One thing that isn't really teachable, though, is strong ankles. But a pair of good, sturdy shoes can do wonders.

FINDING YOUR NICHE

Once you understand the requirements for catering, your next step is to study the market to figure out where you might fit in. By investigating the existing businesses in your area—and the unfulfilled needs—you will be able to more easily target your own efforts.

First, is the area you live in growing? Is the population constant or is there an influx of summer or winter people?

Is it a young population or an older one? Is there a healthy business community? Are more businesses starting or moving to your area? Are there many cultural groups such as orchestras, theater groups, and museums?

Next, look at your competition. Are there many caterers? What kinds of food do they prepare? What range of prices do they charge? If there are a number of caterers already, is there a common theme that many of them share? Do they sell to the same group of people?

Researching the market is all well and good, but how do you go about it? Ask friends and acquaintances for the names of caterers, look in the phone book, call your local Chamber of Commerce, look for newspaper announcements or ads, call charities and businesses and ask who they use. Call local wholesale suppliers of chairs and glasses and other kitchen or serving equipment and ask who their catering clients are. Then call the various caterers themselves and ask them questions. Caterers these days are much more open and forthcoming with information than in the past. Who knows, someone might pass along some overflow business to you once you get started.

Once you know what the competition is up to, turn your thoughts to your skills and tastes. Is there something that you can provide that the competition doesn't? Has anyone caught on to the light food trend yet? Is anyone specializing in regional foods?

There's a company in New York City called Sushi Madness that caters only sushi; while sushi might not have a market in your area, barbecues or clambakes might.

Recently a caterer in suburban Washington came up with the notion of a catered crab feast. Now, the blue crab is much prized in the Chesapeake Bay region, but many people won't attempt to serve them at home because they are messy to prepare as well as eat. But hiring someone to come in and do a feast? With the tables covered with newspapers and the potato salad and corn on the cob all served up (and the whole mess cleaned up afterward), it all seems suddenly possible—and special and fun, too.

Then there's Tom Heller, a south Florida caterer who specializes in picnics. In fact, his business is called The Company Picnic Company and almost all of the business is in barbecue picnics. Heller's operation, the outgrowth of his dream to be a comedian, is different because there are games and entertainment. He provides carnival rides and amusements and organizes guests for games such as potato sack races.

Might there be room to create a market for your services where one doesn't already exist? You don't have to be as flamboyant as Tom Heller. For instance, maybe the idea of in-house business breakfasts hasn't caught on in your city yet. Informal, catered pool parties are another possibility. Or maybe there are a lot of apartment dwellers in the area —is anyone delivering meals to them?

Here is an example of how I would go about discovering my market. I live in a resort area that has recently been discovered by weekenders and summer people from New York City. People are buying property and building expensive houses all around us. They are a well-off lot, with fairly sophisticated tastes. I've checked the service listings in the local newspapers and called some of the local suppliers and asked them if they have any catering clients. I've found out that there aren't many people catering. The local restaurants seem to handle what business there is. The restaurants in the area tend to be good and expensive or cheap and family style (specializing in group foods like pizza).

In short, there are very few options when it comes to planning the big summer barbecues after the fund-raising orchestra performances or the dinner dance after the big fox hunt. I have an ideal seasonal market. I probably cannot expect to work all year long doing parties for a thousand, but I may well be able to tempt people in the summer with moderate-sized and more intimate dinner parties. I may even be able to set up a supper delivery service for the nights they arrive for the weekend, saving them the hassles of cooking. I may even decide to set up a shop in town and cater from there as well as sell take-out.

Do You Need Experience?

You've done your research, you know where you fit in, but you have no experience doing it. Everyone you spoke with seems to know what they are doing. Do you need to train?

Many people feel that you can take no wiser step when contemplating a catering career than working for someone else first. Gary Goldberg says that almost without exception everyone who has worked for his and Martin Johner's firm Culinary Center of New York has trained with them and then gone out and started on their own. He feels it gives them a head start. He also suggests a minimum of a two-year program at a reputable cooking school.

Conversely, Sally Godfrey believes that catering benefits from the spontaneity that good untrained cooks bring to it. She also believes that the standard trial-and-error method is the only one that would have worked for her. Similarly, Ann Vivian and David Hart feel that their idealism and lack of professional experience have helped them take on parties that more traditionally trained caterers would find too much trouble.

Stacy Bogdonoff and Paul Neuman suggest a middle road, recommending that people work for another caterer for a while, even a few months, and get a feel for the pace and timing required, as well as the tricks of portioning, packing, and estimating costs and ingredients.

If you've got the time and access, working for a caterer is a good idea. It might well help you cut down on mistakes and make it easier to get a start. You might also have a chance to meet potential clients. If it simply isn't possible, don't despair, as many successful caterers get started without any actual catering training.

Small Is Best . . . at Least at First

No matter whether you have experience or are a rank rookie, you will probably be starting out on a small scale. It's usually healthy to think big in the long term, but unless you have a large amount of extra capital, a whole lot of experience, and a staff of trained people, it pays to start out small. Being small allows you to learn and grow, establish a loyal clientele, and make mistakes and recover without risking too much more than your time.

Catering is a business that is ideally suited to small beginnings, relying primarily on your service. It is also a business that is usually built by word-of-mouth advertising generated by satisfied customers who've had good experiences.

Sean Driscoll and Christopher Idone say they didn't really accept the fact that they were in business for almost nine months after they started preparing meals for money. Every time they got a call—and they got a lot of them—they looked at each other in amazement. To start Remember Basil, Ltd., Dounia Rathbone and Donald Beckwith simply told everyone they met they were caterers until finally someone hired them. When Pamela Mitchell and Andrea Israel started their muffin business the oven in their apartment was so small they could only bake two dozen muffins at a time. It took them eight hours to bake the fifty dozen they soon needed each day.

Whether you begin as a full-service business or in the specialty-catering area making muffins, cakes, hors d'oeuvre, or ice cream, starting slowly is generally a great advantage. Don't be ashamed at your small beginnings, and don't aim to feed hungry hundreds the first time out. General Foods wasn't built in a day.

Do You Need a Partner?

The decision to start a business solo or with a partner is a personal one. Some people find it useful to begin with a partner, others to bring someone in after the business has grown. Still others prefer to control everything themselves all the way, but there is no consensus about the best method.

Many people get into the business working alone from their own kitchens. Many retain that status indefinitely, only hiring people as they grow to take over some of the tasks they either don't care to do any longer or that they feel someone else can do as well as (or better than) they can. Often, however, people find as the business gains momentum that there is just too much work to do or that the presence of a partner frees them for other aspects of their jobs.

On day one, Fanny Farkas started with a partner, Arlene Cotler, who had been one of her cooking students. To her surprise, she found after a few months that she really liked the business aspects of selling parties, finding rental spaces, dealing with purveyors, and working up price quotations. So now Fanny handles the business and Arlene handles the kitchen.

Stacy Bogdonoff says she loves creating the menus and dealing with clients, while her husband Paul Neuman feels most at home in the kitchen. She tells him what she wants; he and his staff go about creating it.

When Dounia Rathbone and Donald Beckwith started out, Dounia was in charge of the kitchen and Donald helped out with the waiting, business matters, and miscellaneous chores. It must have suited their needs, as they have maintained the same basic division of labor ever since, Dounia handling the kitchen, Donald the business.

Sean Driscoll of Glorious Food has always run the business end of the company, leaving the food to chef Jean-Claude Nedelec. Chef Nedelec devises the methods for creating meals for two thousand that look, and taste, as though they were made for ten.

For these people, partnership worked. Sara Foster, on the other hand, has preferred to keep everything under her own control. She has hired staff, but her operation is small enough that she handles the overall running of the business as well as the actual execution.

Sally Godfrey feels strongly that her catering is entirely her show, yet she wants to be free to concentrate on the food, not the business aspects, so she has turned them over to an "employee" (in her case, her husband).

All of this is to say that you can go either way. You may form a partnership from the beginning, you may take in someone as you grow, or you can stay completely independent. If you don't like marketing and money matters, consider a partner earlier rather than later, or hire someone as soon as you can. If you prefer the business end to the food end, take in a cooking partner or hire a chef.

HOW TO USE THIS BOOK

Are you still interested in being a caterer? If so, then you will find much in the following chapters that will be of value to you as you plan and embark on your catering adventure.

Part One focuses on the business of catering and contains chapters covering the nuts-and-bolts aspects of pricing, marketing, insurance, organizing your kitchen, hiring help, and handling rental equipment.

Part Two is all about the craft of catering and includes chapters on creating menus, quantity shopping and cooking, and food presentation and serving.

Part Three prepares you for an actual catering event from the first phone call through the last goodbye.

Part Four contains a sampling of party menus and their recipes from a broad spectrum, including a business breakfast, brunch, wedding reception, cocktail party, picnic, and dinners. It even includes a ball for over a thousand people.

2

Pricing and Marketing
Your Product

One of the most important things you can do for your fledgling catering company is to plan it as a business from the outset. This does not mean you have to invest in a computer system to calculate portions. Nor am I suggesting you need to have your lawyer handle all your negotiations.

The point is that many people come into the industry casually, and find themselves in business without really admitting it to themselves. They start preparing food for people informally, or as cooking teachers they get inundated with requests to do parties. Then the business somehow gets away from them. Even people who set out specifically planning to cater too often enter with the idea that they'll sort of take it as it comes and deal with the serious aspects later.

A more sensible method is to set up systems for dealing with the business aspects from the start, before they turn into problems. In other words, to start your company in a haphazard manner is to run the grave risk of succeeding as a cook and failing as a business. It isn't necessary to rack your brain to devise a pricing schedule while a potential client waits on the phone for the price—and another is on hold. Getting involved in disputes with a client after the party is avoidable. Perhaps all you needed was a letter of agreement that spelled out your responsibilities.

There are three areas you need to know about to plan your business: you need a system for pricing your food; you need to be able to market your services; and you need insurance and possibly permits (which we'll discuss in chapter 3).

PRICING

Establishing prices for the meals you cater is one of the most important aspects of your business and certainly the trickiest, at least in the beginning. Gary Goldberg, who advises people just starting out in the business, says it is invariably the thing people ask him about first.

Few people use the same method for determining their prices. Pricing must take into account not only the quantifiable costs of ingredients and labor, but other, more intangible elements such as the client's budget, the kind of party to be given, whether it is a rush, the likelihood that the job will bring you new business, whether other caterers are bidding on the job, and a host of other considerations, many of which may be unforeseen. With all of these elements, it may seem a daunting task to establish prices, but there are ways to weave through the web of considerations.

At its most basic, pricing a party depends on the cost of the food, the labor, and the overhead. Most people, in fact, base their prices primarily on the actual costs of the meal: the food and the time it takes to prepare it. If they work out of their homes or a client's kitchen, their overhead (that is, the established costs of the space they work from) is small and often not a factor in the calculating. Value, or what the caterer's service is worth, is much harder to determine.

In the beginning it may seem impossible to assign a dollar value to your own worth. The tendency is often to underprice at first, figuring in the cost of ingredients as the main element, and undercharging for the cost of labor and time. Until you are experienced you may find yourself undercharging for your time, as speed and efficiency are gained only with practice. A certain amount of experience is necessary to gauge what the local market considers valuable yet not extravagantly expensive. But let's look at some specific methods.

Pricing Methods

There are several basic methods for figuring prices that, used together, will serve as basic guidelines for establishing prices that are fair to you and the client. The methods involve:

1. Researching your competition to determine the going rate;

2. Factoring your material and supply costs using a simple formula;

3. Assessing your gross profit margin;

4. Determining the cost of labor.

The Going Rate. You must determine the general market prices in your area. Researching these prices is officially known as "conducting a competition analysis"—in fact, it's a matter of figuring out the other guy's rate and guessing at what the market will bear.

If you plan to feature simple food, call around to other caterers who do simple food, rather than the fanciest haute cuisine caterers. Look in your local yellow pages and newspapers and ask friends, specialty food store owners, and cooking instructors for the names of other caterers. Then call them and get estimates. The answers you receive will give you a range of prices from which you may be able to determine your own parameters.

Consultant and caterer Gary Goldberg uses the example of Wally, a free-lance bartender and waiter with whom he has worked for about fifteen years. Wally has recently become a caterer himself, specializing in his native Southern food. He's catering down-home food, working entirely out of clients' kitchens. Wally found that the most he could charge for his kind of food would be $35 per person, a fairly modest sum for New York City. "I was glad to hear that," says Goldberg. "In other words he didn't say he was going to charge $70 per person for essentially family food. He had investigated other people like himself and decided that was what he could charge." With his top figure in mind, Wally then set about figuring out his prices.

The Raw Costs. The next step in determining a price is figuring out how much the food will cost you. After you've been in the catering business a while, you will be able to estimate the costs of a meal just by looking at the menu. However, instant estimating takes practice, and to start with the best method is the time-consuming but accurate one of carefully costing out your dishes.

Costing out is primarily a matter of recording. First, gather the recipes for one of your sample menus. Make lists of the various ingredients, and the quantities needed. Combine those that are used in several dishes (like butter and onions), to figure total quantities needed. Then research the prices of all items at the grocery store. By adding the costs of the ingredients in each dish you will arrive at the total cost of the ingredients for the meal. Divide by the number of people the menu serves to get a per-head food cost.

Determining the cost of staples used in small quantities can pose something of a problem. For instance, it is very difficult to figure the cost of flour when a dish requires only three tablespoons. On the other hand, a quarter of a bottle of expensive liqueur used in a meal is relatively easy to determine. If you create a special menu for a client that requires unusual and rarely used ingredients you can include the full cost of the specialty items if you don't plan to use them again. When minor quantities of everyday ingredients are called for, make your best guess.

It is difficult at this point to determine your overhead, unless you plan to start from a professional kitchen outside your home. If you do, you will know what your rent and utilities are and can thus consider those a direct cost that must be covered by your final price. If you can't break out the overhead costs, estimate the cost of gas, stationery, telephone, business taxes, and anything else that might not be easily calculable.

Factoring. Factoring involves a simple formula: take the cost of the ingredients of a meal and multiply by three to determine the overall cost. The resulting price should cover your labor and material costs, and overhead, and leave a reasonable profit. (Again, you divide the sum by the number of guests to find the per-head cost.) These figures are for the food and preparation alone, and do not include any extras such as the cost of extra help, decorations, rented equipment, or liquor.

The factoring formula establishes the cost of the food consistently at a third of the cost of the meal, and often it's about right. Say you have a meal that begins with phyllo triangles stuffed with pesto, features stuffed Cornish game hens as the main course, and is accompanied by pecan rice with wild mushrooms, asparagus, green salad, and a cold lemon mousse to close. If your calculator tells you the food cost is roughly $10 per person, then you multiply by three and get $30 per person. That seems a fair price, considering your labor. This system works well when both the cost of your ingredients and labor are fairly modest.

How does it work when the ingredients are expensive? Sometimes expensive ingredients take little preparation and are thus balanced by their ease of preparation. You will also learn how to match up expensive and inexpensive ingredients within a meal. Chances are good you won't be quoting too many meals that start with smoked salmon, move on to truffle-laden miniature vol-au-vents with crayfish, segue into pheasant and then filet mignon finished with fresh raspberries in a Chinese grapefruit champagne sauce. More likely you will need menus that feature one or more extravagant dishes to be combined with others that feature less expensive ingredients, such as seasonal vegetables and fruit, pasta, bread, and cheeses.

Determining Your Gross Profit Margin. If your food cost is high and your research tells you that you are pricing yourself out of the market, as is bound to occur sometimes, you won't be able to rely on the factoring method. At such times, you may want to use your gross profit margin as a guide.

Your gross profit is, quite simply, the difference between your actual costs and your price. If, for example, you are featuring venison steaks at $10 apiece, and food costs for the whole menu reach $20 per person, then the times-three formula brings you to $60 a head, giving you a $40 gross profit. Hence, your guess is that you probably won't get the job at $60.

What do you do? Look again at the cost of the food. Broken down the venison is the most expensive single ingredient. If you multiply the cost of it by three it would be $30, a hefty price for a steak at most any restaurant. However, if you merely double the cost you will still make a whopping $10 gross profit on the cost of the steak. Since the labor required to prepare a venison steak is fairly low, the job can still be profitable at a two-times markup. If you keep the rest of the menu fairly simple in preparation and ingredients, you will make money on the job at, say, $40 or $45.

What's a fair profit margin? John Mossman, a veteran caterer of Bakersfield, California, finds that a gross profit of 30 to 40 percent should yield a net profit of 10 to 20 percent. For many people in the business, such as Linda

Nicol of Red Robin Catering in Larkspur, California, it runs about 10 percent. "It's a good living and we pay all our bills, but that's about it," she says.

Assessing Labor Costs. While your venison steak dinner worked out well at a two-times factor, what if you have a dish that is labor intensive? That's another kind of problem.

Say you have to price both a simple half roast duck and an elaborate boned, stuffed, rolled duck to be served with a reduced sauce. The cost of ingredients for the two is roughly the same, at $4.00 a head.

The simple roast duck takes thirty minutes of labor, but the boned, stuffed, rolled duck dish takes an intense three hours to prepare. If you use the factoring method you would charge $12 for both. That's fine for the roast duck, but you would lose money preparing the more elaborate recipe. Given the increased labor cost and the nature of the dish (it requires special skills and it is something that few people would attempt at home), a more appropriate price might be five or six times the cost of the ingredients, or $24.

Another way to determine the fairness of a price is to take the factored price and divide it by the projected number of hours it takes to prepare. If the resulting figure pays you less than what you consider a living wage, raise the price.

These formulations and considerations can seem intimidating. But try to live by them—if you don't you may regret it. For example, trying to make life simpler than it is by making only cheap and labor-saving meals, you will keep your prices way below the average. You may appear to be a great bargain and perhaps everyone will want to hire you. One outfit that succeeds at this is Bonifer's Catering Service. At Bonifer's, in Ferdinand, Indiana, their most popular meal is also their least expensive. It consists of fried chicken and baked ham, three side dishes (such as potatoes, green beans, baked beans, dressing, slaw, or cake), bread, coffee, tea, or lemonade. It costs $3.00 per person.

That works for Ray Bonifer because of volume—but the chances are good that if you start by underpricing you may go broke or, at best, make a minimal wage.

People hire caterers because they want to serve their guests special food, whether it's fancy or just simple and well prepared. Be prepared to offer it to them.

Most people know, particularly astute shoppers, that what they are buying is your expert service. You can do something better than they can, and they are expecting to pay a fair price for it. Don't worry about always bringing in a low price. Figure some meals at a low price, others at higher prices. That way, you'll have a range. You may want to weight your menu to the meals you like to prepare: price them a little lower, and you may get to cook what you enjoy most.

When establishing prices, you will want to consider all of the methods mentioned: factoring your ingredient costs; determining your gross profit margin; considering your labor costs; and comparing your competition's prices. If you consider some (and often all of these) when preparing your figures, you will develop prices that are fair, both to you and your clients.

Miscellaneous Extras

Your basic food, labor, and overhead calculations are the heart of pricing, but once those basic costs are established you also have to think of the extras. For instance, if you provide full service, will you charge extra for arranging for rentals, decorations, entertainment, and such? Some people add in an extra small fee or percentage (up to 10 percent, depending on the number of extras), while others consider it part of the cost of overhead. If you provide limited service, how will you be reimbursed for the cost of delivery, in the price or as an added fee?

Sometimes these matters can be dealt with very simply and straightforwardly. For instance, if you don't like delivering and would prefer customers to pick up, you might

add a separate delivery charge as a method of discourage-
ment. Conversely, if you want to be known for the lavish
service you provide you might take any extra time you
spend and consider it overhead.

The costs of rentals, decorations, and entertainment can
be paid either directly by the client, or indirectly when they
pay you the fees along with a small percentage markup or
fee you add in for your trouble.

Many new caterers prefer to break the costs out separately, while most well-established caterers prefer to make
an all-inclusive price. Fanny Farkas, of Panhandlers Catering Service has noticed that in times of economic hard-
ship clients tend to want an all-inclusive price so that they
know what the overall price will be, rather than having to
add the elements together. (In chapter 5, we will talk more
about rentals, and other such extra costs, and tailoring your
final price.) One last, but important, note on extras: if you
intend to run an official business you may have to charge
sales tax on your food. If so, that must be added to the final
price (see chapter 3). Talk to your local Chamber of Commerce to find out the requirements in your area.

ALTERNATE PRICING ROUTES

If you plan to cook in a client's home using the client's
equipment, your pricing will probably be based entirely on
your labor as a service accommodator, so called, and it is
easier to figure your prices than if you offer full service.

As far as the food costs go, itinerant cooks often give the
clients the sales slips for direct reimbursement. Some people even have the clients do the shopping, from a list they
compile together. You do lose some control over the food,
however, if you have a client do the shopping, since you are
relying on them to make decisions.

The procedures for establishing your price structure are
not all that different from establishing full-service catering
costs, but they are simpler. First, call around and find out

PRICING YOUR SAMPLE MENUS

1. Call around to determine the going rate in your area.

2. Research the cost of ingredients for each dish.

3. Multiply ingredient costs by three.

4. Divide the figure by the number of servings to reach a per head cost.

5. If the resulting price seems too high, look at the ingredients and their preparation time. Compare the markups: can you charge a lower markup for an expensive dinner and still make as much money as with a standard markup on an inexpensive meal?

6. If the sample menu is especially time-consuming to prepare, divide the factored price by the number of projected labor hours. If the resulting number seems particularly low, raise the price.

7. Compare all prices to those the competition is quoting.

8. Establish the costs for additional services such as serving, delivery, and rentals.

what the going rate for in-home accommodator service is. Make sure that you compare prices of comparable caterers, those that do food of roughly the same quality as yours. A person who comes in and cooks hot dogs and beans will charge a different rate from someone whose meals take half a day to prepare.

Second, estimate how long your meals will take to cook. Your sample menus (see chapter 6), will be composed of practiced dishes, and should help determine your labor time. It may take the experience of a few parties to determine the actual time it takes to prepare particular meals for certain numbers of people, but this is part of the trial-and-error process of learning the business. In the beginning you are likely to find yourself underestimating or overestimating the amount of time it takes to carry a meal through the stages of planning, shopping, and preparation. Probably the over- and under-estimations will balance one another off.

Third, decide upon your per-hour wage. Planning, consultation, shopping, and cleaning up are most often figured at a lower rate than the actual task of cooking. For instance, you might charge $10 an hour for planning and consultation, $15 an hour for cooking, and $10 an hour for shopping and cleaning up. The actual amount you charge is up to you, and at least partly predetermined by the going rates in your area. Add up the time it takes to perform various services to determine your overall time. (See table below for a sample calculation.)

The Fixed Fee

There is an alternative pricing method if you would like to be less dependent on the variations of an hourly rate: you can charge a fixed fee.

A PRICING CALCULATION
FOR THE SERVICE ACCOMMODATOR

The event is a pre-concert supper for 12. The fee required is as follows:

Consultation:	2 hours @ $10 per hour	= $20
Shopping:	3 hours @ $10 per hour	= $30
Cooking:	4 hours @ $15 per hour	= $60
Cleanup:	1 hour @ $10 per hour	= $10
Total:	10 hours	$120

Average hourly rate: $12

This is a particularly good method if you are a fast worker or are preparing a simple meal since no matter how long it takes you to prepare the meal, you know what your day's earnings will be (rarely will you be in a position to cook for more than one party). Clients often like this method, too, because they know in advance of a party exactly how much your services will cost.

To calculate your overall fee, all you do is add up the estimated number of hours required to prepare the meal (including planning, shopping, and cooking) and then determine a package price. If you were to prepare the same meal under the terms of a fixed fee that is figured in the sample calculation on page 24, you might want to keep the price at $120 or you might want to increase it to include more of a profit or to cover any unforeseen time needed (a small additional markup or margin for the unknowns is always a sensible idea, if the price allows). The price for the meal will be the agreed-upon amount, no matter how long it takes. To charge for the ingredients, you attach the receipts to your final bill.

You may want to use both methods, the package price and the hourly rate, depending on the particular requirements of a party, or a customer's preference. Whatever method you use, try to charge enough so that you make a decent professional wage, at least $10 an hour.

Regarding taxes, as an itinerant cook you provide only service, so in most states you charge no sales tax. As a self-employed or free-lance person, you report the income you receive only on your own income tax returns.

PRICING IN PRACTICE

Bidding for a Job. Many people who call for an estimate and menu will be merely shopping around. Sometimes they will be calling for themselves, at other times they may be representing an organization or business. Try to determine if the person will be getting other quotes and always make it clear that you can offer suggestions to cover a variety of price ranges.

Bidding on jobs can be a little nerve-racking, particularly if you don't know who your competition is. The tendency is to think that if you could just bring the price in low enough you would be assured the job. Indeed, if they tell you they are interested only in the lowest price, you have to consider how much you want such jobs and bid appropriately.

Often, however, price is not the entire story. The potential client is most likely interested in the best meal at the best price and you may have a little more leeway than you think. Here you will need to sell the potential client on your meals in a manner that makes it clear they are a good value.

One technique is to make your food sound especially interesting. You can do this by devising imaginative menus and describing the dishes in appetizing detail. Special touches such as miniature cheese muffins, or your vegetable curls, can be a surprisingly effective selling point; they distinguish your services from those of other caterers. Anything that sets you apart bears mentioning when selling your services, especially when you are bidding for a job.

Valuing Volume. Another major factor in pricing is how many people are to be fed. The basic formulas may apply, but sometimes must be modified.

The cost of food is constant: food for one hundred costs roughly ten times more than food for ten (although you can get discounts on some large volumes of food). On the other hand, the time spent shopping, cooking, and cleaning up does not increase tenfold (as you know from entertaining at home, cooking for eight does not take twice as long as cooking for four).

The bottom line is that on a high volume job, you can take a lower markup and still make more money than on a small job. Sometimes you can cut your price per head nearly in half. When you figure your sample prices they will naturally be based on a fixed number of people. Explain this to a potential customer when you give them sample prices and let them know that the per-person cost of the same meal would be proportionately lower for a large party.

When quoting prices, make clear to your clients that should they change their minds and lower the number of people they invite to save a few dollars, the price per head will increase. Conversely, should they expand the party the price per head will drop.

Special Considerations. While the above methods of pricing will probably carry you through most situations, occasionally you'll find that something seems left out. For instance, how do you charge for a rush job? How do you cover yourself when you know a client will be picky and intrusive and will need a great deal of attention? Sometimes a party is difficult to do, because of the personalities of the people involved, or where it's being given, or its general nature. This is the great gray area, but one in which you will learn to rely on your judgment in marking up your prices.

One of the methods that Neuman and Bogdonoff use with an habitual last-minute customer works well. When the client calls, he wants a party immediately. Since they have a full-time kitchen and shop, they can usually accommodate him with a last minute crash (as Stacy says, "It's unbelievable what you can do in an hour. It makes me wonder what we do the rest of the time"). The customer expects to pay a premium for special service. "We don't double the price," Paul says, "but we also don't give him the discount he would be entitled to based on the volume ordered."

What do you do when you know a client will need an inordinate amount of attention or coddling, or the party will be particularly difficult to execute? Stacy recommends building an "aggravation factor" into the price. It can be a percentage, or a dollar amount, which you decide, but it will serve to cover you under extraordinary circumstances.

By adding an aggravation factor into your prices, you can also tell whether a job is economically viable for you.

Assessing Your Profitability

The best way to learn to price profitably is to evaluate your costs after every party—and do a profit-and-loss calculation for every event you cater. That's not much help before you have your first client, but, in fact, you use the same methods for preparing sample prices as you do for the post-party P & L.

To determine how successful your pricing has been, you compare your actual costs with the money received (or estimated costs with anticipated receipts). Gather the receipts after every job and total them, then subtract the total from the fee paid to determine your gross profit. You probably won't have too many other expenses to start with besides food, but as the business grows you will probably have other expenses to add, such as kitchen space and hired help.

The gross profit at first may look hefty, but when you consider your overhead (gas, electricity, rent, etc.); the hidden costs of staples used (such as the few tablespoons of flour in a sauce, shortening for greasing pans, salt and other seasonings); and the cost of any specially acquired equipment, the impressiveness of the figure will probably dwindle. This "profit" also includes the cost of your skilled labor not only in cooking the food, but in planning, consulting with the client, surveying the site, and shopping.

To determine just how profitable the job really was, divide the gross profit figure by the number of hours it took you to create the meal. Include the non-cooking hours such as planning, shopping, and consulting. The resulting figure will give you your wage per hour.

Another method for determining profitability—and advance pricing, too—is to set a dollar figure or a percentage of the gross profit that you feel you must earn to make money. According to *Catering Today*, the magazine of the catering industry, the net profit margin for the industry averages from 10 to 20 percent. Use it in your calculations before the party, and look for it after, as you subtract all your costs from the gross profit.

Whatever method you use, don't be discouraged if the number looks low at first. It should improve over several parties, as you gain experience and speed. It may also become apparent at some point that it would be cheaper for you to hire someone to help prepare the food, thereby cutting down on the number of hours you spend of your more valuable time. Having help can give you the freedom to take on larger parties or schedule events more closely.

Determining a fair wage or profit is a personal matter. The decision of how much you wish to earn, or how much you need to keep your business afloat, will be dictated by all kinds of factors including what you are used to making and the standard of living in your area. Don't forget for a moment that your labor is highly skilled and should be treated as such, and that to run a successful business, you need to do more than just break even.

GETTING THE WORD OUT

"A successful caterer is made by marketing," says Donald Beckwith of Remember Basil, Ltd. He should know, since he and his wife Dounia Rathbone have built their business from the bottom up, starting in their own kitchen using their own pots and pans and gradually growing into a much sought-after business.

How do you market yourself and where do you find your first client? The following are some helpful methods and tried-and-true techniques for attracting business.

Selling Tools

Before you begin contacting your public, it's helpful to have a few selling tools.

The Name. Whether you choose a name that describes

your services, describes you, or is just fanciful, it helps to know who you are. As mentioned earlier, Dounia Rathbone and Donald Beckwith attribute some of their early success to their company name, Remember Basil, Ltd. Glorious Food got its name when a lyricist friend of Sean Driscoll and Christopher Idone dropped by. She was asked to come up with a name and replied that Christopher's food was "fresh and glorious." Sally Godfrey named her business Gallimaufrey because it means "stew, ragout, or hodgepodge, and that's how I like it." Tom Heller's The Company Picnic Company tells you exactly the kind of parties they do. Similarly, the name Culinary Classics evokes images of conventional French food rather than the casual or trendy.

Many people prefer to use their own names. David Ziff Cooking is a perfect example, as it tells you exactly who and what the business is. Neuman and Bogdonoff has almost a rhythmical, and thus memorable, ring to it. Whatever you choose, a descriptive name, a clever name, or just your own name, it should be fairly short and to the point.

Business Cards and Stationery. Have them nicely designed and printed with the name of your company, your name, address, and phone number. You may want to use a visual image as a logo. Even something as simple as a utensil or a pot may make your outfit more easily remembered. If you're really lucky you might be able to barter with a graphic artist for the service. Some printers design stationery and cards as well.

The Presentation Book. A presentation book is another good tool. Starting out, you won't have newspaper clippings or menus from successful parties to show off. However, now is the time to set up your book. As your business grows, you will constantly add to it. Gary Goldberg considers his presentation book, comprised largely of menus attractively designed and executed in calligraphy, an essential tool. He suggests having a few sample menus duplicated on printed stationery, interesting cards, postcards, or notepaper. As a special touch, he often has menus made as souvenirs for his clients and their guests, one gracing each place setting. He keeps an extra for his presentation book.

Gary also suggests bartering services with someone who is just setting out as a food photographer (another growing field) for food shots for your book. You may want to wait until your business is established in order to use food that you have actually prepared for a party. (If you choose to use photographs, be wary of using snapshots that don't show your food to good advantage. A picture of nice food looking ugly is much worse than no picture at all.)

Pamela Mitchell's market for her muffin business was primarily bed and breakfasts in Carmel, California. She printed up a list of her muffins and enclosed it in a flyer of rhyming verse introducing Sweet Satisfaction. "We approached with our flyers and with half a dozen each of two kinds of samples. And that did pretty well for us. Then we got business cards and, boy, did that carry us a long way." The bed and breakfasts then spread the news about Pamela and Andrea by word of mouth and the business began to take off.

Many people find brochures useful. When Greg Crafton of Cinderella Catering in Jefferson, Louisiana, started out, he decided to have his menus and brochures professionally printed on ivory paper using brown ink. At the time he was the only caterer in the area to give his advertising pieces a professional look, while his competition used only photocopies. Soon they, too, had their menus and brochures beautifully printed. Now Cinderella prints a four-color, sixteen-page brochure to set themselves apart.

The Word-of-Mouth Approach

It is never too early to start the process of attracting business. Most people start out gathering business by word of mouth—they let their friends know they are setting up in business and ask them to pass along the word to other friends.

"We started by just telling people we were caterers," says Donald Beckwith of Remember Basil. "Everywhere we went we told people. Finally, out of the blue, someone called and asked us to do a Thanksgiving dinner." It took Beckwith and Dounia Rathbone about a year to establish themselves as caterers. To keep themselves going during that time, they started a cooking school out of their apartment. To attract customers for their school, they stood on neighborhood street corners and stopped people, asking them if they would like cooking lessons. It's been ten years since they had to scramble so hard for clients, and today even corporations come knocking. But their perseverance and patience gave them their start.

Friends and acquaintances can be one of the best sources of business in the beginning, as they already know what a good cook you are and can vouch for you to others. By using the word-of-mouth approach you also save time and money on promotion and publicity. Another advantage is that you may be able to start out slowly, honing your skills and testing the market as you go.

While talking yourself up to people, don't forget other caterers. Perhaps you already know a caterer or two, or have struck up an acquaintance in the course of doing your research. If you do know other caterers, or can meet some, they often are a good source for referrals of jobs that they cannot handle either because they are too busy or because they do different kinds of work.

In the end, the best word-of-mouth advertising possible will be the referrals of satisfied customers. If your food is good and your customers happy, they will recommend you to anyone they know. Ted Smith of International Caterers feels that if you put your advertising money into the food you prepare, your customers will sell your product. Indeed, Ray Bonifer has found the word-of-mouth approach so successful that he is curtailing his newspaper advertising. Of course, both of these caterers are now well established, and in the beginning you may need to hustle a little more to bring in the jobs that will establish your reputation.

Other Marketing Methods

When you rely on word of mouth, you are tacitly acknowledging that while you will take business of almost any kind, it will probably come from people somewhat like yourself. However, there are other more direct ways of targeting specific kinds of clients.

Do you want busy working people who like special food and entertaining and who have the money but have neither the time nor often the inclination to create it themselves? Do you want to cater the food concession at the local charity crafts fair, or a local business's monthly breakfast or a women's club's spring luncheon? Maybe you want the chance to cater all of these.

Whichever clientele you decide to concentrate on, there are methods for marketing yourself to them. To attract discriminating private clients start by going to specialty food stores and asking to leave your card and menu. Ask the store owner if you can create a special event for them, and don't be surprised if he or she is delighted, as they too are often looking for good publicity and something special to entice customers. You will probably want to start with the ones with which you already do business and thus have some sort of a relationship established. You may want to offer to recommend the merchandise that you use from them in return for displaying your card and menu. People often ask at such stores for recommended caterers. You might offer to bring in samples for them to taste or to display to customers as a method of demonstrating the quality of your food.

Visit party supply stores, rental companies, bakeries, bridal boutiques, and florists. Talk with the owners, describing the kind of food and services you provide and leave cards and menus. Here again, if you particularly like the products of these shops, you might want to use them for your jobs.

To solicit other kinds of business, such as charities, begin by scouting out the various churches, schools, and clubs in your area and then target their annual or seasonal events, such as hospital book fairs, antiques shows, benefit luncheons, gala dinners, and parent-teacher nights. You probably already know about some of them, but make sure you check the notices in the newspaper. Try to find out who the organizers are and approach them about contracting the food out to you.

Frequently, such organizations rely on volunteers to cater their events, but not always. Some have food booths for raising money, other times they just need to feed the workers, and it's a real hassle for the volunteers to handle it. Offer to provide the food at a very modest amount or offer to donate all the profits from the sale of the food to the organization in exchange for use of their mailing list or free publicity from them. You probably won't make any money, and may well lose some, but the exposure may more than make up for any losses. Also, the food you provide for a charity is tax deductible.

Museums and businesses that hold regular events often are good sources for jobs. Some museums may be accustomed to volunteer labor, but others will have an events budget and may be looking for outside caterers to provide meals for them. Call to find out the name of the special events coordinator. Write a letter, enclosing a sample menu or two and follow it up with a phone call to make an appointment to pitch your business in person.

Publicity and Advertising

Call the local newspaper food or business department and interest a reporter in doing a story on you. Think up an angle for the story and propose that you and the reporter get together to sample your food. You might also consider having some good photos taken of you in your kitchen and send these to food and business editors along with a press release.

Another method for attracting customers is to advertise. Placing ads in local newspapers and "pennysavers" is inexpensive and can be a good method for familiarizing the public with your name and services. Alan Bell placed an ad as a surprise for David Ziff in the New York *Times* under gourmet services. Once the calls began coming in, the business was begun. He also took out small ads in *New York Magazine*, then the most influential local magazine. The ad caught the attention of Paula Wolfert, the magazine's restaurant reviewer at the time. After attending a party they catered, she wrote a glowing review of their services. That, too, greatly helped establish their business.

Teri-Woodard Polster of Laguna Hills, California, finds, like many caterers, that a well-designed ad in the Yellow Pages is valuable for attracting customers. Ads in a number of local publications may well reap substantial benefits but, as with most aspects of the business, don't spend beyond your means before your business is making money. Also keep in mind that responses from a blind ad are more expensive—and generally less reliable—than the clients you get through word of mouth.

Publicity can really make your name known but be aware that it also attracts official attention. If local regulations require that your kitchen be licensed be sure it is before seeking public acclaim. If not, you could be subject to fines or closing of the business before you really begin.

In the beginning, one of your most important tasks is to establish a clientele. At this stage you need the business and the exposure, so be prepared to trade on the publicity opportunities by giving clients a particularly good price. You may well make up in exposure what you lose in dollars. Ask event organizers, particularly for fund-raisers, to mention your name in any publicity material such as posters, newsletters, newspaper announcements, and bulletins they may be preparing. This can be presented as a trade for your full rate. Once you have customers and have proven your worth to them, you can begin charging market rates. This is not to say you should work at a loss for very long or that you should ever conduct yourself in less than a self-assured and businesslike manner. You may not wish to do discounted business, but if that big public opportunity appears, consider it.

Hearing the Word. Whatever method you choose to stimulate business, you must be available to accept the inquiries that come your way. Many people starting a small business from home tend to forget that their image as a business is all-important. For instance, there must be someone, or something, to answer the phone when you're not there. If you're generally home, you probably won't have a problem. However, if you are frequently out for long periods during the day you are likely to miss calls, and you can't expect prospective clients to keep calling back. Buy an answering machine and tape a message that briefly describes your service. Or subscribe to an answering service.

3

Insurance, Taxes, and the Law

Pricing and marketing are not the only aspects of your business that appear far removed from your culinary creativity. While becoming a caterer may seem like it should be an outpouring of your heart and soul, in the eyes of the law your company is a business just like any other, subject to rules and regulations.

Before you begin you need to learn the basics of running your business. This doesn't mean that you need earn an MBA, although a course in small business management would be very useful. It does mean that you need to be aware of the legality of your venture, and the need for insurance and contracts.

ARE YOU LEGAL?

You may find yourself running afoul of the law before you even begin. Most people just starting out cater from their own kitchens and, unless you have a large personal fortune or backers, you probably won't be able to afford to set up a commercial kitchen. The problem is that in some towns it is illegal to cater from your home kitchen. In many places you must register with the local health department, and in some towns you need a permit to prepare food.

The rules vary greatly: some municipalities have regulations requiring that all food for sale be cooked in a commercial kitchen, while some cities will allow you to cook food at home and sell it in another jurisdiction, but not in your own town. Others allow you to cater in your town but not in the neighboring one. Some places prohibit preparation of food in a client's home for pay, which rules out itinerant cooks and even technically rules out a full-time cook.

Almost everyone I've spoken with started out at home and moved to a commercial kitchen as soon as their businesses were established enough to pay the rent on a commercial space. No doubt some of them did so in violation of local ordinances, as the practical reality is that very often people can get their businesses established before the local government notices them. Occasionally, local officials are indulgent toward the fledgling caterer, and perhaps there are enough loopholes that you or an attorney may be able to design your venture so that it is a legal exception to any statutes. Ask other caterers about their experiences and check with your local Board of Health for information on local regulations. Find a way to do it legally. It's the only way to go.

If you find that there is no way you can prepare food from your kitchen and sell it to another person, there are alternatives which do not mean investing in a commercial kitchen. One thing you may be able to do is become a service accommodator, one who cooks for others at their homes or places of business (see earlier discussion of service accommodator, in chapter 2). It is also possible that the letter of the law will allow you to finish the last stages of cooking on site, having done the bulk of the preparation at home. Since many dishes require some last-minute cooking you may already qualify as a service accommodator. You might also investigate renting a church, school, or club kitchen. These are usually properly equipped and often the rental costs are very reasonable. Church kitchens, in particular, are often underutilized.

Again, check the local requirements when preparing to rent space in someone else's kitchen. Pamela Mitchell and Andrea Israel started Sweet Satisfaction, their muffin company, out of a tiny apartment kitchen in Monterey, California. It was so small, in fact, that the mixing bowl covered the sink. Since California regulations are very stringent, they set out to find a proper commercial kitchen as soon as they could. They approached restaurants and hotels asking if they could rent space during off hours, but to no avail. Finally, they found two fellow caterers doing their preliminary cooking at a local Elks Club. They were willing to share their space with Pamela and Andrea. Relieved at finally being able to be strictly legit, the two women muffineers went to register as a small business with the local health department. Then the health department came to inspect and closed everyone down because the club was zoned for on-premise catering only.

If you have the resources, and are fairly sure of your business acumen, it is best to work from a proper commercial kitchen from the start. Beginning with a properly equipped and inspected kitchen assures your being in good graces with the authorities.

Health Inspections. Not everyone's experience with the health department has been as problematical as Pamela and Andrea's. Most, if not all, towns will require that your kitchen be inspected, but health inspections are for the good of the public and generally the inspectors' concerns are sensible. They are interested in proper lighting, appliances, plumbing and sewage disposal, washing facilities, garbage disposal, and ventilation.

Inspectors are most concerned with the safety and cleanliness of the premises and of the people who work there. Typical standard requirements are that all food be stored up off the floor, that there be separate facilities (sinks and chopping boards) for preparing food and cleaning dishes, that the facilities for disposing of garbage be adequate, that there be enough light for people to work easily and without strain, and that there be adequate refrigerator space to cool and keep foods.

It is essential to know what the health code in your area requires. Inquire at City Hall.

INSURANCE

Your catering outfit is like any other small business, complete with its own attendant risks and liabilities. Since you are dealing with people's health, both via the food you feed them and the people who help you prepare it, the last thing you want is someone to get sick from something you made. Among other risks you face are helpers who hurt themselves while working with you or a kitchen fire. These are nightmares, of course, but they can happen, and you should be covered for such eventualities. Your home insurance is unlikely to cover such possibilities, so investigate business insurance.

Liability Coverage. It may be difficult to get, particularly if you work out of a home kitchen, but call a broker before you hire your first helper or serve your first meal. If you have trouble finding full coverage, consultant Gary Goldberg recommends investigating one-time coverage for particularly large functions. It's expensive, but for a large party the cost can sometimes be amortized by the volume. Some places (the famed Radio City Music Hall in New York is a particularly grand example) require such special insurance before booking any party.

Another thing people are concerned with today is the responsibility of the caterer when alcohol is served. You may face this, and there are no easy solutions to it. Some states have assigned responsibility for drunken behavior not to the drinker but to the barkeep. Find out whether you are at risk in your state, and whether you are or not, discuss the issue with any client whose event involves alcohol.

There are some things which you, as a responsible caterer, can do to limit alcohol consumption, and these are covered in chapter 7.

Insurance will cost you some money, but, on the bright side it is a legitimate overhead expense and thus is tax deductible. It should also be figured into your overhead calculations when you are determining your fixed costs.

TAXES

Taxes seem to be with us no matter what we do and, as a business selling a product and service, you will probably have to pay any state or local sales tax (which should be figured into your pricing). Contact the Small Business Administration—or an accountant—for information regarding setting up a tax schedule.

You will need to pay personal income taxes as a self-employed person. It is a nuisance to set up the quarterly payment schedule, but your accountant can help you establish a system. You will have to keep records and receipts. On the positive side, as a self-employed person you are entitled to a number of deductions, including the food you buy to test recipes, the equipment for your business, any kitchen renovations needed to serve your business needs, the business-related miles you put on the car, the gasoline used while shopping, part of your phone bill, any rent you pay for a kitchen or a separate room if you have an office in your home, the services of your accountant, and business expenditures such as stationery, printing, and advertising.

Unless you are particularly adept at bookkeeping, talk with an accountant when setting up your business. He or she will be able to advise you on planning profit projections, as well as setting up an accounting system for your company.

You might want to hire the regular services of an accountant, or you might find one who will consult with you on a one-time basis. You will need to begin keeping separate files for each area such as recipe testing, equipment, and utilities to help calculate your taxes. Keep a log of gas purchases and miles traveled to use for tax deductions as well. Once you get into the habit of keeping records, it becomes an accepted part of the ritual.

CONTRACTS

The decision to use a formal contract or rely on an informal understanding with clients is an individual one. Most caterers in large cities work with contracts and a deposit of anywhere between 20 and 50 percent of the total cost. When the client is an organization or business, it is generally more convenient to work with a contract, for the people involved are familiar with paperwork, indeed, often cannot operate without it.

Overall, both you and the customer are probably safer with a contract because it confirms in writing the full understanding of responsibilities of the two parties. On the other hand, caterers in small towns or with repeat customers often will forego the written confirmation in favor of a more casual verbal understanding. A third alternative is to do both, working with a contract on large jobs for which you will have to extend yourself and your resources and not bothering with them for smaller events.

June Jenkins and Angelique Graziano, restaurateurs and caterers in Fort Worth, Texas, remember ruefully the wedding reception they catered in which the responsibilities weren't properly stated. They had understood that the client would handle the bar and they would do everything else. "He had never mentioned the bar," says Angelique. "I got there and they didn't have an ice cube, they didn't have

SAMPLE LETTER CONTRACT

FINE FOODS CATERING LTD.
999 West 55th Street
New York, NY 10000

June 12, 1986

Ms. Luann Smith
1924 S.E. Second St.
Quicheville, Michigan 22222

Dear Ms. Smith:

This will serve to confirm our understanding regarding the Bastille Day picnic party for twelve guests you will be giving on July 15th at your home. I will be providing the meal which will consist of Pain Bagne (a Mediterranean seafood salad sandwich), French potato salad, and apple tart with vanilla ice cream. I will deliver the food, set up the tables, serve the food and clean up. I will arrive an hour before the party at noon and stay until the party is through at approximately 4 o'clock.

The total cost for food, labor, and service will be $300, plus state tax of 7½ percent, payable one-third upon signing of this letter of agreement and two-thirds at the close of the picnic. You will be providing any bar setups and drinks as well as all dishware, cutlery, glassware, and decorations.

If this reflects your understanding please
sign below and return one copy to me, along
with the $107.50 due.

I look forward to July 15. We will be speaking
between now and then to finalize last-minute
arrangements.

Sincerely,

Jocelyn P. Caterer

AGREED:

_____

Ms. Luann Smith

SAMPLE FORM CONTRACT

Date:

Caterer: Name:

Street Address:

City, State, Zip:

Phone number:

Client: Name:

Street Address:

City, State, Zip:

Phone number:

Date and time of party:

Hours caterer to be on duty:

Menu:

Tentative number of people to attend (to be confirmed):

Special requests (e.g., refrigerator will be cleared):

Service:
  number of serving people
  bartenders

Rental equipment:
  tablecloths
  glassware
  cutlery
  serving dishes, etc.

Equipment to be supplied by client:
  itemized list as above

Other services:
  decorations, music, etc.

Costs:
  Food
    \$_____ × _____ guests = _____
  Services
    _____ servers   @ \$_____ per hour = \$_____
    _____ bartenders @ \$_____ per hour = \$_____
    _____ in kitchen   @ \$_____ per hour = \$_____

                               Estimated total:

                                     Sales tax:

                                       Deposit:

The above estimated total price is subject to change
upon revision of the menu, the confirmation of the num-

---

ber of guests, or other changes in the above specified terms.

The balance of the bill will be payable on receipt after the party. Gratuities are not included.

Signed: _____   Signed: _____
Date: Date:

---

a bottle of club soda. He had bought one bottle of whiskey and a few bottles of champagne—not nearly enough—and that was it." Had June and Angelique used a simple letter agreement, the question would have been raised automatically and the nervous groom wouldn't have found himself in a spot.

Creating a contract is not a difficult matter. All it really needs to be is a written understanding of what you and the client have agreed upon verbally. You don't have to spend thousands of dollars in legal fees having a contract drawn.

"I would tell anybody starting a business that they should develop their own contract and then see a lawyer," says Gary Goldberg. He gives the example of Wally, the new caterer, coming in to show him the contract that his lawyer developed for him. Since the lawyer naturally felt obliged to protect his client, the contract was full of complicated clauses. "You can have 150 clauses in a contract that foresee every eventuality and it will be so intimidating that no one will sign it," says Goldberg.

A better contract is one that gives the caterer's and the client's names, along with the date of the agreement, the date of the party, the site, the schedule, the menu to be served, any additional services to be rendered, and the price and how it is to be paid.

A contract can be set up in a number of ways. It can be as

simple as a letter outlining the various details of the party or it can be a standard-looking form. The letter-style agreement included here is the kind favored by Goldberg and many caterers as it sets out the understanding and the menu in a non-threatening manner. A more formal agreement option is also included.

The Small Business Administration publishes a number of helpful and inexpensive publications on running a small business called Management Aids. Write to them at P.O. Box 15434, Fort Worth, TX 76119 for a list of titles.

4

Organizing Your Kitchen

No doubt you've gathered by now that laying the ground-work for a business venture—even in a creative area like food—requires a systematic approach. The importance of advance planning and preparation involves not only the external factors of pricing, contracts, and publicity, but also the organization of your working habits, and the tools and equipment of the art.

Organizing yourself and your work area will save you a lot of time and effort when you actually prepare for a party for money. Since we all hear that time is money, let's get going.

WORKING METHODS

You may already be a disciplined and orderly sort of person. If so, the task of studying your movements to improve efficiency will probably come naturally. If not, now is the time to rethink consciously the manner in which you work.

Lists. Many people find that making lists forces them to organize their thoughts and tasks. Actually writing down the to-do's and what-to-buy's can have an amazing impact on one's organization.

Lists help you organize tasks and the time you need to do them. They also serve to make concrete what is in your mind, either lessening the feeling that there is too much to do, or allowing you to plan for the needed extra time. Plus, once something is down on paper you no longer need to remember to remember.

Lists can be organized in many ways, and you may well have your own methods already. One way is to make separate lists for each of the days leading up to a party and divide the tasks among the days, weighting them as heavily toward the beginning as possible. This does not mean you should end up having all the food prepared days in advance of an event—the chances of that are pretty small. But you can do such tasks as arranging for rentals, making calls to find ingredients, and placing advance orders earlier rather than later. Then, as the big day draws near, you can swing into action in the preparation of the food.

Another method is to make up work lists for each dish to be prepared. Then cross reference each one to the other where tasks interweave—if you have three dishes needing chopped onions, it only makes sense to chop them all at once. A fuller discussion of preparing shopping lists and work plans is to be found in chapter 5, but the sooner you start listing (if you don't already), the easier it will be when faced with your first party.

Task Efficiency. Sounds a little like a business school word, doesn't it? It's really only a matter of thinking through the everyday tasks you perform and figuring out ways to do them more quickly and with less effort.

Many kitchen chores like peeling and chopping a carrot are automatic to the practiced cook. However, peeling forty carrots and chopping twenty onions is another matter. Modern equipment can be a great help, but machines go only so far—you still have to peel the carrots. If you trot back and forth to the sink every few minutes to wash a handful of carrots, you will waste a good deal of time and energy.

The Assembly-Line Method. If you have organized your kitchen around efficient work stations, you are already part way to minimizing your movements. If your work surfaces are clear, you will have room to set up your equipment before you begin the task.

Line up everything you need for a task in advance. This is known as assembling a *batterie de cuisine*. Putting them in order of use or at specific stations we all recognize as an assembly line.

Creating an assembly line is useful in all kinds of catering, and essential when preparing large quantities of food. For one thing, you are less likely to forget an ingredient if you have everything lined up in advance. Assembly is quicker, particularly when creating multiples of a dish, whether you are making eight beef tenderloins to serve two hundred people or making finger foods for twenty. Equally important, the precise look of plated dinners, each of which is arranged and garnished in the same manner, benefits from good assembly-line technique.

Clean as you go. Once you've prepared a dish, proceed to the next. However, before you pass Go, you must stop and clean.

For many cooks, cleanup is an odious word. It must be done, of course, but creative and satisfying it is not—it seems so pointless sometimes to clean up when you know full well you will be messing the same areas up with something else in about two minutes. However, until you are well established and have enough space and equipment that you needn't reuse anything and can hire someone to clean up for you, you are stuck with constant cleanup.

Cleaning up after each major step of preparation not only keeps the kitchen neater, it ultimately saves time and increases enjoyment in the actual cooking. There are few things more frustrating and concentration-breaking than trying to find the spatula only to discover the one you need is soaking in a bowl. The bowl is under a pile of plates in the sink and full of water, so of course your floury hands will need to be washed, dried, and refloured before the dumb spatula can be put to use. Now, where were you in that recipe again?

Create Cold Storage Space. A clear refrigerator is an absolute must in catering. If you're lucky you will have an extra one, but if like many people you don't, you will do yourself a favor by cultivating the habit of pitching and organizing. Many of us compulsively save leftovers, and then let them grow green before we throw them away. It's as though it's morally wrong to throw them out until they are inedible. If no one has eaten them in three or four days, the chances are great that no one will.

One thing you can do to cut down on the number of leftovers is to ask yourself (or whoever is doing the saving) if there is enough to warrant using a fresh container. And how appetizing will those cold beans be in a day or two? If the answers are no and not very, pitch them.

If you can learn to keep the refrigerator uncluttered with leftovers the task of clearing it to receive party supplies will be much easier. When it comes time to prepare for a party, move all your own food to one shelf or area.

Organize the party supplies on the shelves for maximum efficiency by making up designated areas. Keep the carrots together, the butter in one area, and so on. Place the ingredients you will be using first toward the front, those you will need last at the back. Items that will be used more than once should be placed within easy reach. This kind of organization takes a little practice if you are not already accustomed to it. It is also not absolutely foolproof, since occasionally the order of preparation changes for one reason or another.

EQUIPPING THE KITCHEN

Visions of beautifully stocked kitchens with walk-in refrigerators, miles of counters, and lots of help may dance in your head. Having really proper equipment would make the business so much easier, you think. However, unless you have a private income or corporate backers, you probably won't have the luxury of creating a brand-new state-of-the-art professional kitchen, at least not right away.

Take comfort: remember, very few of even the most successful caterers started out on a grand scale. Most started slowly and small with the equipment they already had. In fact, that's one of the appeals of the business. "You don't need that much to begin with," says Fanny Farkas. "I think it's foolish to run out and buy before you've gotten the business because you don't know what kind of business you're going to get."

Fanny speaks from experience, for when she started eight years ago, she started in the smallest way possible, doing small dinner parties in clients' homes. "I would just go in and cook the dinners using whatever the client or I had. Whenever I needed a piece of equipment, such as a mandoline, I would go out and get one." Donald Beckwith of Remember Basil, Ltd. told me, "We used pots and pans and everything else of our own. Little by little we started accumulating." Fanny and Donald and Dounia had a certain amount of equipment to start with, as you probably do, too. That's what this section is about, looking over what you do have and being alert to what you might need when the jobs begin rolling in.

Large Appliances. Begin by assessing what you have already. Of course you have the two most important appliances, a stove and a refrigerator.

The bigger the oven the better, and if you have a second oven, terrific, your life is already made easier. If you have a fairly large refrigerator, good. If you have a second one, you're in clover, as most caterers seem to agree that having a second refrigerator makes life much easier. But don't go out and buy one just yet. See how the business goes. For their first few years of business, Christopher Idone and Sean Driscoll cooked on friends' stoves and used many other people's refrigerators.

The only other large appliance that is particularly useful is a freezer. If you have one you will be able to lay in supplies of certain foods such as chicken and seasonal fruits when the prices are good. Certain breads and pastries can also be made in large quantity and frozen until needed. As time goes on you will probably find that having a freezer is indispensable. But to begin with, it's nice but not essential.

Mixer. When Fanny Farkas was asked what equipment was essential to start out, she promptly answered "A Kitchenaid and a Cuisinart." The fact is, she herself started with only the Kitchenaid mixer.

People joke that a good mixer can do everything but wash the dishes. It's true, a sturdy mixer is practically indispensable, but you probably won't need one with every possible attachment. It should be a good solid one, complete with several bowls that fit it, mounted on a heavy base. The hand-held models bear little relation to the more useful big boys, but the smaller ones have their purposes, too (whipping egg whites or cream or mixing sauces on a job, to name a couple).

Food Processor. The food processor has changed the way Americans cook. As Pierre Franey, the 60-Minute Gourmet, says, "It improved amateur cooking forever." With its help, turning pro is made easier.

Food processors save chopping and puréeing time. If you thought your food processor was handy before, you will be delighted with it the first time you shred ten pounds of cabbage or grate five pounds of carrots. However, food processors shouldn't replace hand chopping where the texture is important, such as delicate garnishes of parsley, other herbs, or vegetables.

Blender. A blender is useful for making fine purées. It can also add air to a mixture (whipping egg whites or cream when your mixer is occupied) while a food processor can't.

Portable Convection Oven. Convection ovens are great as an extra oven, particularly at a party site. They can be used for most kinds of oven cooking, and are especially useful for baking.

Pots and Pans. For some people the question of pots and pans is even more important than that of appliances. Here again, if you like to cook, you probably already have a basic selection of them. If you find you need something to do a particular party, then buy it. (See table on page 62 for list of pots and pans you may need.)

Utensils. As usual, you get what you pay for: Good quality utensils tend to be more expensive, but give longer and better service than cheap ones. And speaking of cost, it is possible to spend your life savings on utensils as there are utensils for doing just about everything in the kitchen. Buy only what you need, as usual, but do make sure that good sharp knives are to be found in your equipment drawer. They may be the most essential utensils, yet are often the most neglected. (See table on page 64 for a checklist of utensils.)

Serving Dishes. When equipping your kitchen for catering, you also need to consider serving dishes. If you will be doing all preparation at a client's home, you will probably use the client's own dishes; if you intend to drop your food off, you are likely to use disposable plates and pans. On the other hand, if you will be providing general service you will need to have some dishes yourself. Here again, don't rush out to buy them before you have the need, but it helps to know what you will need when the time comes. The following guidelines may help steer you when you decide to invest.

Keep it simple. Simple serving dishes blend well with most kinds of dishes. These days there are so many kinds of well-designed inexpensive dishes available in cookware stores, discount outlets, and department stores that they need not be heavy and institutional-looking. White porcelain dishes and glass bowls are probably the most versatile, as they can be elegantly simple yet plain and cheap.

Simplicity aside, you may want to make a special trademark of some of your dishes. For instance, if you specialize in salads you might want to serve them in a particular type of wood or glass bowl. Fanny Farkas and Arlene Cotler have made their lacquer serving trays a Panhandlers' feature. You will probably also want to have a selection of baskets for serving crackers and breads. (For more about food presentation, see chapter 8.)

Useful serving dishes include: round and oval platters in several sizes; serving bowls in several sizes; salad bowls, in glass and wood; casseroles in several sizes; wooden boards for cheese; and baskets.

Buying Equipment

Almost anything can be rented. If you are scheduled to prepare a blanquette de veau for seventy people on your first job, you may well not have the money or time to shop for a ten-gallon pot before the party. Don't change the menu, rent the pot.

When you find yourself ready to buy equipment, be it for the first party or the tenth, do some homework. Consumer guides are a great place to read evaluations, as are cooking magazines that test equipment, such as *Cook's Magazine* (it tests everything from cookie sheets to charcoal grills). Investigate local restaurant supply houses, cookware shops, and department stores.

Whatever you buy will probably get hard use, so buy equipment of good quality that will stand up to frequent use and lots of travel. Fanny Farkas suggests that whatever you buy, make sure it's good and sturdy and then "buy it one size larger than you think you will need it." This does not mean that you must buy everything in commercial grade. Unless you are setting up a commercial kitchen, you may find that some commercial appliances are ill-suited to a

A PANOPLY OF PANS AND POTS

You may need a great variety of pots and pans. Compare the contents of your cupboards and pot racks with the following:

ASSORTED SKILLETS: They should be heavy cast-iron and non-stick. Have at least one very large one, a deep skillet, and a couple of medium-sized ones.

SAUCEPANS: You need several good quality saucepans of different sizes, including at least two deep ones.

LARGE POTS: Useful for quantities of stews, sauces, and so on.

FISH POACHER

DUTCH OVEN: Good for stews, and occasionally to serve as a deep saucepan.

DOUBLE-BOILER

STEAMER

ROASTING PANS: A minimum of two.

OMELET PANS: Optional, depending upon the nature of your menus.

WOK: Also optional.

BAKING EQUIPMENT: Several good heavy baking sheets (the light ones stay flat for only a matter of minutes, it seems); several long, multipurpose baking pans suitable for sheet cakes or lasagna; springform, bundt, loaf, jelly roll and pie pans; loose-bottomed tart tins; quiche dishes; muffin and round cake pans; at least two large cooling racks.

BOWLS: You'll need numerous bowls, in varying sizes, shapes, and materials, including glass, ceramic and, if possible, at least one copper one (for beating egg whites).

PLASTIC CONTAINERS: You will find a use for about as many as you can find. Cottage cheese cartons, large yogurt and ricotta cheese cartons are cheap and disposable. Large plastic boxes and trays are good for storing hors d'oeuvre and prepared vegetables and garnishes.

home kitchen, no matter how professionally you run it. Unless you have a very large kitchen, for example, a Garland range probably won't fit.

Commercial quality pots and pans have advantages (in particular, size and durability), but keep in mind that oven temperatures and cooking times may have to be adjusted to accommodate their weight, so they must be tested before you go out on the job. It may seem obvious, but make sure that the baking pans you buy will fit in your oven. Some commercial lines are being marketed for home use, and these are scaled to fit twenty-seven-inch ovens, but if you buy directly from a commercial supply house, you may find some pans too big. Measure before you buy.

Treat the commercial equipment with the attention it requires. Commercial baking pans often have a non-stick silicone glaze over their tin coatings. They are made to be used without washing, and if you immerse them in soapy water or scrub them the porous glaze will deteriorate and the tin coating will be damaged.

Commercial-grade equipment is generally more expensive than consumer goods. If you find you really must have commercial pots or pans, it will pay to shop around and ask questions. Commercial supply houses will often sell used equipment at reduced prices. You may come across the deal-of-the-year, as Sally Godfrey did. "The kitchen supply place said you can have this Garland stove for $50 if you just get it out of here. So we did." Inspect all merchandise carefully before buying, no matter how good a deal it is.

Go to restaurant auctions, as they are another good

ESSENTIAL UTENSILS

KNIVES: You need a variety of sizes, including a chef's knife, a cleaver, several paring knives, a carving knife, at least two serrated knives, and a sharpening steel.
MEASURING CUPS: Glass cups in 2, 4, and 8-cup sizes and a nested set of smaller metal ones for dry measuring.
MEASURING SPOONS: At least two sets.
FLOUR SIFTER
SPOONS: Several wooden spoons and a miscellany of others, including a runcible spoon and ladle.
WHISKS: At least three, in varying sizes.
RUBBER SPATULAS: At least one large and one small.
VEGETABLE PEELERS: A minimum of two.
SPECIALTY UTENSILS AND GADGETS: You probably won't need all of these right away, but if you do a variety of events you will probably need them all eventually. Check your shelves and drawers for: meat, candy, and oven thermometers; kitchen scales; pastry brushes; two colanders; salad spinner; kitchen and poultry scissors; funnels of several sizes; melon baller; metal and bamboo skewers; cutting boards; four-sided grater; corkscrew; pastry bag with dessert and hors d'oeuvre tips; cheesecloth; molds; kitchen twine; tongs.

source, but be careful to inspect all the inventory thoroughly before the bidding and to note down the lot number. A lot number is the surest way of distinguishing the item you want when it comes up on the block.

Make a second and possibly a third choice just in case you lose out on the bid. And after you have marked down your choices—but before the bidding begins—establish the price you are willing to pay for each item. If it sells for more, let it go. This will help keep you from getting auction fever and outbidding your budget.

Luckily for all of us, one of the benefits of today's cooking boom is that good heavy equipment that used to be made only for restaurants and institutions is now being sold retail for home use, often modified for home kitchens. If you buy good, solid equipment (not always the most expensive), you will be making an investment in your business that will be paid for over and over again as your business grows and expands.

Setting Up Your Kitchen

It may seem odd, but for some people a principal determinant of what they cook is where they cook it. If you have a large commercial kitchen, you can do almost anything; if you are confined to a tiny apartment kitchen with two burners, you will be limited. Yet you may not be as limited as you think.

Begin by studying your kitchen. Most kitchens built within the last few decades use a triangle as the basic arrangement of major stations: the points of the triangle are stove, sink, and refrigerator. Counters, cabinets, and any other surfaces generally form a rectangle around the triangle, while other surfaces such as tables and work islands are usually placed somewhere outside of it altogether.

Having the kitchen arranged in the basic triangle makes the movements between the major appliances efficient. However, if your kitchen is not arranged in this manner, there is little you can do, aside from moving the refrigerator or remodeling the room. Whether you have the built-in advantage of proper placement or not, the trick to making your kitchen work efficiently is to organize the areas around the major work stations.

Work Surfaces. When you begin cooking food in quantities, you will need large open surfaces. No matter how big your kitchen, in fact, you will probably feel you can never have enough counter space. While most of us try to keep our counters clear, it's surprising when you really look at them just how many gadgets you have around that aren't used very much.

On a typical cook's counter, you are likely to find a coffeemaker, a coffee grinder, a toaster oven or toaster, a mixer, a food processor, a blender, a set of canisters, a dishdrainer, a chopping board, a knife block, and an electric can opener. This doesn't even include slightly more esoteric items such as spice grinders, juicers, ice cream machines, pasta makers and marble pastry boards, not to mention the odd bread box. Add to those the effluvia of everyday life that seems to accumulate in a kitchen, from pads of paper, pens and pencils to half-eaten boxes of crackers, partial loaves of bread, and cute decorations. Add a plant or two and stray pieces of mail and you've got clutter.

Clutter can do you in when you're on a tight schedule. Clear the counters of all but the essentials. Obviously, the effluvia goes first. Then the appliances that you don't use very often. For instance, do you really use the blender now that you've got a food processor? Could you mount the knives on a magnetic bar instead of keeping them in a bulky countertop knife block? Put the appliances you know you'll never use in deep storage, and those you use occasionally within easy access.

Work Areas. Set up work stations with the remaining appliances in logical working-arrangement spaces. Some appliances will require more counter space around them than others. The coffeemaker and toaster oven won't need much, but the mixer, food processor, stove, and sink will.

The next step is to organize the resulting areas by task. The area surrounding the stove is probably your most used surface. The key is to locate conveniently the things you use while at the stove. Herbs and spices should be on open shelves at eye level. They may not look as neat, and they may get a little dirty in such an exposed spot, but it's better to wipe them with a cloth every month or two than leave them to lose their strength sitting unused on a forgotten dark shelf, or to have to spend five minutes looking for the chervil while the sauce bubbles away. Keeping staples such as oil, vinegar, and salt and pepper on the counter by the stove saves time and is less of a nuisance as well.

Locate utensils near the stove, in crocks, hanging from racks, or in a kitchen carousel. It will save time otherwise spent searching through messy drawers. Pot holders hanging near the stove and oven (nowhere near open flame) are much handier than those that live in a drawer, even an accessible one.

Hang pots and pans on the wall or put them in cupboards near the stove. Organize them by size and frequency of use. Store the lids on the pans or in a rack nearby, organized in the same way. Instinctively, people seem to stack pots and pans, perhaps because few people have the room to spread the pans on shelves. But if you weed out seldom used pots and pans, you may be amazed at the difference in efficiency. Your cooking may be improved by not having to hunt for something at the moment the sauce needs to be stirred.

The counter near the mixer is a natural for baking. Baking takes up quite a bit of room. Space is required for mixing, rolling, and assembling pans, so, if you can, reserve a fair amount of counter space. Next, locate the baking equipment nearby (pans, sifter, rolling pin, pastry cloth, cutters) and baking ingredients (flour, sugar, baking powder, and spices). When equipment and ingredients are kept near the work areas, they tend to be used more often. I know I forget I have things if I can't see them every once in a while.

The same theories of cupboard organization apply to the baking cupboard. Organize your baking pans and sheets by frequency of use and size, try not to stack pans and bowls, and locate your spices and ingredients within easy, visible reach.

The food processor vicinity is a natural for chopping and cutting. Since cutting and chopping tend to be messy, this area should be located near the sink. For many people accustomed to tiny kitchens, the old cutting-board-over-the-sink trick is a familiar and easy solution. In any case, cutting boards and knives belong in this area, with knives in the aforementioned wall rack. They are convenient there, and they stay sharp longer, too, when they are not banged around with other utensils.

Store pots and pans that don't fit in the cupboards near the stove near the cutting area, since they will be needed there. In fact, you might want to divide pots and pans into those that tend to be used near the stove, and those that are needed before you reach the stove.

Organizing your kitchen is important to the main business of catering. The more you do to prepare yourself for the work to come, the easier it will be. Besides, once you get going, you probably won't have time to do it, nor will you be able to afford inefficiency. You will also find that adapting on-site kitchens to your needs can be done more quickly when you have established efficient patterns and systems at home.

But enough of getting your kitchen and yourself in shape; it's time to talk about how to fill it with activity.

5

Preparing for Service

Since catering is by definition a service industry, part of
your preparations should include thoughts about hiring
staff as well as managing extra services like rentals, decorations, and entertainment so that once you find yourself
faced with a need you'll be ready to act.

Part of this planning will be determined by the type of
catering you intend to do. If you plan a business based
solely on muffins, you won't need too much in the way of
service. But what if a client asks you to do an afternoon tea?
Then you might need to rent china and linen, and, depending on the size of the crowd, hire someone to help serve
and clean up. You don't necessarily need to line up your
help and develop rental accounts before you start, but
knowing how to before you begin can save time and effort
down the line.

HIRING HELP

In the beginning, your staff may consist of one (you) or two (you and a partner). At some point, however, you are going to find yourself needing help to serve, cook, and clean up and later on possibly to help plan and manage. It may be for the first party, or for the fifth or tenth, but whenever it is you will need to be prepared to hire the people who will help you build your company. Indeed, Ted Smith feels he owes much of the success of International Caterers in South Portland, Maine, to his staff. "I only have this because of the good people I have working for me," he says.

Many caterers feel that finding people by word of mouth is the best method—a good thing, too, since in the beginning this is by far the easiest and cheapest route to follow. A friend's teenage daughter or son may be happy to serve, or a neighbor to help in the kitchen.

If you live in a metropolitan area where young people are trying to make their living in the arts, or that has a college or two, you may have a good source of willing help. One way to find it is to post notices on the job boards at colleges or acting schools or inquire of administrators if there is a part-time job placement service.

Sally Godfrey of Gallimaufrey in Providence, Rhode Island, gets almost all of her help from the student body at Brown University. One of her most valued cooks is a premed student she has worked with for four years. Students tend to have wide circles of friends, and by finding one good worker access to others is almost assured.

You may feel that all you need are bodies to help you, but the fact is, you are establishing a network of people you can draw on for years to come. What you really want are pleasant people who are willing and happy to work for you, employees who will take orders well and won't get easily flustered. They need not have vast amounts of cooking or serving experience, but it helps if they like food and are familiar with working as members of a team.

The people you hire will need to be trained to your methods and standards. Most of them probably won't have too much experience and you may not either. In fact, you may not know what your needs are until you find yourself thoroughly planning a party. And even then it can take several parties, each with its different set of problems to solve, before you establish a comfortable management style and a clear understanding of how tasks and responsibilities are to be divided and delegated.

At first, you will probably have more call to hire serving staff than kitchen help, unless your first party is really large, so let's look at how to create a serving team that will do you proud. After all, the service staff is a reflection of you. As Stacy Bogdonoff says, "They represent us when they're at a party."

Serving Staff. When hiring serving staff you should have in mind what your expectations are, how you want your workers to act, how you want them to look, and how you want them to think. This sounds a little like a Marine recruiter "looking for a few good men," but such considerations shouldn't be deemed restrictive. The best managers know what they want out of people and communicate it to them.

For Sean Driscoll of Glorious Food, this begins with explaining his demands to waiters at training seminars. "We're not tyrants," he says, "but I tell them 'I don't care what you were before you came to me and I don't care what you do when you leave the site of the party, but for those hours you have to do what we say.'" While someone is employed by you, particularly since it's only for a few crucial hours, you must be able to rely on them for total cooperation.

You and your staff must be able to work together as a unit. You need team players who are more interested in the job they are doing together than anything else, at least during their working time with you. They will also need to be flexible enough to switch from one task to another at a moment's notice, to respond quickly, even instinctively, in emergencies, and generally pitch in as needed.

For the team to work effectively they need to know what their responsibilities will be. They need to know the basic plan of action, as well as their specific tasks. Paul Neuman has the highest regard for his serving staff, and they for him, and one of the main reasons is that their duties are clearly laid out. "We don't throw them curves. The food is prepared, the garnish is ready. They know what they're getting into. A lot of caterers don't make the responsibilities clear-cut and the waiters are frazzled. They have to do the food, and then they have to do the dishes, and then they have to serve the customers, and they feel they're doing everything."

One way to keep serving people from feeling pressured, thus giving them "a chance to do a great job for you," as Paul says, is to tell them exactly what they will need to do. For instance, if they will be working a cocktail party of seventy-five people, the three servers rotating with platters of food will need to know how often to come back to the kitchen for refills, and how to coordinate hot foods with cold foods. One or more of the servers or one of the two bartenders may also be assigned the task of picking up empty glasses. In other words, everyone will need to know his or her specific job and how to fit into the team.

With the specifics of a job in mind, you have to make a judgment when interviewing applicants: will he or she follow orders, or is there an evident streak of obstinance? If they are independent, are they likely to come up with imaginative solutions to problems and pitch in?

What other qualities should you look for when hiring people? They should be pleasant and willing to help, but unobtrusive. Neuman and Bogdonoff's waiters embody these ideals. "We always take compliments on our help. They're attentive, and friendly. Even if they don't clean every ashtray, they're helping out. They make us look great. They get raves on the job. And then they like to work for us."

As you can guess from Paul's comments, the mutual respect of manager and workers helps to create a good working relationship. Another way is to project a calm, organized image yourself. Some caterers are notorious for appearing well in control to the client and taking their anxiety out on their staff. Such behavior does not make for good or long-lasting relationships, and one thing you want to cultivate is a trained, even loyal staff. The better prepared you are the less likely you—and your staff—are to get frazzled.

Dressing the Part. One of the easiest things to decide is how your staff should look. Wisdom dictates that serving staff be neatly and quietly dressed. Dark slacks or skirts with a plain (often white) shirt or blouse and comfortable shoes make good sense. Ann Vivian and David Hart dress their serving staff in cream-colored oxford cloth shirts and navy slacks or skirts. They feel that such a style reflects not only the traditional marketplace of Boston, but their general service attitude, which is professional, efficient, and unobtrusive, but also friendly.

Whatever you choose, make it something basic that most people will have, or won't cost them a great deal. If you choose to go with tuxedos, and sometimes you may have to, the tuxedo is usually the responsibility of the waiter. Sean Driscoll, whose waiters are always dressed in tuxedos, recommends thrift shops as good sources for inexpensive suits.

If you wish, you can add a signature apron, tie, or pin to distinguish a basic uniform. Any such extras are your responsibility.

Special costumes can add a distinguishing touch to certain parties, but they need to be planned with a degree of sensitivity to the surroundings and the occasion. Gary Goldberg remembers fondly the party he and his partner

Martin Johner catered at The Cloisters Museum, a fortress housing the Metropolitan Museum's collection of medieval art, in New York. Through the courtesy of a friend, an ex-Franciscan monk, the waiters were dressed as friars. The effect was charming given the setting, and the guests were delighted by the whole show. What works once, however, doesn't always work: when Gary and Martin took the same show down to the South Street Seaport development in lower Manhattan, an area of shops and eating establishments set waterside on an old wharf, the "friars" looked ridiculous amid the swarm of fifty thousand people. "People called us 'brother' and assumed that the proceeds of our sales were for the Franciscans," Gary remembers. They quickly shed the robes.

How Many to Hire?

For full-service parties, the rule of thumb is one server for every ten guests. This ratio of one staff person for every ten people includes waiters and waitresses, bartenders, and a pantry person who works full time in the kitchen. However, the ratio of servers decreases as the number of guests increases, depending on the type of party. Parties of over a hundred people tend to be cocktail parties and buffets, where there is not as much need for personnel, so you can decrease to something like one for twelve or at most fifteen people. The following shows how this would break down for three sizes and kinds of parties:

Seated dinner for 20
1 bartender/server
1 server
1 pantry person

Buffet for 50
1 bartender
3 servers
1 pantry person

Cocktail Party for 100

2 bartenders
4 servers (if hot and cold foods are to be passed)
1 pantry person

It's important for people to feel that the party you cater for them is the best it can be, and part of what they will be buying is the good service you provide. The only way to give good service is to have enough people working the party, yet the first economy measure clients often suggest is limiting the number of people on staff.

Clients may not realize how much more difficult such false economy makes your job. They also don't realize that the extra fifty or a hundred dollars they save would be more than made up in the smooth-flowing service that only enough staff people can provide. Guests waiting for drinks or trying to nab a morsel of food from waiters who pass by with empty trays are spending their time in frustration (albeit mild) when they should be enjoying themselves. Be firm with clients about staffing. As Stacy Bogdonoff says, "Skimping on service is bad for the party, and it reflects badly on me."

How much are these people going to cost, you ask. Are they paid by the hour or by the party? Who pays them? Are they tipped, and by whom?

Rates for serving people vary from place to place. You would be safe in estimating anywhere from $7.00 an hour to $15 an hour. That's a big range, and the $15 reflects trained people in big cities working for the most sought-after companies. Bartenders often earn a little more than waiters and waitresses. The best way to find out the going rate where you live is to call other caterers and ask.

One thing to keep in mind when considering fees is that as a rule, people who are paid well work harder and better. Generally serving people work on a fixed fee for a specific number of hours. This is the figure that goes into your final quotation. If for any reason they are requested to stay longer, the extra time will be added on at the hourly rate.

Service staff are paid at the end of the party, before they leave. If you have hired them, you pay them. Even if you haven't been paid for the party, it is your responsibility to pay promptly. Gratuities are usually the responsibility of the client. Make sure you state this when you discuss staffing with a client (see chapter 9 for a discussion of meeting with a client). If he or she asks how much would be appropriate, explain that 15 or 20 percent is not unusual.

If a party is particularly large, too large for you to handle all the cooking yourself, the kitchen staff you hire are your responsibility, and their cost (usually less than the serving staff, but up to you) will be covered in your overhead, and thus reflected in the cost per head for food.

Kitchen Staff. The primary reason for hiring someone is fairly obvious: there is too much work for one person to handle. An added benefit is that you can actually increase the amount of work you can take on, and thus your profits, by having one or more people helping to do the work of chopping, peeling, and washing up. Having help in the kitchen also cuts down drastically on the amount of time it takes to prepare for a party. All cooking can be handled on the day of the party. You will be allowed more time to be a normal human being, or to take on more work, and the food for the party will be guaranteed fresh.

Hiring kitchen help does not mean that you need to give up any of the creative aspects of catering. An extra pair or two of hands can take care of peeling and slicing five pounds of carrots, or shucking fifty ears of corn, leaving you free to concentrate on the creative aspects of cooking and presentation.

Ah yes, you sigh wistfully, how do I go about finding the perfect people to help me without interfering with what I like to do? First, treat hiring help as a business decision. This means try not to hire friends, unless you are pretty sure you can work with them on a professional level, which is a difficult task. Anybody you hire has to be able to work with you and for you. Friendships have been ruined over criticism of work methods.

The above notwithstanding, you probably will have to hire friends in the beginning. To reduce the possibilities for friction, set up the arrangement in as businesslike a manner as possible. State what the wages will be up front. Money among friends is one of the most difficult areas, so get it over with. Also state what you expect them to do and when you need to have it done.

Whoever you hire, unless you have the resources to tap into the increasing network of free-lance cooks and chefs, will probably be most useful if they have some kitchen experience, but are flexible enough to learn how you like your vegetables chopped or your sauces made.

Like service help, you also need people you feel comfortable instructing and ordering. They must be dependable and hard working, able to keep to a schedule. You need not fear that you must become a martinet, as in almost any working situation there can be room for a pleasant and relaxed atmosphere within a framework of hard, occasionally frantic, effort.

Within any environment, even one of blissful cooperation, there will undoubtedly be frustrations. You are most likely able to chop onions, peel apples, and wash lettuce faster than anyone you hire. Some of your staff may be too chatty for you or sloppy in some way. Occasionally, you may feel that if you did it all yourself you would be through in half the time. But whether you can do a job faster or not, if you did it all yourself you would be exhausted and less likely to be up to dealing effectively with the elements of the job that only you can handle.

One of the best methods for encouraging people to become efficient workers is for you to become a good manager. The payoff will benefit both your workers and yourself. The following is a list of suggested techniques for increasing productivity and happiness.

• Divide tasks by what people like to do. If everyone just loves to peel asparagus (hard to imagine), rotate the chore. In any case, rotate the tasks occasionally to keep people from becoming tired and bored with monotonous chores.

• Set up work stations for the various tasks. Place any equipment needed at the spot. For instance, if carrots are to be prepared arrange a setup of a cutting board, swivel peeler, knife, garbage bag, bowl of water, and empty bowl. This will keep someone from having to hunt up the peeler, borrow a knife, or trot to the sink every few minutes.

• Show people how you like certain tasks done. If you like your onions chopped finely, show them how you do it. Encourage them to devise efficient methods of their own. You have more experience, but you may be doing some chores out of habit which can be improved upon. For instance, you have two tomatoes that need peeling and your method of dropping them in boiling water seems time consuming for just two. Your helper always skins hers by skewering the tomato on a fork and running it over the burner for a few seconds. A happy solution for both of you has just been reached. She stays interested in the job and also helps improve the overall efficiency of the operation.

• If you have more than one person working with you, assign two people to the really tedious tasks, such as shelling shrimp. This not only makes the chore go faster, but it keeps people from getting tired or bored.

• Set up a break-time for lunch. Hard as it is, everyone works more efficiently if they take a break away from the kitchen, eat food other than that being prepared, and talk about life in the big world.

• Reserve the important aspects of creating dishes, particularly the seasoning, and special cooking for yourself. That way you won't have to worry about them being done to your satisfaction.

• Try to relax. In all probability the work will get done and it will get done more efficiently and pleasantly if you can act as the leader of the team.

The ideal number of people to hire varies from job to job. Smaller jobs often don't require any help, while really large ones will require many people. The number of people you can manage is an individual question dependent on the size of your kitchen, the number of dishes to be prepared, and the number of people you can supervise while still being able to cook yourself. Some caterers find that they can handle no more than three other people in their kitchens, others five or six. You may need to experiment to see how many you can handle before you spend all of your time supervising and no time cooking.

PART TWO
The Craft of Catering

6

Creating Menus

If you love food (and why else would you go into this business?) you probably already have a sense of how foods go together, the timing necessary to bring off a meal, and how the assembled food should look on the plates.

Menu planning, which is the sum total of all of these elements, is often one of the more creative aspects of starting out. It is work for active imaginations, and to some people, very much an adventure. As Stacy Bogdonoff puts it, "Menu creating is really a lot of fun. It gives me a chance to try out ideas."

Wait a minute, you say, I'm only planning on muffins, so why do I need menus? The simple answer is that if you are doing only one kind of food, then all you need are lists of the dishes. However, if you expand into doing afternoon teas, as Pamela Mitchell did, you will need more varied offerings. To cater an event, whether it's a cocktail party or an eight-course dress dinner, you need menus.

Don't worry about every last sprig of rosemary, at least for now. At this point your menus need only a point of origin. In fact, you will probably find as your business develops that your menus change constantly, perhaps with every party you give. To start out, however, you must have well-planned sample menus, together with cost calculations, for use as selling tools for your new business.

Catering is in part about fantasy, since people often use caterers to help them create out-of-the-ordinary events. As a result, part of your task in creating menus will be to make your food special. Maybe it will be in the choice of a few luxurious dishes, or the newest of the new, or maybe old favorites updated or given a little dash by a new method of cooking, serving, or presentation. The dishes you choose will distinguish you from the other cooks in town as well as lend you the aura of expertise you need to start out.

Begin with a simple premise: work with what you know and be confident of what you have. The "C" in catering might as well stand for confidence, as it is the basis on which all else rests. Catering is a public business, and it will be obvious to the first client who calls if you are trying to do something unfamiliar and you talk haltingly about it. Sell the dishes that you feel most comfortable with and the ones that are your most successful. These dishes need not be your own inventions, they can be your grandmother's tried and true, or straight out of a cookbook or magazine. But if you know them, your confidence will show through.

BASIC PLANNING METHODS

Many people plan meals around one key element, perhaps a dish that has won oooohs and ahhhhs over the years, a real showstopper. Christopher Idone, co-founder of Glorious Food, suggests that one limit oneself to one "bravura course" in a meal. That way, the rest of the meal can be constructed around it. Also, as Idone points out, good cooks can prepare tricky recipes, but they needn't show off their accumulated knowledge and skill in every course. After all, fireworks begin to look a lot alike after you've seen a few. As a practical matter, too, creating six or eight remark-able courses is such time-consuming hard work that you probably can't charge enough to justify them.

You may wish to start with a favorite dish as the focus of a meal, perhaps even a dessert like strawberry shortcake or a first course like trout pâté, but that's just the start.

Think back to your most successful parties. After you've picked your way through the unrepeatable elements that made them great, such as the company or the occasion, focus on the food. What was the combination of flavors and aromas? Did the flavors play off of each other? Were sweet things balanced with savory? Were smooth and creamy tex-tures set off by crisp or chewy foods? Did the aromas blend together to give an overall flow to the meal? Was there a variety of color on the assembled plates?

Was your timing such that the courses flowed smoothly from the appetizer through the main courses of the meal to the dessert? Were there no long pauses between courses while the sauce reduced? Was the soup hot and the ice cream softened?

In an ideal world everything always turns out perfectly but rarely so in the real, so there may be elements of many meals but only a few complete ones that stand out. One of your tasks as a caterer is to design menus which can achieve perfect balance and timing.

Balance is essential to menu planning. At its most ele-mentary, a balanced menu is composed of a range of ele-ments from the four basic food groups: meat, poultry, fish, or other protein; fruits and vegetables; breads and cereals; and milk and dairy products. We all learned this in the third grade and most people include, automatically, a represen-tation of these foods when planning a meal.

But balance is also about creating a meal of complemen-tary flavors, textures, and colors served in a manner that the courses can be enjoyed together (at cocktail parties and buffets) or serially (as with seated dinners). All menus should be viewed as complete meals in this sense, even tea parties and receptions.

No doubt everyone has experienced the party where things were a little out of balance. I remember vividly the brunch I gave that featured fruit salad, sweet Swedish pastry rings, pancakes, and sausages. The liquid refreshment was Bloody Marys and Mimosas. Everything was so sweet that the guests wolfed down the sausages at a record rate, and there was a line for the tomato juice.

I learned how not to plan a brunch from that meal in the same way that anyone who cooks a good deal learns the techniques of balancing. It becomes a matter of instinct after a while that a sweet dish needs to be balanced by a savory, that a crunchy dish is offset well by a smooth or soft one. This may already be second nature to you, but if it isn't, start thinking about balancing dishes as you plan.

Consider the following menu for a simple but elegant autumn dinner:

CHEESE PUFFS

VEAL STEW WITH WILD MUSHROOMS, CARROTS, AND PEARL ONIONS

IN A RED WINE SAUCE

WILD AND WHITE RICE PILAF

SAUTÉED BRUSSELS SPROUTS

TOSSED GREENS WITH BALSAMIC VINAIGRETTE DRESSING

GINGER PEAR TART

The cheese puffs, served with cocktails, are light in flavor and substance—no one is likely to have their taste buds deadened or their stomachs filled too early. The stew will be fairly delicate in flavor in keeping with the veal, and it will need something to catch the juice, thus the bed of white and wild rice. The slightly crunchy texture of the rice goes well with the smoothness of the sauce. Brussels sprouts sautéed with a little garlic and olive oil add contrast in color to the pale stew and rice as well as an earthy, slightly bitter flavor. French bread with sweet butter goes well with everything and can serve to catch any extra sauce. A green salad with a vinaigrette dressing served after the main course or as a first course adds color, a crispy texture, and a pleasing tartness. A ginger pear tart served with ice cream finishes the meal simply but elegantly in keeping with the tone set by the veal stew.

Consider Time vs. Cost

The meal described meets several criteria important to caterers. First, much of the meal can be made ahead, needing only last-minute heating or sautéing. The stew can be made up to three days in advance. The rice takes only twenty minutes to prepare (it can be precooked and reheated on site). The Brussels sprouts can be lightly steamed and then chilled in advance of the last-minute sauté. The salad greens can be washed a day ahead and stored until ready to be cut and combined about an hour before serving. The salad dressing can be made several days in advance and chilled. The pear tart can be made hours ahead, but should be made the day of the party.

The only cooking that must be done right before dinner is the reheating of the stew, the rice preparation, the quick sauté of the vegetables, and the warming of the bread and the tart. With only a slight variation in preparing the vegetable, in fact, this meal could even be dropped off and reheated by the client.

The autumn dinner also can be made profitably. The combination of ingredients is both luxurious and humble. Wild rice, wild mushrooms, and veal in any form are luxuries. Brussels sprouts and winter pears are seasonal and likely to be found at good prices. A combination of luxury ingredients and more humble ingredients is ideal, as the luxury elements make a relatively expensive price tag not unreasonable and the more affordable foods help your margin for profit. Furthermore, while requiring time to prepare, the meal is not particularly labor intensive. Any excess cost in ingredients is balanced by the ease of preparation. The resulting meal is special, but it can be produced at a reasonable cost.

As you create menus, evaluate each dish for the amount of preparation time required and the cost of ingredients. Within each category you should try to strike a balance between expense and time involved. Sometimes expensive ingredients take less time to prepare than inexpensive ones. For instance, broiled salmon with a mustard wine sauce takes little time to prepare, while an exotic but cheap Bosnian ragout might require fifty steps. When you serve the Bosnian stew just make sure that other dishes on the menu can be prepared fairly rapidly to balance out the cost of your time. When you serve the salmon, you may want to spend a little more time on one of the other dishes, perhaps by carving the humble carrots into lozenges before cooking.

Plan with the Seasons

Try to put to use seasonal fruits and vegetables. These days, with so many people interested in good fresh food, the amount of seasonal produce is practically unlimited, and foods in season have better flavor than those out of season. They also tend to be more reasonably priced.

Full-flavored tomatoes, for example, are available only in summer, when they are also inexpensive. At any other time of the year their flavor is such that they are best used only as decoration. Thanks to air freight, asparagus can be gotten most of the year, and asparagus is always considered luxurious. But in the spring, it is not only a harbinger of the greening days ahead but reasonably priced as well. Strawberries are a similar case (served in midwinter they look spectacular but have little taste). So instead, why not buy citrus fruits, which are at their peak at mid-winter, and skip the strawberries till springtime?

Dishes vary from season to season, too. A hearty beef stew tastes wonderful in the winter, but is too hot and heavy in the summer. A cold fish salad doesn't seem substantial enough in the winter. Even though people eat lighter year round than they used to, they tend to eat heavier and richer foods in the winter and lighter foods in the summer, particularly in hot climates.

Try an Occasional Special Effect. There are instances where making exceptions to the stand-by-the-season rule make sense. Sometimes, a specialty item served off-season can make a particular statement or add a special fillip to a meal. Raspberries, which do have flavor when shipped from South America, seem doubly special served in midwinter. Exotic tropical fruits and vegetables such as passion fruit, guavas, star fruit, cherimoya, and daikon, whose seasons often bear little resemblance to ours, can make a meal stand out above others.

When used judiciously, the expensive extra can add a special, even romantic element to both simple and elaborate meals. You may even want to provide one element of the exotic or luxurious in fairly modest meals.

A little bit of an expensive ingredient can go a long way to enliven a modest meal or increase the luxury of an expensive one. Everyone acknowledges a bowl of fine beluga caviar on ice as the ultimate in luxury, but how about a tiny dollop of relatively inexpensive caviar—it can make even common stuffed eggs or boiled potatoes special. Or garnish a basic fruit salad with a few slices of star fruit and people forget they're eating just apples, oranges, and grapefruit.

You also aren't required to use expensive ingredients to achieve special effects. Often you can use common ingredients in an unusual way, like cutting oranges and lemons into the shape of baskets and filling them with ice cream, fruit ice, or mousse. It takes time, but this and other techniques that rely on a combination of ingredients in a dish can achieve a special effect. (Summer tomatoes served with basil is a classic combination of this kind; pork roast smothered with fresh rosemary is another.) No doubt you have your own favorite combinations that win compliments every time you serve them.

What to Plan for

Much of the planning of actual meals must be dictated by your own interests and talents, but you should tailor menus to fit anticipated occasions, themes, and price ranges. If you plan to offer a full range of catering, it makes sense to plan at least two types of wedding reception food, several cocktail parties, and a number of kinds of dinners, all ranging in price from modest through moderate to luxuriously expensive.

Since customers hire caterers to provide something out of the ordinary, it's up to you to make your menus sound appealing. If clients wanted plain roast chicken, they could probably handle that themselves. However, if you suggest a chicken roasted with fresh herbs and stuffed with pâté, or cooked with a dried fruit stuffing, you may clinch the deal. If you have a specialty likely to become a signature item, such as miniature corn muffins, baby cheesecakes, or a special chutney, these will also add an element of the special. Be sure to work them into your menus.

Gathering Recipes

We've agreed: you start with your old favorites, the successes of last night and last year. You add some imaginative tricks here and there, as a fresh new dish or two can make even a fairly conventional menu up-to-date. But what happens when you run out of your own store of recipes?

To begin with, you don't need a repertoire of hundreds of dishes. You need enough to offer an interesting selection, but you need not feel you have to offer limitless alternatives. Where do you go for recipes? Cookbooks, naturally, food magazines, and newspapers are the most accessible sources. Once you find something you like try comparing it with other similar recipes. Fashions in food, as

CREATING MENUS 91

in all things, tend to be disseminated rapidly and you can find new twists to tailor dishes to your own methods just by reading several sources.

There are a number of other sources of food ideas, as well, besides the printed page. Sara Foster finds that eating in restaurants is a good source for inspiration. David Ziff and Alan Bell like to travel, and they encounter new food combinations in other parts of the country as well as in the food they eat in restaurants at home. They also recommend talking to other food people, like other caterers, restaurateurs, and cooks.

Practice

Practice any new recipes you choose and that you think you are likely to use frequently. Only by using them will you discover if something really works for you, or if it takes too long or should be modified.

When Pamela Mitchell started her muffin business, she wanted to be the Baskin-Robbins of muffineers and offer thirty-one flavors. To accomplish this, she adapted English tea bread recipes. She developed her own, too. Remember, part of practicing involves experimentation, naturally enough, and if you have good instincts about varying recipes, try improvising upon the new recipe you incorporate into your repertoire at any stage of your business.

Improvise if you wish, but practice you must. You don't necessarily have to test a recipe four or five times, but you do need to try things you've never made. Paul Neuman remembers his first party as a new caterer. The hostess asked if he could prepare roast lamb. "Naturally," he replied. Actually, he had never made it, so he went home and looked it up in Julia Child.

On the evening of the party, Paul, who was cooking the meal in the client's kitchen, put the lamb on as directed and continued preparing the meal. When he checked it after twenty minutes, the thermometer showed the meat was done. "Funny," he thought, "according to the recipe, it

FREE ADVICE
ON EXPENSIVE INGREDIENTS

SHELLFISH AND SEAFOOD

Shrimp and crab. Shrimp are expensive, unless you live in a Gulf state; they can also be a nuisance to prepare. However, shrimp are without doubt the most popular food known to party-going humanity.

One way to provide shrimp (or crabmeat) at reasonable cost (both in terms of time and money) is to use baby frozen shrimp or crabmeat in canapés mixed with other ingredients. Another is to use shrimp as a highlight for other less expensive ingredients.

Keep in mind, however, that any dish in which shrimp is the primary element requires fresh shrimp if at all possible.

If you live in an area where fresh crabs are available, the time invested in preparing them can be amply rewarded. Soft-shell crabs are both easy to prepare and elegant.

Lobster. Lobster is undeniably extravagant and often a nuisance to prepare. However, some people think that the ultimate compliment they can pay their guests is to serve them lobster. This sort of thinking means you can usually charge proportionately for the extra cost.

Caviar. Caviar is considered the epitome of luxury, and to play to that feeling, you can use small amounts of lumpfish caviar in dishes to great advantage. Remember, too, that caviar requires no preparation—just open the jar or carton and serve it up.

Salmon and swordfish. Fresh salmon and swordfish are fairly expensive but when grilled as steaks they are easy to prepare—their cost may be balanced by the saving in prep time.

A little smoked salmon can go a long way in flavoring dishes, or it may be presented in such a simple manner that the cost is made up in the time you save.

FISH, FOWL, AND GAME

Smoked trout and other smoked fish. Smoked fish, other than salmon, can be surprisingly reasonable, especially considering how exotic most people think they are. Often, they can be easily prepared for presentation, in such recipes as smoked trout with horseradish cream.

Duck, pheasant, and quail. These days, game birds are the chic alternative to poultry. They are expensive, though duck can sometimes be found at fairly moderate prices.

Rabbit and venison. These meats have both gained a trendy popularity and are becoming increasingly available, as both rabbit and deer specialty farms increase in number.

FRUITS AND VEGETABLES

All kinds of heretofore rare fruits and vegetables are now available in many cities, indicating that there is a new breadth of taste out there for the once exotic and slightly mysterious. Some of these foods, like kiwis, have become almost commonplace, while others, such as cactus pear and passion fruit, are still seen as a delightful novelty. The following is a short list of out-of-the-ordinary fruits and vegetables that are likely to meet with an appreciative public.

Fruit. Star fruit, papaya, kiwis, passion fruit, casaba melons, raspberries, wild blueberries, ginger root.

Vegetables. Asparagus, artichokes, fancy mushrooms (shiitake, straw, and morels), truffles, chestnuts, miniature vegetables of any kind, Belgian endive, radicchio, lamb's lettuce (also called mâche), and arugula.

---

shouldn't be done for another hour and a quarter." Relying on his thermometer reading, he took it out, remembering that he liked it pink himself.

He finished preparing the meal, and after serving the first course, began to carve the lamb. Needless to say, it was far short of rare but was practically raw. Panic set in as he wondered what to do. He couldn't delay the meal by having the hosts serve another round of cocktails, since the guests were already seated and were eating the first course. All he could do was crank the oven up high, carve the meat and cook it as quickly as he could. He beseeched the gods on Olympus to get him out of this mess and promised them if he could just eke this one out, he would never cater again.

The guests lingered over the first course an extra fifteen minutes. They never noticed the delay, and Paul went on to cater many more meals, though never again was he quite so ill-prepared.

CONSIDER THE EVENTS

Once you have assembled your tentative list of menus, you need to consider a number of other factors. Some of these considerations can be anticipated in advance (see table on page 97 of "Guidelines for Foods Requiring Prompt and Special Care"), while others must be dealt with when you make a quote on actual meals (when you know more about the number of guests and the physical setup of the client's kitchen, for example). The following are some important "situational" elements to be considered.

Kind of Party. Every party, be it a seated dinner, cocktail

party, wedding reception, luncheon, beach picnic, or a
sweet sixteen celebration, has its own requirements for
amount as well as type of food. At the same time, however,
there are some generalizations about categories of parties
that are helpful in planning.

For one, people tend to eat fairly lightly at cocktail parties, heavily at wedding receptions (the nervous guests tend
to make up for the scant appetite of the principals). When
sports are involved (particularly participatory ones), appetites are somehow enhanced.

People at buffets generally eat less than at seated dinners
—they tend to be talking, or it is too much trouble to go
back for seconds. Naturally, there are exceptions. One way
to be sure you will be covered for ravenous buffet eaters at
receptions is by having large cheese boards and plenty of
dips and vegetables in addition to elegant hors d'oeuvre.

In general, luncheons and daytime parties require lighter
and smaller quantities of food than evening parties. People
show more self-restraint and seem much more conscious of
their weight during the day. A notable exception is Sunday
brunch. (While it has its own distinct foods, treat it as an
evening meal with regard to richness and quantity.) Working business lunches have changed considerably over the
last few years. Once known for heavy cocktails followed by
heavier food, they tend now to be more streamlined and to
feature sumptuous but light food.

Size of Party. The number of guests will help determine
certain menus. Some dishes expand well to feed large
crowds; others are better suited to smaller intimate parties.
The first rule of number is, the larger the group, the more
conservative the menu, because the logistics of preparing
intricate food for twenty is far simpler than for five hundred. Also, the more people you have, the more food idio-
syncracies you are likely to encounter. If at all possible, try
to serve at least two main entrées to large groups. You will
have more breadth to show off and will more neatly fill the

KINDS OF MEALS
AND THEIR COURSES

Whether you are planning on full-service catering, or to specialize only in small dinners for the rich and famous, make sure the sample menus you have prepared offer the standard courses people expect—and that you have figured the cost of each into your estimated prices.

Below is a breakdown on the meals you may be offering and the fundamental parts of each.

COCKTAIL PARTY
Snacks
Hot hors d'oeuvre
  (at least two)
Cold hors d'oeuvre
  (at least two)
Fruit or dessert

SIMPLE SUPPER
Hors d'oeuvre
Main course
Vegetable
Bread
Salad
Dessert

BRUNCH
Main course
Vegetable
Bread
Salad (optional)
Dessert

PICNIC
Appetizer
Cold cuts/main course
Vegetable
Bread
Dessert
Beverage

LUNCHEON
First course
Main course
Vegetable (optional)
Bread (optional)
Salad
Dessert

DINNER BUFFET
Hors d'oeuvre
Main courses (two or
  more)
Vegetables (two)
Bread
Salad
Dessert

MIDNIGHT SUPPER	FORMAL DINNER
First course	Hors d'oeuvre
Main course	First course
Vegetable	Fish course
Bread	Main course
Dessert	Vegetables (two)
	Bread
RECEPTION	Salad
Punch (optional)	Savory
Sandwiches (at least two)	Dessert
Hot hors d'oeuvre	
(at least two)	
Cold hors d'oeuvre	
(at least two)	

needs of all the Uncle Joes who won't eat potato salad and the Aunt Susans who don't like chicken.

Certain kinds of food are difficult to prepare for large crowds as well. For instance, unless you will be working on a strict time schedule and from a large kitchen, you will be unable to serve cooked soufflés. Save your chocolate mocha soufflé for a small seated dinner. Similarly, hollandaise sauces must be made in small batches and served shortly after making, and thus are better suited to small parties. As Fanny Farkas points out, hors d'oeuvre are primarily a matter of assembly. Therefore, they tend to be well suited to large crowds.

Large parties and gatherings where people will be standing up to eat rather than sitting dictate certain types of food to avoid. This may seem obvious, but it is a major consideration when planning menus. Food that is difficult to chew or awkward to handle makes for embarrassing situations. We all know stories like the one about the wedding guest who, neat and tidy in appearance and movement, tried to cut the chicken on the paper plate in her lap using a plastic knife. The knife broke, the plate flipped, and the food spilled all down the guest's skirt. You can't be responsible for clumsiness, but you need to consider the guest's convenience.

Time of Day. A cocktail party that starts at 7 o'clock is likely to require more substantial food than one that starts at 5 o'clock. Make sure a client understands this when you discuss menus. If a client is feeling particularly concerned about money, you might suggest that the party start a little earlier in the evening in the hope that guests will be less hungry and less inclined to treat the party as dinner.

Parties that have specific beginning and ending points are far easier to plan for than those that can trail on and on, such as brunches and cocktail parties. An after-dinner surprise birthday party will be very straightforward, probably requiring little more than dessert and champagne or coffee while an open house can run at any time of the day, requiring several kinds of food. Suggest that the client choose a clear-cut time for the event, such as open house from 2 to 5 P.M., if they are concerned about cost, or cocktails, 6 to 8 P.M., if they are not. In any case, you will need to determine specifically how much will be needed.

Time of Year. The season is another consideration in menu planning. Winter food is different from summer food, as people change their eating habits to suit the seasons. At Christmastime, people often join in the elation present in the air, and eat and drink with more abandon than they would at other times. People at summer pool parties usually eat more lightly for a number of reasons, including the fact that they are more aware of how they look when they are wearing bathing suits.

The kinds of foods to be served varies greatly with the season as well. As we discussed earlier, hearty stews and meat dishes tend to be less popular (and are considerably hotter to fix) during summer months. Yet some of the traditional summer foods do not keep well in hot weather (foods such as melons, sandwiches, vegetables, anything made with mayonnaise or gelatin, as well as such old standbys as cheese). The key to successful summer food is both in the planning, so that ingredients can be combined at the last minute, and in the choosing of foods that can be served cold or lukewarm.

The Guests. The age group attending the party is another important factor. The eating habits of different generations are simply different. According to statistics as well as general experience, younger people are less accustomed to eating "three squares" a day. They tend to eat more casually, often making the food at a cocktail party their dinner.

As you might expect, young women tend to eat more vegetables and other lighter, less fattening foods. Men of all ages eat more substantial food, young men more than anyone. It's a good idea to have a selection of cheeses and meats with bread and crackers at a cocktail party when you know there will be a number of young men. Younger people of both sexes consume larger quantities of nibblings such as nachos, and chips or vegetables with dips. They also are more likely to choose wine and beer over hard liquor. Older people tend to prefer less rich and more easily chewable dishes.

People in their early twenties and those over sixty tend to be less adventuresome in their tastes. Children are, of course, least interested in unusual food, so don't try out your anchovy surprise at a child's birthday party.

Logistics. Plan according to the time needed to prepare the various dishes. Trying to juggle the execution of four or more dishes at once is difficult in the best of circumstances, and almost impossible in catering quantities while guests float through the kitchen. Menus composed primarily of dishes that can be prepared completely in advance and of a few that can be begun before and finished off at the party will probably be most successful. This is not to say that nothing can be prepared at the last minute on site, just that you should limit the number of such dishes.

You will also find that the facilities available to you will vary. Some clients will have beautifully equipped kitchens, others will have nothing. You may also find yourself doing parties in unusual settings that have no kitchen facilities. Alan Bell and David Ziff remember very fondly the party they catered to celebrate *A Chorus Line* becoming the longest-running musical on Broadway. The party was held outdoors for two thousand people in Shubert Alley, a broad pedestrian way between buildings in New York's theater district. The alley was covered by a tent, and the caterers rented a dark theater to serve from. But there were no kitchen facilities whatever. The food they chose, primarily hors d'oeuvre, was all assembled and arranged on platters at their kitchen.

When Glorious Food catered the Liberty Weekend festivities in New York, they faced an even greater logistical challenge. They had to serve dinner to almost three thousand and breakfast to a thousand—from no kitchens. Everything had to be brought to the island by boat, and all the food had to arrive fully prepared.

7

Quantity Shopping
and Food Preparation

If you love the process of food preparation you'll feel right at home in this chapter. In the following pages we will talk about the familiar steps of getting ready to entertain your guests. Only this time, they're your client's guests.

The old saying "time is money" is no less true in the catering business than elsewhere: profit in catering is determined in part by how efficiently one plans and works. As a result, an essential skill for you to master is shopping economically and efficiently.

SHOPPING

Understanding Economy. One secret to efficient shopping is appreciating that practical economics is a matter of balancing money-saving and time-saving. It is never economical to buy everything at the convenience store next door, nor is it to drive twenty miles to save four cents a pound on potatoes. It is uneconomical to underbuy and to overbuy, unless you can be sure you will use the extra.

Sometimes time rules, sometimes not. At first it may seem uneconomical to buy whole chicken breasts when you need boned breasts: boned breasts cost three times more than whole, but you have to bone them. However, given the price differential, and that with a little practice boning chicken breasts is short work, (plus the fact that you can use the bones for chicken stock) it makes sense to buy whole breasts. On the other hand, buying dried kidney beans to use as one of many elements in a salad isn't truly an economy, as canned kidney beans are quite inexpensive and require a whole lot less work for similar results.

Shopping decisions can't always be made solely on the basis of time or money. Some things, though they are labor intensive to make, really are better when homemade. If you have the time and inclination to make them, good jams, preserves, relishes, and preserved fruits are really worth the effort. They keep for months, so you don't have to invest time in making them before every job. Don't hesitate to feature them as a specialty. You may not have enough for every party, nor will they always be appropriate, so save them for the events that will best feature them.

The Stock Question. Anyone who cooks a good deal has at one time or another faced the issue of making his or her own stocks. Homemade stocks are definitely cheaper and better than store-bought, but they do take a certain amount of time. The classic method for keeping stock on hand is to keep a pot going on the back of the stove almost all the time. Whenever vegetables are peeled for a dish, the trimmings go in the pot; whenever a chicken is cooked the gizzards and other pieces are added. You might consider reducing the stock and freezing it in ice cube trays so you have a ready supply of concentrated stock on hand that requires a minimum of storage space. Keeping a stockpot going is a good method for keeping stock on hand, but it is time consuming.

Some caterers feel that anything less than a homemade stock is cheating, others think it doesn't make that much difference; still others wish they had their own but feel they don't have time to make the quantities needed. If you feel good stocks are important but just can't see your way clear to making them in large quantities you can compromise as Sally Godfrey does. She takes good quality canned consommé and doctors it with fresh vegetables and a little wine. While it's not quite as good as homemade, it's a lot better than most. This allows her to concentrate on other aspects of her cooking, such as making her own baking powder.

Watch for Specials. Watch the newspaper for specials and stock up on them when available. If chicken is a particularly good bargain one week and you have a freezer, buying enough for several meals or parties makes good sense. Even if you don't have a freezer you can lay in supplies. Canned Italian tomatoes last a long time and are almost guaranteed to be used. On the other hand, flour, seemingly forever fresh, goes stale and should be used within a few months of purchase.

Using Shopping Lists. While making jams, preserves, and stocks can be both economical and provide a special element that sets your food apart, most of your food planning will be figuring how to buy the right amount at a good price. People tend to buy too much at first, falling victim to impulse buying—I don't believe there is a person alive who has not done this. However, a good shopping list, strictly adhered to, can cut down drastically on panicky impulses.

Everybody knows how to make a shopping list, right? Most of us scribble things down as they occur to us, but a less haphazard approach must also be used. Since shopping for food is part of the cost of doing business, you need to learn to make lists that will make the most of your time and energy and will serve to organize your thoughts. A proper shopping list is more than a random listing of ingredients.

Making good lists can be a several step process. Begin by

organizing the list in sections for each type of food: fruits, vegetables, meat, poultry, fish, dairy, staples, bakery, and specialty items. Then check your recipes and the supplies on hand (will you need to supplement the chicken you bought on special and froze?) and enter the ingredients and amounts needed under each heading of the list, imagining how each dish will look when presented, including any garnish or decoration. This list will serve as both your shopping guide and as your master list of all the ingredients needed for the party.

Next, organize the list by making a second list. This may begin to sound like a chain letter, but it makes sense. Your second list will be organized by store and by traffic patterns within the store. If you plan your lists first by the stores at which you buy different ingredients such as the supermarket, fish store, delicatessen, and bakery, and then by the general traffic pattern you follow in the shop, you will be less likely to find yourself zigzagging the store, or skipping over items.

For example, in my supermarket the entrance is in the produce aisle. As I enter, I encounter the staple vegetables such as carrots, onions, and potatoes. Leafy green vegetables are next, special seasonal vegetables and herbs, and the fruit section follow. The end of the aisle runs into the meat counter, which runs all along the back of the store. If I plan my lists according to my traffic pattern it not only saves me time in the store, but I am more aware and relaxed, and better able to make decisions because I am not as frazzled trying to make sure I'm not missing things on the list.

Once your lists are organized as to what you need and where to find it, it is time to think about when to buy. In general, the fresher your ingredients, the better your food. Many caterers prefer to shop for the bulk of their ingredients the day before, or at most two days before the party. They leave a few things such as lettuce, bread, and fragile fruits and vegetables to the day of the party. Your particular time schedule and menu will determine just when you shop.

Try to plan your shopping trip for a time when you are fresh and alert. It is awfully easy to leave the shopping to the end of a day, or after a frazzled morning of errands. Easy, you think, if my lists are well prepared, I won't need to make decisions. Not so. You will find you need to make choices constantly. If the supermarket is out of a brand you usually buy, can you substitute with another brand in a different size? Should you buy extra? People who are tired are more likely to overbuy, overestimating the amount people eat or feeling that the extra will somehow be used. Sometimes the extras do keep, but if such items are in any way perishable, you may find your profits dwindling as your garbage grows.

Another trick that many people use to keep their decision-making faculties sharp is to shop on a full stomach. Everyone overestimates the amount of food needed when we find ourselves starving at the grocery store. We tend to overstock either on everything or on what we are craving at that moment. The one thing you need to be careful of when shopping on a full stomach is assuming that everyone who comes to the party will be full like you are at the moment. Stick to your lists; they will not let you down.

Another helpful method for utilizing your time wisely is to observe the best times for shopping. Deliveries are usually made twice a week in supermarkets; question a clerk to find out when the shelves are restocked. Simple observation will quickly show you the least crowded, and thus less frustrating times. Obviously, if your cheese shop does a roaring sandwich business at noon, you don't want to be there.

In many areas, such information is common knowledge. Zabar's, a popular New York delicatessen, is busy in the bakery department early in the morning for the breakfast trade, and in the whole store from 4 P.M. until closing for the dinner crowd. Weekends are an absolute madhouse at all times and virtually no one who feels rushed for time or likes a little breathing space can afford to shop then. The best time to shop there in relative peace is between 9 and 12 weekday mornings.

Whenever you choose to shop for the party, plan it so that you make the fewest number of stops in the smallest possible area. Driving across town to save twenty cents per pound on asparagus is a false economy unless you buy a number of other ingredients at the same time.

Just as you plan your shopping within a store by the traffic patterns, plan your stops in the same manner. Many people find it helpful to begin with the supermarket where the basics are found, then they feel the core of the meal is taken care of. When you check out, pack your own bags or boxes. That way you can organize them yourself. Make sure that cold and frozen foods are kept together. They will stay cold longer and you won't find yourself hunting through five other parcels to find that last container of sour cream when you get home.

If you live in a city and don't own a car, it is even more important to plan your shopping route. You are probably already used to planning your stops, but you may also be accustomed to hopping out at the last minute for one or two forgotten items. Unless you have plenty of people around to help, you won't have time to keep running to the corner. City dwellers have a tendency to skip items on a shopping list, thinking that there is probably some at home, not wanting to take up the precious space to store two. They also tend to buy fewer things in an effort to limit the bulk and weight of the bags they're carrying home. The result is extra trips to the store when the cream has been forgotten, then for the butter, or the bread crumbs. If you haven't already done so, now is the time to start using the delivery service that most city supermarkets and other stores provide.

Stores you are likely to frequent will be a good delicatessen, an import store for specialty items, a greengrocer, butcher, and fish store, if available. Each of these stores, despite their higher prices, can provide not only the ingredients you are unlikely to find elsewhere but sometimes invaluable information. The people at the fancy cheese shop should know which of their cheeses are at their peak and can often make suggestions of good combinations. The deli owner may be able to steer you to a new kind of salami or recommend an interesting variety for a charcuterie platter. The butcher may be able to tell you something about which cuts to buy and how to cut meat to the best advantage, not to mention cut it for you. The greengrocer can tell you what is the best buy on any particular day and may be willing to order specially for you. The fancy food shop owner may have a new shipment of special European crackers that would be interesting to try.

Learning about the features of small shops means, of course, spending some time and money at them. Developing a rapport with the small shopkeepers does not mean that you have to buy all of your goods there. If the supermarket is having a special on asparagus that the greengrocer does not, buy them at the supermarket and don't feel guilty. Absolute loyalty to your suppliers, forsaking all specials elsewhere, is unnecessary. Just because you didn't buy the strawberries from Joe at the wholesaler's doesn't mean that you can't next time.

Taking the time to comparison shop is another matter altogether. If you feel you have it, great, you will save yourself money. It probably makes sense on large orders most of the time. On smaller items that you buy regularly, comparison shop on one or two a week. Before you know it, you will be a walking, talking pricing expert.

Shop Yourself. Resist the temptation to have someone else do your general shopping unless you know the person's buying habits and can anticipate them in your planning, or unless you can organize your lists so carefully that there is no room for choice.

Even those of us who list every conceivable item carry a

certain amount of information around in our heads. For instance, let's say I need canned tomatoes for a pasta dish. I usually use Italian plum tomatoes of a certain brand. Today, however, there is another brand of peeled Italian plum tomatoes on sale for half the price of my usual ones. My stock of tomatoes also happens to be low, so I buy a case of them. If I send someone else out to shop I can't reasonably say to them "If you see a sale on imported Italian plum tomatoes stock up on them, but be sure not to get the kind that have tomato sauce, and be sure that they have basil, but not onions. Now, if the store is all out of them, buy two extra cans of the regular tomatoes, but make sure they are not the stewed variety." Presumably you have particular feelings about a number of foods and if you try to explain all this to someone else he or she is likely to find themselves paralyzed, stuffed with information which may or may not be useful—and that they may or may not remember.

Buying Wholesale

Buying food from wholesalers is another option. There are two schools of thought among small caterers about

SHOPPING TIPS

• Stock up on meat and poultry on special and freeze until ready to use.
• Do the majority of the food shopping one or two days before the party.
• Buy bread, fish, and fragile vegetables such as salad greens the day of the party.
• Separate foods that need freezing or refrigeration and either buy them last, or pack them in a cooler in the car.
• Resist buying on impulse.
• Keep family items separate from job items when shopping.

whether it is worth it to buy wholesale, as prices are not always lower unless bought in large quantity. The right answer is different for different people in different places.

The value of using a wholesaler is primarily for the discount prices and high quality of food they provide. However, unless you can place large orders, you sometimes won't see great savings. On the other hand, some purveyors carry items difficult to find in average stores. One definite service that wholesalers provide is delivery, usually for free.

To determine if ordering wholesale is a good option for you, look in the yellow pages for wholesale suppliers and make some calls. When speaking with a salesperson, find out who else the company supplies. If they supply good restaurants you can be confident of the quality. Ask if they can handle the kinds of orders you are likely to place. The salesperson will tell you whether they can or not, and often will be able to direct you elsewhere if they can't.

Find out what the minimum orders are for certain goods —do they sell chickens only by the dozen or can you buy six? Can you buy two cases of raspberries but only three heads of lettuce? Can they guarantee delivery on the day you request? Can you open an account or do they require payment COD? Don't be surprised or put off if the policy is COD. Check the prices and policies of several places.

If you decide to use wholesalers for some of your food, it pays to get to know the company a little. Try to deal with the same people when you call, as that way they get to know what you like and you get to know what they mean. You will also be better able to bargain with them and, unlike supermarkets, wholesalers can strike deals on large orders.

Getting a good deal depends on your negotiating talent. Many people love haggling, an equal number dread it. Whatever your style, don't expect special deals or service unless you do a fair amount of business. Follow your own instincts, but in all dealings try to be professional and firm but friendly. Suppliers must know that you cannot tolerate substandard goods delivered late; indeed, your livelihood depends in part on their service.

If you are lucky, you will be able to find suppliers in your area, rather than across town. Often this is not possible, but if you do find one nearby it is worth considering developing a relationship with them even if you don't plan to use them all the time. Inevitably, at some point, a delivery won't arrive or it will be too late to change something from across town. A close supplier can be a lifesaver at such times, even if the price is a little higher.

Try to visit the wholesale suppliers you consider using. Only by visiting will you be able to see firsthand the quality of merchandise they offer. Also, you can actually show your salesperson what you mean by lean beef or ripe strawberries. Many people pay closer attention to the needs of someone they have met in person.

Once you have developed your sources, wholesale and retail, you can relax a little, confident that you will have the ingredients for a successful party. You are also one step further along toward an organized business and can now begin thinking about preparing the food.

FIGURING QUANTITIES

No doubt you already have a fairly clear sense of portions to serve, particularly if you like to entertain. But how often do you serve two entrées at your own dinners, or six kinds of hors d'oeuvre, as may be the case at many of the events you cater? And how do you advise a client on drinks to serve and setting up a bar?

There are no absolute rules when it comes to figuring how much people will eat. It depends on many things, such as the ages of guests, the time of year, kind of event, and a multitude of unknowns. As Neuman and Bogdonoff point out, "You can serve the same meal at Sunday brunch and Thursday dinner and people will eat differently, and you

TIPS FOR DEALING
WITH WHOLESALERS

• Have your complete order prepared before you call.

• Speak with the same person each time you call.

• Discuss the availability and price of ingredients you need.

• Don't hesitate to call elsewhere if the prices seem too high or prompt delivery seems chancy.

• Stress that you will not accept anything but the best merchandise and if they deliver substandard goods they will be returned.

• Get a guaranteed delivery time.

• Be prepared to pay in cash on delivery.

• When the order arrives, check every item before the delivery person leaves. If the fruit is unripe or the chicken parts not what you asked for, return them; next time the supplier should do better.

don't always know why." The following are a few guidelines to help you plan.

Hors d'Oeuvre. The number of appetizers that people eat can be tricky to figure. However, as a guide, allow around a dozen per person for a cocktail party, six to eight if dinner will follow. The more kinds you serve, the more people will eat, sampling most varieties at least a couple of times.

Meat and Poultry. The general rule for figuring meat or poultry as a main course is to allow half a pound (boneless) per person or one and a half to two chicken pieces. If you have two meats, say a roast and a ham, figure a half pound total. If you use meat in a stew, you won't need as much, so figure a quarter to a third of a pound per person—a quarter if there are a lot of vegetables, a third if the emphasis is on the meat.

STOCKING UP

Foods with long shelf life

Canned Italian tomatoes
Tomato paste
Pickles
Canned chicken and beef
  broth
Artichoke hearts

Olives
Prepared mustard
Soy sauce, worcestershire
  sauce, ketchup
Commercial mayonnaise

Foods with 3-to-6-month shelf life

Flour
Sugar: brown, white,
  confectioners'

Dried pasta

Foods to be frozen up to 3 months

Chicken
Beef
Lamb
Puff pastry, sheets and
vol-au-vents

Phyllo pastry
Butter
Cream puffs
Berries

Another exception to the rule is determined by the size of the crowd. People eat less at large parties (say fifty or more), so figure about a third of a pound per person, or one and a third pieces of chicken. If the gathering is primarily of people over the age of fifty, figure a quarter to a third of a pound of meat or chicken, as you would with a stew, since older people eat less meat.

Fish and Seafood. Here again, figure half a pound per person for small groups and a third of a pound for large crowds. Fish and seafood can be tricky, however. You may have a crowd that loves it, or you may have one that prefers landed protein. There's one thing certain, though, they will eat as much shrimp and as much smoked salmon as you can put out. You'll need to choose an amount that the budget can handle when figuring shrimp. Smoked salmon is a little easier, in that you can figure two to three slices as a general rule, and anything extra you provide will undoubtedly be eaten.

Vegetables. The general rule for vegetables is to allow half a cup of beans, peas, and such; one potato; and four asparagus stalks per person for the average party. At large parties, figure a quarter cup of vegetables, half a potato, but keep the asparagus at four stalks.

Salad is figured by the handful. Allow one moderate-sized handful per person for average parties, one smallish one for large groups.

Pasta, Grains, and Bread. Most of us tend to think people will eat up pasta and grains at the same rate as everything else. For some reason they don't, and again, the larger the party, the less they devour. When figuring rice, you will be safe if you allow up to an ounce of uncooked rice per person. Depending on the dish and how it is used (whether main dish or side dish), you can figure anywhere from eight to sixteen people per pound of dried pasta. Bread can be popular or not, depending on the crowd. The average loaf of good bread will serve twelve to fourteen people.

Dessert. Allow a third to a half a cup of desserts such as mousses, puddings, and compotes, depending on the richness of the dish and the meal it accompanies. A ten-inch pie will serve eight, a ten-inch cake ten, and a two-quart soufflé ten.

One final note about quantities: when figuring the number of people to prepare for, be sure you allow enough. You don't want to swim in the extra, as you can kiss your profit goodbye, but it's probably even worse for you to bring too little. Any good host would prefer to have too much rather than too little, and you may need to feed a few more than intended. Fanny Farkas remembers her first party for four hundred people, not because of the food, or the logistics of preparing it, but for the portions. She had thought that food for four hundred meant just that, and she took the exact quantity, not figuring in the volunteers who worked the party. She was mortified when she discovered that there wouldn't be enough for the large staff.

Figuring the Drinks

One of the areas you will probably find yourself asked about frequently is that of the drinks. Clients often need guidance in figuring quantities, as novices are likely to greatly overestimate or underestimate amounts needed. How many old-fashioneds has the client really served in the last fifteen years and do they really need setups for every imaginable drink? Conversely, will all their guests be drinking scotch, or might some have switched to wine or soft drinks? Would a punch be appropriate? As the expert you can suggest the range of beverages to include. Most clients provide the liquor themselves, and in most states you need a liquor license to sell it to them anyway. But you can place the order as one of your services.

As for drink quantities, figure one to two glasses of wine or cocktails before dinner, two to three or possibly four for a cocktail party, depending on the drinking habits of the crowd and the duration of the party. Cocktails are generally mixed using one and a half ounces (one jigger) of liquor to several parts mixer, depending on the size of the glass, the amount of ice, and the guest's preference. About six ounces of wine is allowed for each person, making four servings per standard-sized bottle of 750 ml. Jug wines come in varying sizes from two to three liters. (The chart on pages 116–17 is a handy reference that you might want to give to clients.)

As a side note, the issue of alcohol at parties is increasingly important these days, particularly in the way of liability. Gary Goldberg suggests that clients serve wine instead of hard liquor. This makes sense for several reasons. First, food tastes better when the taste buds aren't dulled by hard cocktails. Second, it's easier to serve, as waiters can pass through crowds with trays of glasses, eliminating crowded bars. Third, the client can make a specialty of the drink served, like Gary and Martin Johner, for example, who create wine drinks especially for parties. One of their current favorites is a little reminiscent of a Bellini—it's composed of champagne and peach schnapps, and is both light and festive.

Tips for Cooking in Quantity

Cooking in quantity is a technique like any other and requires a certain amount of practice in order to feel comfortable. At first, you may find yourself using pots that are way too large or small because until you've done it a few times it's difficult to gauge physical quantities. You may also find that certain things, like making sauces or reducing stocks, take much longer than you're used to, which makes sense given the increased volume, but can't really be figured until you've done it. The following are a few suggestions that may help as you learn.

Seasoning. Add salt toward the end of cooking to avoid oversalting a dish. Also, make sure not to double the seasonings when doubling a recipe. Taste it instead, as some foods require more salt than others when increased.

Herbs need not always be doubled and, here again, go slowly and add gradually until the proper taste is achieved. Sauces need not be doubled when doubling the size of a casserole or stew, as one and a half times the sauce is usually plenty.

Sweetening. Sugar is another ingredient that shouldn't automatically be doubled. For some reason, it goes further than you would imagine. When doubling recipes, go easy, adding more as needed.

Accenting. Occasionally you will find that a dish needs perking up, or toning down. Often a squeeze of lemon juice can enhance the flavor of vegetables and sauces, while a

STOCKING THE BAR

A Fully Stocked Bar for 25

The Basic Summer Bar	The Basic Winter Bar
1 quart scotch	3 quarts scotch
1 quart bourbon	2 quarts bourbon
3 quarts vodka	2 quarts vodka
3 quarts gin	2 quarts gin
2 quarts rum	1 quart rum
4 bottles dry white wine	4 bottles dry white wine
2 bottles dry red wine	2 bottles dry red wine
1 dozen bottles beer	1 dozen bottles beer

If the crowd is particularly young, increase the amount of vodka, rum, and beer and decrease the amount of scotch, bourbon, and gin.

Figuring ice: Allow 1 pound of ice per person plus 10 pounds for every 25 people.

Mixers

Summer	Winter
10 quarts tonic water	5 quarts tonic water
6 quarts club soda (10 if serving white wine spritzers)	10 quarts club soda
2 quarts ginger ale	2 quarts ginger ale
2 quarts orange juice	1 quart orange juice
3 quarts cola	2 quarts cola
4 quarts diet soda	3 quarts diet soda
5 limes	3 limes
5 lemons	3 lemons

At all times:
  1 small bottle dry vermouth if martinis will be served.
  Ice bucket, water pitcher, jigger, paring knife, bottle opener, corkscrew, cocktail napkins.

little bit of sugar can smooth out the acidity of tomato-based dishes.

Mixing. Take care not to overmix flour when cooking in quantity. This is one of the reasons cake recipes are not easily doubled. The same holds true for soufflés. If you make soufflés, make them individually.

Combining. It's easy to overmix and thereby break down

STORING FOOD COOKED IN ADVANCE

When cooking food in advance of a party you must be sure to store it properly.

• **Hot foods** should be cooled rapidly, covered, and refrigerated to prohibit the production of bacteria. Cool foods in the refrigerator or in shallow pans of ice or very cold water.

• **Hot cooked foods** ready for transport should be carried in insulated boxes or bags to maintain food temperatures at 140 degrees.

• **Cold foods** should be stored at a maximum of 45 degrees.

• **Mayonnaise-based sauces** must be refrigerated immediately after making.

• **Breads and cakes** should be cooled and frozen, if made more than a day in advance.

• **Washed greens** should be dried and wrapped in damp paper towels before chilling.

GUIDELINES FOR FOODS REQUIRING PROMPT AND SPECIAL CARE

Raw cut fruits and vegetables. They tend to wilt or dry out if left uncovered and unrefrigerated for more than thirty minutes or an hour. Since cutting time immediately before serving is usually hard to schedule, make sure you have plastic wrap and plenty of refrigerator space.

Hot soufflés. They are hard to make in quantity and timing the serving is difficult. If you are not a very practiced soufflé chef, skip them, or only try them with small dinners—at a patient client's home.

Hollandaise and other sauces. Most sauces are difficult to make in large batches and tend to curdle when kept warm for a long time. Prepare as close to serving time as possible.

Pastries and sandwiches. These tend to become soggy easily, particularly when filled with moist ingredients, unless they are to be served as they come out of the oven or off the board.

Deep-fried foods. Batter-fried vegetables need to be served immediately, as do most deep-fried foods. Fried chicken can be prepared in advance if it is to be served at room temperature.

Gelatin mixtures. Gelatin salads, aspics, molds, and bavarians tend to soften and can even melt when kept in a warm room for long.

Melted cheese. Once melted, cheese toughens. It should be eaten just out of the oven; if precise timing of courses will be a problem at a job, melted cheese dishes should be avoided.

delicate mixtures such as soft vegetables and fragile salad greens. Try to keep a light hand.

Sauce-Making and Reductions. When making large quantities of sauce or reducing large quantities of liquid, leave extra time, up to two or three times the expected time, or pour the liquids into shallower pans to speed up the process.

8

Making It All Look Great

Catered food must look as good as it tastes—it's one of the things that distinguishes the special from the everyday. It should look appetizing and not overly fussy, as though it came from the client's kitchen prepared by a master hand. It is as important that a simple ragout look as inviting as a trout in aspic. Equally important to the look of the food is that it be served in a manner that will highlight or enhance its beauty.

DECORATING, GARNISHING, AND ARRANGING

Presentation and flavor go hand in hand. For some people, if the food looks beautiful it tastes wonderful. Others of us reserve judgment until the results of the taste tests come in. But everyone responds to good food beautifully presented.

Sean Driscoll of Glorious Food tells of an elegant dessert that they serve regularly to large parties—from four hundred to a thousand—called "The Three Berries." It is a dish of fresh berries served imaginatively, sometimes arranged on clay platters or on leaves. A simple sauce of crème fraîche, Grand Marnier, or raspberries is served separately. Even though the dessert is simple, the presentation of it makes it seem special. "People get a very big kick out of it," Driscoll says, "and they forget that they are eating strawberries, raspberries, and blueberries." This is the secret of serving food with style, to make anything, even the most humble berry or chunk of cheese, seem special.

Some foods look better than they taste and others taste better than they look. The crestfallen feeling of biting into a gorgeous-looking cake only to taste nothing but sugar and shortening is universal. Conversely, who hasn't been surprised by unenthusiastically tasting a dull brown something, maybe it's a casserole, only to discover to one's intense delight the most marvelous flavor. You feel guilty for having doubted it.

When you cater a party you don't want anyone to feel guilty for having doubted your food or worse yet, pass it by because it wasn't pretty. Luckily, simple presentation techniques can help make the humble-looking look great and the great-looking stand out.

The Overall Presentation. One of the things that becomes apparent when you think of food as visual art is the maxim that less is more. Nouvelle cuisine presentations seem to best typify this. An exquisite carrot chrysanthemum posed with a tiny sorrel and scallop soufflé on a nest of beet purée can make a breathtaking picture. Of course such effects can be taken to silly extremes with yawning expanses of plate surrounding minute portions of improbable food.

On the other end of the spectrum, a giant bowl overflowing with tempting fruit looks exaggeratedly large and inviting while a platter decorated with fourteen kinds of fluted vegetables and piped decorations is confusing and fussy-looking. More or less food on a plate or platter is not the key to a good presentation: rather, it is that the food be interestingly arranged with a sense of scale and proportion and a minimum of fuss.

A light hand and careful planning of a table, platter, or plate is all you need to show off your food to best advantage. You can use ingredients sparingly or in abundance, but the result should be that the food looks as though it was prepared effortlessly. You may rely primarily on placing your food in interesting patterns, or choosing one exquisite garnish, or lavishly decorating with a single ingredient.

In all probability you will use all of these techniques, as different dishes call for different presentations. If you are creating a buffet table, you will want a range of looks, depending on the dishes being served—nothing is more static than seeing all the dishes on a table arranged in the same manner. Clearly, no thought has been given to the particular dishes when all ten are arranged with a neat rim of parsley. Conversely, a table set with ten different motifs is confusing. Arrangements should be made with attention to the different kinds of dishes being presented, their size and containers, with foods simply and appealingly decorated.

Often it's hard to visualize just how a plate, platter, or table will look when laden with food. Caterers often create diagrams in order to better organize their thoughts on food presentation. They need not be drawn to scale, or even very realistically, for the purpose is to help in placing, sizing, and shaping the foods.

The following are some techniques that will help set your food apart as special and appealing to look at as well as eat. Appetizing presentations of food can make the difference between just good food and really special food because they help create expectations of the delicious flavors to come.

Serving Dishes. When choosing serving platters, consider the occasion. A formal party deserves formal dishes, just as a casual one is best served by informal serving ware.

This does not necessarily mean you have to keep Limoges platters on hand along with rustic wooden bowls. If you want to, that's fine, but you don't have to. Plain white china of classic design tends to blend with the widest variety of dinnerware. The food and decorations can dress it up or down.

You may want to develop a signature look. Some people collect interesting baskets to use, others, special trays or bowls. David and Mary Ellen Shubbert of Top Bananas in Atlanta are always on the lookout for unusual serving containers, using all kinds of baskets, bowls, and trays, including pizza paddles and mirrored trays. Their rule of thumb is that if a rental supply house has it they won't use it.

One of the secrets to using special serving dishes and containers successfully is knowing when to use certain pieces. Your rustic whiskey keg would look out of place next to the swirling silver candelabra on a formal buffet table. But delicate Chinese baskets would harmonize nicely. An informal supper featuring hearty food is a terrific time to show off Mexican platters, Italian crockery, Bulgarian bowls, and handmade wooden trays and baskets. Gleaming copper pans look smashing on almost any kind of table. Occasion notwithstanding, sometimes an unusual juxtaposition of food and serving container can make an exciting statement.

Keep in mind the size and shape of foods when choosing serving dishes. A long platter accents the shape of a rolled cake better than a round one, which tends to foreshorten it. A special country ham or roast looks more luxurious resting on a large platter than on a formfitting small one. The shape and texture of most bread loaves makes them ideal for serving in oval baskets.

Consider also the color of food when choosing serving dishes. Contrasting colors tend to heighten the visual impact. For instance, dishes with cream sauces are set off well by dark-colored crockery. A round burgundy bowl can elevate a head of steamed cauliflower to the exotic.

Vivid dishes stand out against white backgrounds. Hearty peasant food such as chili, cassoulet, and dried bean dishes look terrific in earthenware. Bright-colored sauces look beautiful served in glass bowls. Here again, the kind of food you serve will lead you to the kinds of dishes to serve it in. Choosing containers that show your food to best advantage is part of the art of presentation.

The Food. The presentation of food on plate, platter, or bowl is the aspect of good presentation that people worry about the most. For many people, radish roses, spiced red apple rings, and miles of piped mayonnaise are the symbols of the old-fashioned decorated plate. Today one is more likely to see a nasturtium blossom gracing a fashionable platter than an iceberg lettuce leaf. All you need to create attractive presentations are a little imagination and the ability to use a variety of ingredients.

The secret to enhancing the appearance of food is the same as the creation of dishes and menus in that you must balance and highlight taste, color, and texture. Not all dishes, of course, benefit from accenting all three. A stuffed egg, for instance, subtle in flavor and color, stands out when garnished with a tiny sprig of Italian parsley, but it does not need a crunchy contrast to its smooth texture. A handful of slivered almonds sprinkled over the top of a trifle add both taste and texture and, more incidentally, color.

Your style of garnishing and decorating food can become a personal statement—not so wild that it detracts from the food or surroundings, but something that signifies how you feel about the food. Perhaps you arrange food in a particular manner, or use certain ingredients in an unusual way. Perhaps it is the use of a lemon slice, a method of twisting edible garnishes, or some other food like a traditional corn fritter, a special roll, bread, or other baked product. The choice is yours.

There is one rule that caterers seem to agree on: whatever you use to garnish a plate, make sure that it is edible.

Food is most beautifully enhanced by other food, as the colors and textures are naturally harmonious, allowing the star, the food on the platter, to stand out. A perfect rose, resting decorously on a plate of appetizers can easily over-shadow the food itself. It's bad enough when a food garnish takes over, but when it is something else, it is even more disconcerting. Stone sculptures do not enhance a platter of food. Nor do plastic umbrellas, or paper frills around indi-vidual canapés. (Doily-lined platters are another matter.)

To bring the esthetic down to the practical, the last thing you need to worry about is that someone might accidentally eat a nonedible garnish. This is not to say that you intend for people to eat the chive flowers on the plate with the cucumber canapés, but it won't hurt them if they do. For both esthetic and culinary reasons, bunches of plastic grapes nestled among beautiful cheeses are out. Instead of a parasol in a drink, how about a wedge of fruit? It's both tasty and beautiful.

Taste. The best decorations and garnishes are those that enhance the flavor of the food while enhancing the appeal. Not all dishes require or benefit from a tasty decoration, but some do. The classic combination of salmon with dill is a good example. The fresh flavor of dill complements the richness of the fish, while the green of the herb points out the intense pink of the fish.

Texture. Some decorations and garnishes add texture to dishes. Croutons floated on soup add such a touch, as do crumbled fried bacon and chopped cucumber. They all add flavor as well.

Color. For many people, determining the color to perk up a dish is of paramount importance. The principal food colors are red, yellow, brown, and green. By highlighting the overall color of the dish with a second color you create excitement. Red foods, such as tomato-based sauces, natu-rally call for green as an accent to make them stand out. Brown food such as stews, grains, and vegetables like egg-plant and potato look well with bright shades of red, green, or yellow as highlights. Yellow dishes such as saffron rice, curries, and rutabagas look pretty with red or green accents. White dishes such as rice, peeled potatoes, turnips, and dishes with cream-based sauces, or mayonnaise provide a neutral base that look good with almost any color.

Intense shades of colors also make food stand out. Float a slice of tomato on a pale tomato or shrimp soup, a thin slice of artichoke heart or a sprig of watercress on a pale green soup and the dish becomes alluring.

The art of decorating and presenting food need not be daunting. Indeed, many people find the final preparations for a dish most rewarding, a fitting send-off before the food faces public scrutiny. Sometimes an imaginative new garnish can make a standard dish seem updated.

Food magazines and slick full-color cookbooks are good sources for the newest decorating ideas. Once you have an idea, practice it, arranging platters and plates, or making a quick sketch. All you really need to remember is that the food is the focal point and the garnish is there to accent it, not overpower it. With that in mind, refer to the table that follows with its suggestions of garnishes and decorations. Feel free to invent your own. Once you've developed your own sense of the garnishes and decorations suitable to the meal, you'll be ready to move on to preparing it.

SERVING

There are few things sadder than seeing lovingly made and beautifully arranged food badly served. This applies to all kinds of food, from platters of salmon-topped cucumbers to plates of fried chicken and slaw. If food is not thoughtfully served, it can lose much of the effect of your time and effort. Of course, sometimes you may not control the serving, in which case you can't worry too much, and should just try to plan foolproof beautiful menus, but for the most part you will be in charge and can control the pacing as well as the plating of the food you serve.

No matter what kind of serving will be done, you have to coordinate the food and courses to make sure they flow evenly. If cocktail food will be passed there should be someone circulating with a tray at all times. If you are setting up a buffet, make sure all the courses appear on the table before the guests line up. June Jenkins has one unpleasant memory of the time she catered a party in Hawaii in which a curry was the main course. First, she dished the rice onto the serving platter. As she dished up the curry, one of the waiters took the rice and headed for the service table, which was in another tent on the beach about a hundred yards away. As soon as she was finished, she hustled to the service tent with the curry, only to discover that the crowd, despite a huge selection of cold appetizers and cheeses eaten before dinner, was ravenous and had already eaten all the rice.

Cocktail Parties. In the case of cocktail parties, you will probably be coordinating much of the cooking and warming of hors d'oeuvre. You should keep a watch on how fast the food is going, and what seems to be particularly popular, and see to it that trays are replenished as needed. Also, unless you are working with someone whose garnishing eye you trust, put the finishing touches on each plate yourself (or at least check someone else's) before it leaves the kitchen. It's not enough that the first plate look good; each one must look fresh.

Set aside a plate or two of the most popular foods, such as shrimp and salmon to serve later on in the party. This reinforces the feeling that there is a gracious plenty, even of the expensive stuff.

Make sure the host or hostess sees a plate of each dish when it looks its best, before it's been devoured. It lets them see how beautiful the food is, and thus increases their pleasure. Also, make sure the staff knows who the hosts are and make sure someone occasionally asks if they can do anything for them.

Instruct your help that when passing a tray of food, it is to

GARNISHES AND DECORATIONS

VEGETABLES

CARROTS: Curls, cutout shapes, shredded

SCALLIONS: Chrysanthemums, brushes

CUCUMBERS: Sliced, chopped, julienned, skins curled into flowers and shapes; pickles: sweet, sour, dill, chips, cornichons

ONIONS: Cut in rings, chopped

PEARL ONIONS: Pickled, steamed

SQUASH FLOWERS

SUMMER SQUASH AND ZUCCHINI: Sliced, cut in shapes

BABY POTATOES: Steamed and oiled

PEAS: Shelled raw, steamed

SNOW PEAS: Raw, steamed

MUSHROOMS: Fluted decoratively

TOMATOES: Halved, quartered, sliced, cut into decorative shapes; cherry tomatoes whole, halved and sliced

PEPPERS: Sliced into rings, chopped, packed in oil and cut into strips

RADISHES: Sliced, halved, cut into decorative shapes

BABY BEETS: Boiled and oiled, pickled

OKRA: Pickled

LETTUCE: Leaves used to line bowls, shredded, chopped

CABBAGE: Shredded, chopped, hollowed out to hold dip

RADICCHIO: Leaves used as accent, formed into flowers

BELGIAN ENDIVE LEAVES

ASPARAGUS: Whole, tips, peeled, sliced

PICKLED BABY CORN

BROCCOLI FLORETS

CAULIFLOWER FLORETS

CELERY LEAVES

FENNEL: Halved, quartered; leaves

HORSERADISH: Prepared; fresh shredded
WASABI (JAPANESE GREEN HORSERADISH)
WATER CHESTNUTS: Sliced and whole

HERBS

PARSLEY (CURLY AND FLAT): Sprigs, leaves, bunches, chopped, fried
BASIL: Bunches, leaves whole and shredded
ROSEMARY: Leaves, branches
SAGE: Leaves, branches
SORREL LEAVES
MINT: Sprigs, leaves, chopped, shredded
LEMON BALM LEAVES
CAPERS
DILL: Sprays, chopped; seeds
MARJORAM: Sprigs, chopped
THYME: Sprigs, chopped
CHIVES: Chopped, whole; flowers
TARRAGON: Sprigs, leaves, chopped
WATERCRESS: Leaves, sprigs
OLIVES: Black (plain and cured), green (plain, pimento stuffed, almond stuffed); whole, pitted, sliced, quartered, chopped

FRUITS

LEMONS: Sliced, quartered, fluted, cut into baskets and other shapes; rind peeled, grated, curled, candied
ORANGES: Sliced, quartered, fluted, cut into baskets and other shapes; rind peeled, grated, curled, candied
GRAPEFRUIT: Cut into baskets and other receptacles, fluted; rind curled, candied
KUMQUATS: Fresh or preserved in syrup

APRICOTS: Fresh whole, halved; dried halved, plumped in water, juice, or brandy

PEACHES: Whole, sliced, quartered; poached

STRAWBERRIES: Whole, sliced; crystallized

RASPBERRIES

BLUEBERRIES

PRUNES: Dried and plumped in water, juice, or spirits

PLUMS: Whole, halved and pitted, quartered

APPLES: Whole, sliced, cut into shapes

PEARS: Halved, sliced

CHERRIES: Whole, halved and pitted; preserved

GRAPES: In clusters or singly, crystallized

RAISINS: Dried or plumped in liquid

COCONUT: Grated, shredded; hollowed as receptacle

PINEAPPLE: Whole studded with other fruits; fluted, sliced, cut into fans and chunks

MELONS: Cut into balls and chunks; carved into animal and flower shapes

NUTS AND SEEDS

ALMONDS: Whole, blanched, slivered, shredded, toasted, chopped, caramelized

PECANS: Shelled whole, halves, caramelized

WALNUTS: Shelled halves, chopped, caramelized

PEANUTS: Roasted whole, halved, chopped; roasted Spanish; salted and plain; caramelized

PINE NUTS: Raw, toasted

SESAME SEEDS: Raw, toasted

POPPY SEEDS

CARAWAY SEEDS

DILL SEEDS

ANNATO SEEDS

CARDAMOM SEEDS

STAR ANISE

Anise
Roasted coffee beans

MISCELLANEOUS FOODS

Bread: Croutons, bread crumbs, toasted slices, fried shapes
Miniature choux puffs
Hard-cooked egg: Sliced, quartered, sieved, chopped
Caviar: Black, red, golden
Crème fraîche
Whipped cream: Plain, sweetened, salted; piped
Butter: Molded, curled, whipped
Cream cheese: Whipped, piped
Cheddar cheese: Sliced, grated, shredded
Grated Parmesan cheese
Crumbled blue cheese
Bacon: Fried strips, crumbled, chopped
Anchovies: Strips, curled
Grape leaves
Ginger: Fresh grated, sliced, curled; preserved; crystallized
Crushed ice
Gelatin: Molded, chopped; as an aspic glaze
Miniature meringues
Chocolate: Chunks, chips, curls; slivered, grated, shaved, rolled into cigarettes, molded into shapes, dipped with fruits
Sugar: Confectioners' (sifted through paper doily); granulated, brown for sprinkling and glazing
Glazes: Sugar, fruit, chocolate, butterscotch, rum

be presented to each guest in a group, engaging their attention for a split second, so that they feel they are being served. Also, the tray should be held at a height so that the guests can see it without having to look too far up or down.

It's also a good idea to carry a little plate or have a pocket that guests can drop toothpicks into. It's a little service, but one that is often appreciated. How often has each of us wadded them up in a napkin, while searching for a convenient stashing place?

Wedding Receptions. The principals at wedding receptions are often too nervous and too busy to pay much attention to the flow of the food and the party. They may look to you to provide the signals, such as when to move from one kind of food to the next. When the food is elaborate, set up a system with the hostess whereby you can coordinate the start of the next event, from the serving of appetizers and drinks, to the seating and serving of dinner, to the cutting of the cake.

Even simple receptions can occasionally get out of hand. I once attended a wedding reception on an unusually hot day in New England. The reception was an afternoon affair, with light hors d'oeuvre, punch, and champagne. The guests arrived at the club where the reception was being held and somehow, nothing was ready. The club wasn't air-conditioned, and, worse yet, the room was designed to trap the bleak winter sun, and was doing an even better job with the strong summer heat. In other words, the place was sweltering.

Guests loitered for a number of minutes, getting thirstier by the moment. Finally a big bowl of sweet children's punch, with a floating ice cream sculpture, appeared. Everyone dove toward the punch, which was drained in a matter of minutes. Then the adult's punch appeared, and they dove toward that, the sweet punch having made them all the thirstier. It, too, was gone in no time, an awkward half hour before anything else appeared.

Buffets. Unless you deliver food and provide no service, buffets should be attended and the food plated for each guest. Beautiful food should be presented as such, even in the sometimes informal setting of a buffet. Serving the food rather than having people help themselves also helps promote the feeling that the guests are special. By asking how much they would like to be served, you are paying them individual attention.

On a practical level, whoever is serving the food, either you or your service people, can gauge the portions so that each guest will have a full portion of food. In general, it's a good idea to serve fairly lightly, unless a person requests more (which you gladly provide). If left to their own devices, some guests will experience acute symptoms of "big eyes, small stomach." This doesn't mean you should be stingy, but people can always come back for more.

Seated Dinners. In some ways, the coordination of a seated dinner is easier than that of a cocktail party. Less last-minute fiddling and garnishing is required, and courses flow logically from one to the next. However, that also means that each course must be just right. If something happens to a dish, like with Paul Neuman's undercooked lamb, you can't very well substitute or drop it from the menu.

Similarly, when serving dinner to seated guests, if the waiter trips, the dish is lost. Donald Beckwith remembers with amusement that when Remember Basil first started, he was the waiter and, he confesses, "I wasn't such a good one." One of the first parties they did was a seated dinner for ten people. "I was carrying a tray of hot food, with a napkin over my arm to protect it from the heat. I got to the table and everyone looked up, expectantly. Slowly, the tray slid toward me, and away, and back again. The people's mouths were agape." Luckily, he didn't drop it. But he did give up waiting table.

PART THREE
The Catering Event

9

Getting the Job

Once you've done your homework and you're ready to go, your phone will bring you your first potential customer. When it rings it is important that you project a calm, competent, relaxed image. You should have your sample menus and price lists at hand. You listen to the client's requests and needs, taking notes all the while, and offer suggestions. Finally you set up a meeting, and sign off, pleased at having reached a happy meeting of minds. Sound easy? Here's how to do it.

THE FIRST PHONE CALL

As we discussed in chapter 6 it is imperative to create menus which offer the promise of a special event. A special event can be defined in as many ways as there are people who want one, but a key step in preparing to start your business is to develop menus that will entice—but not intimidate—customers.

You should have several menus available for your easy

reference, and each one should be accompanied by interesting descriptions of the food. You may want to have an extravagant (and expensive) menu or two to indicate how proficient and versatile your cooking skills are (some people simply want to be wowed), but your menus should offer a range in prices from the very simple and inexpensive on up. If you plan to do general catering, you should also be prepared to serve a variety of events including cocktail parties, formal buffets, seated dinners, wedding receptions, breakfasts and brunches, picnics, boxed lunches, teas, or any other events you think up.

Having created menus and costed out dishes, you will be prepared to offer specific information when the phone rings. It's possible that your prepared menus will be all you need, but it is more likely that you will find yourself using them to guide you as you create menus tailored to the needs of your clients. Flexibility in your menu planning is important: Mrs. Jones may love the idea of your shrimp-stuffed pea pods, but not the chicken satay.

Flexibility in general is important, particularly in the beginning. Your potential clients may know only vaguely what they want, they may want you to sell them with a pitch, or they may know precisely what they want. It is your job to listen and extract information from the caller in order to be sure you are as responsive as possible.

Here is a possible scenario. The phone rings and it is a friend of a friend named Jane Smith. She has heard about your cooking and your fledgling business from your mutual friend. Jane Smith is having a get-together in three weeks for about a dozen people and she says she would like some "nice food." You check your calendar, you are free Saturday, April 14 (at this point you are probably free most days).

What kind of a party will it be, you ask, hoping to discover the time of day the party will be held, the age group, and type of activity involved. In fact, try to fill in the "Checklist for Client Calls" as you talk (see page 140). She tells you it is to be a dinner for friends before a fund-raising concert. She wants it really nice but fairly light and not too exotic. This gives you a clue to the kind of food the client is probably looking for: the newest of the new is probably not the thing, something more traditional but with modern elements probably is.

You ask her what she particularly likes, and what sorts of things her guests like. The answers to such questions will sometimes tell you the general age of the group, which can give you clues about the kinds of foods to serve, without having to ask directly. Her responses may help guide your suggestions. Mention a few possible dishes to get a range of both her tastes and her budget.

Jane Smith has already hinted that she would like a fairly traditional meal, but she has also hinted at a moderate price range by saying "not too exotic" and "fairly light." But don't rely on her clues to discover a caller's budget—this is a question you can ask outright. As Stacy Bogdonoff says, "I can do any party, just tell me your budget. We can always juggle the menu to fit, but I need to know what you want to pay."

Don't be surprised, however, if people aren't too forthcoming with their budgets. Paul Neuman attributes this to human nature. "Everybody wants a fifty-dollar shirt for twenty-five. But when we price a catering job, we try our best to bring it in at a price the client can afford. If they say they have twenty-five dollars to spend, we put together the best meal we can for that. If they then say, I have only twenty dollars, we can adjust to fit the budget."

Ms. Smith also gave us a clue to her guests. People attending fund-raisers generally tend to be well established and often are fairly sophisticated. They are unlikely to be straight out of school with gigantic appetites, but are probably somewhat older. The time of day gives you an estimate of the kind of food to prepare as well.

The client's answers to your questions will no doubt spark ideas in your mind, which you then discuss. Ms. Smith

Make copies of this checklist, and keep a few by the phone. Whenever a client calls, use one to remind you of key questions to ask, make notes as you talk, and, voilà, you have the beginning of an easy record-keeping system.

CHECKLIST FOR CLIENT CALLS

Name:

Address:

Business phone: Home phone:

Best time to call:

Date of party:

Time of party:

Beginning: Ending:

Address of party:

Phone:

Type of occasion:

Number of guests:

General age group of guests:

General mix of guests:

Type of service: (buffet, seated)

Foods client would like to have:

Dishes to avoid:

General budget of client:

Special services needed:

Will call/visit:

sounds enthusiastic, so you make arrangements to call back or, better yet, to meet in person with suggestions for a more definite menu and prices. Try to set up a specific time to meet at the party site (in this case Ms. Smith tells you it's to be at her house).

Whenever possible, avoid quoting prices during the first conversation. If you must give specific examples and prices, refer back to your prepared sample menus and price list and tell the client that the dishes and prices quoted are only examples. Make sure that the client understands that the price on a sample menu is only an approximation and may not be the cost per head for a complete party, which might require extras such as service, rentals, and other such non-food factors. You can promise to give exact costs to assure the client that she is not being asked to sign a blank check. Tell her you will provide a written estimate after you've worked out the details of the arrangement to her satisfaction.

With menu changes and variations in market prices, you may discover significant costs not considered in an initial fifteen-minute conversation. Sometimes having to revise prices later, particularly if you have to do it more than once, can be embarrassing or fraught with tension for both parties. If, after deflecting her price question she still insists on a price for the meal under discussion, give a price range. That way the client has a notion of your general prices without your being locked in to a firm quotation.

You should also avoid creating a new menu on the phone. Well-thought-out menus take time. This is not to say you shouldn't give the client your initial ideas based on her responses to your questions in order that she can get some idea of the kinds of things you can do. For instance, as you talk with Jane Smith about her spring party, you can make suggestions of some of the dishes you might include. You might suggest lamb, veal, or ham as traditional spring foods. "Oh, yes," Ms. Smith says, "a leg of lamb would be lovely." You might also ask what sort of thing she would like to start with, such as soup or pâté, and what sorts of spring vegetables she might like to include. This way you can get a general idea of the kinds of foods to plan, without being distracted or locked into specific dishes.

The first conversation with a client is not necessarily the one you use to conclude the deal. More often, it is the discussion in which you check each other out. The client presents his or her needs and wishes and you present yourself and your services. Your manner should be friendly and relaxed, yet professional. You know your food; be confident of it. If you and the client like each other, you probably can come to an understanding with ease—Jane Smith became quite enthusiastic during your conversation, so we'll be paying her a visit shortly.

Handling Difficult Calls. Most calls from clients will resemble the one from Jane Smith, but unfortunately, there is another kind of discussion. In this second category you'll meet the problem caller: the demanding one who will require all of your attention until the party; the one who wants a beautiful meal without paying for it; or the one who is primarily comparison shopping.

The demanding client is the person who can't let go and trust you to do your job. These are the people who call five times a day for two weeks before a party. "They are the ones who look up your home phone number in the directory and call at eleven o'clock the night before a party to tell you they think the tablecloths are the wrong shade," says Paul Neuman. Every caterer gets these clients, and they all seem to agree that, as David Bell puts it, you develop a "radar" for them, that allows you to recognize them in the first phone call. The best way to deal with them is to make everything as clear as possible, put as much as you can in writing, and practice forbearance.

The second problem client is the person who wants an expensive meal on a low budget. This variety is easy to deal with if you can find it in your character to be gentle but very firm. Fanny Farkas smiles when she tells of one caller who had rather unrealistic requirements. She started off by saying she had talked with a lot of caterers and hadn't liked any of their menus. "Maybe I can help," said Fanny. "What are you interested in?" "Well," the caller said, "I want a dinner featuring Spanish food and Italian food. There will be a hundred-and-thirty people." Fanny asked what her budget was. The answer was $900, which was to include food, service, and rental of china, cutlery, crystal, and linens. "I'm not surprised she couldn't find a menu she liked," says Fanny. Fanny made some suggestions for a more modest meal, but finally had to decline from quoting.

Then there was the memorable time someone came into Sally Godfrey's take-out shop to discuss catering his party for one hundred. "I want a caterer who can tell me the cost for x number of pounds of roast beef and how much for a quarter-pound of pasta salad." Gallimaufrey took the job, but Sally regretted it, because the client's penny-pinching ways naturally left him short of food. "He insisted on ordering only five quarts of pasta salad for a hundred people!" Sally remembers. "And then he blamed me when he ran out, saying I had cut him short." She sent back to the shop for more food, but it didn't help. The client was furious.

The comparison shopper can be the most frustrating in some ways. This is the caller who wants a price on a specific menu. This is the caller who is not particularly interested in hearing your suggestions and wants to know only what the party will cost. You are at an obvious disadvantage, having been consulted in the middle of the planning. You have a simple choice in handling the situation: you can politely pass on quoting, or you can take the challenge. At this point in the startup of your business you probably have little to lose except time, so selecting the second route is likely the best bet. Later on you may not be so free with your time, as the chances of landing such a job are smaller, and the job itself may be less satisfying to do than if you are in on the menu planning.

The comparison shopper usually wants instant prices. This isn't really a problem if the menu consists of three platters of hors d'oeuvre. Your sample menus and prices may be all you need. However, anything more elaborate requires more thought and effort.

When someone is pressing for a price, the temptation is great to give a hasty quote, but try to resist it. Ask lots of questions regarding the party, the guests, the food, the service. Then try to make an appointment as you would with any client. The caller may want just numbers and will not want to meet with you, so make arrangements to call back with your prices. That way you can prepare them properly. Often a caller's unwillingness to meet with you is an indication that he or she is not very serious. If that seems to be the case, don't spend hours on your quotation.

When you call back to present your prices, make it clear that the quotation is based solely on the specifications given by the client in the initial conversation and would be binding only as such. Then, don't be too disappointed if the client thanks you, hangs up, and is never heard from again.

Sometimes, no matter what the caller is like, how well you have presented yourself, or how much a client may have liked what you said, your services may not meet his or her needs. If you have made a good impression the chances are good that you will be called again, or be recommended to a friend. Remember, every contact you make with a potential client can be good advertising, so be courteous and helpful throughout even if it becomes obvious that there isn't an immediate booking in it for you.

MEETING THE CLIENT

Most caterers consider it essential to visit a client and the party site in advance of the booking. It is the best way both to win the job and to establish the rapport necessary to a good working relationship. A visit gives you the opportunity to present yourself and your business, but it is also the working session that will establish the menu, the price, and the services you will be providing. It is also your chance to check out the working facilities.

One of the most enjoyable parts of a visit can be the opportunity to develop ideas. Sean Driscoll of Glorious Food tells of one party that, several years ago, opened the way for a new kind of catered entertaining. The client called Glorious Food about an informal party she wanted to give. Driscoll went over to meet her and see the apartment. She had a very formal living room and dining room and they puzzled a little about how to make it work informally. Then he saw her kitchen. "It was a sleek commercial kind of kitchen," Driscoll remembers, "and when I saw that I said, 'Forget about the dining room, why don't we do it in the kitchen?' " The kitchen buffet they devised was, needless to say, a great hit.

You always hope that the client meeting will produce an automatic meeting of minds. Sometimes it does. At other times, you will need to bring "silk boxing gloves," as the droll Sean Driscoll says, to negotiate your way through.

Always remember that one of your services is coddling. The client has called you to provide expert advice on his or her party and you are there not only to sell your service as a creator of fine food, but also peace of mind. You are also selling your special attention and concern for detail; for your fee, you are assuming a portion of the responsibility for making the occasion special.

In order to assure the client that you can provide what he or she requires, you need to be fully prepared for the meeting. Develop a specific menu and price along the lines of what you learned in your first conversation (see chapter 2 regarding establishing prices). After all, presenting the menu and discussing it will probably be the main order of business when you meet. You may also find that a considerable part of your consultation will be spent considering alternatives, so make sure that you have substitute dishes to offer. The client may not care for something you suggest, you may discover that a dish will be difficult to prepare given the facilities, or your understanding of the party or its budget may change after further discussion. Be flexible and ready to respond with some suggestions.

Some people want to be fully involved in choosing the menu, and having several alternatives for them to select from makes this possible. Others do not want to have to choose, and will leave the menu largely up to you. You may already know which kind of client you have from your initial conversation, but don't have your mind too set, as some people are quite different in person than over the phone.

Appearances Count. Think of the client visit as a job interview: it is exactly that. How you appear and act is vital to the success of each job. Unless you are interviewing for a large corporate account, you need not go the extreme of wearing a business suit (indeed, it can be intimidating to the average client) but you should dress neatly and appear well groomed.

Be on time for your appointment. This is vital because it is a signal of your responsibility. If you are late for a visit the client will immediately think you might be late for the party, too. If, for reasons beyond your control, you run late, call to say you will be delayed.

Conducting the Interview

You've designed a menu with alternative dishes, given yourself a professional pep talk and are at Ms. Smith's door, on time. The interview is about to begin.

Each person's style is different, of course, and the purpose here is not to tell you how you should walk and talk and act, but it is safe to say that, as with the telephone contact, you should try to be relaxed but businesslike, friendly but competent. Chances are good that the client already considers you the expert on food, so you start out with an advantage. But, of course, you still need to sell yourself.

Some people find selling themselves is very difficult, others love it, but for both types the first few times are almost invariably nerve-racking. One sales technique you may want to use to try to help create a favorable impression is to take along a sample of your food. I know a number of caterers who do it, and not only does it give the client an idea of the quality of the food, it suggests the importance that you, as the caterer, attach to the client and her occasion. Some people find it gives them an easy entrée into the discussion of the party. If the meeting is in the morning, they will take along muffins or pastries; in the afternoon a sample of an hors d'oeuvre or dessert. Whatever they take, it is self-contained and ready to eat. (It is unprofessional to presume the use of a client's kitchen to heat something up.)

Take along a portfolio of your menus and food, if you can (see chapter 2). Gary Goldberg suggests creating handsome handwritten menus. They need not be printed, though using attractive stationery or note cards adds a professional touch. He suggests creating a number of different kinds of menus on several kinds of paper, some large, some small, some intimate, some formal, to create a visual image of the kind of mood you evoke with your food. As we discussed in chapter 2, as your business develops you can add actual menus to your portfolio (a great souvenir for a client) and newspaper clippings or even high quality food photographs to illustrate particular dishes.

Presenting the Menu. Once you've gotten through the pleasantries, describe your proposed menu in detail. When a dish has a foreign or unusual title, first give it the official name, and then give it a more colloquial form. For example, if Ms. Smith was having an Italian-style supper you might suggest "Bucatini all 'Amatriciana," and then identify it as bucatini with pancetta, tomatoes, and hot pepper. If the title inadequately describes the dish, tell briefly how it is prepared: "Thick, hollow pasta served in a spicy tomato-based sauce flavored with Italian bacon." Avoid cutesy, kitschy titles such as Leg of Lamb Surprise that give no indication of what a dish is about.

As you describe the menu, you will probably find that Ms.

Smith has reactions to the dishes. Be aware of them, listening attentively to suggestions, trying to pick up on inflection. If the client hesitates over certain suggestions, it may be because she is unfamiliar with a dish, has had an unpleasant experience with it in the past, or just doesn't like it. Try not to take it personally if you meet with a grimace or negative comment; the client is not judging your food. Instead, ask questions and describe alternatives where appropriate or make a note to return with further suggestions.

If Ms. Smith asks you about dishes you have never made you have a choice. You can be candid and say "I'm not familiar with that but I'm happy to find out" or not let on you don't know about it and research it when you get home. It is often considered more professional not to let on, as many clients, intent upon the one particular dish they ask about, may unnecessarily lose confidence in you if you admit to being unfamiliar with it. On the other hand, you can look just as foolish if you pretend to know about an obscure and extremely difficult dish that only people who have visited Reykjavik are likely to know about. In other words, the decision about being frank is left with you, and you can probably gauge when it is appropriate and when not.

This first meeting is also the time to establish firmly Jane Smith's budget and your general prices. Here again, your alternative dishes may be needed to tailor the meal to the client's budget. For instance, for Ms. Smith's party you have suggested a menu of cheese straws to serve with cocktails, mussel soup to start, lamb stuffed with pork and mushrooms, red new potatoes baked with cream, steamed asparagus, radicchio with watercress dressing, and chocolate dacquoise with raspberry sauce. The food for this meal would probably cost about $100; using the factoring method ($100 × 3) plus the cost of the serving people ($30 × 2), you get $30 a head for Ms. Smith and her eleven guests.

Ms. Smith looks nervous, and says that she can pay no

more than $20 per person, but that what you've suggested is just the kind of meal she had in mind. "We can work something out," you tell her. To keep the menu luxurious-seeming yet less expensive, you can juggle cheaper dishes with more costly ones. For instance, you can make the lamb a simple roast with lemon and herbs. You can also change the mussel soup to fiddlehead soup, which is both lighter and cheaper, and particularly seasonal. If Jane Smith finds that too exotic, you could change the soup to fresh pea soup. You can change the asparagus to peas, or broccoli, the radicchio to Boston lettuce with a simple vinaigrette dressing, and keep the dessert the same. Jane then says, "That sounds good, but I always associate the spring with strawberries." Strawberry shortcake seems the perfect choice.

Once the general menu is established you can move on to the subordinate elements such as drinks to be served. Now is the time to ask what will be served and who will be responsible for it. (A discussion of bar setups and their alternatives is in chapter 7). These days many people find offering wine a simple alternative to the full bar, in which case you can be prepared to offer the services of waiting staff to pass and pour and to advise on quantities.

Jane Smith, however, has chosen to offer a full range of cocktails. Her party for twelve people won't require an elaborate setup, but she does want some advice on where to put it and what to include. The menu presented and discussed, it's time for a quick look around her house.

SCOUTING THE FACILITIES

Checking the premises where you will be working is another important part of the client visit. You will need to know how accessible the kitchen is to the dining area, how much space you will have to work in, what facilities are included, and how the serving spaces are to be arranged.

The first place to check is the kitchen. Jane Smith's is

fairly well equipped. She has the basic equipment and it looks workable. However, don't assume everything works. Fanny Farkas tells of one long evening when she delivered a meal that included a stuffed fish that was to be baked at the last minute by the client's own staff. On arriving she discovered that not only had the crucial member of the staff failed to show up for work that evening, but that the oven didn't work. She ended up unstuffing, filleting, and poaching the fish in batches on top of the stove.

Don't learn the hard way. Check every piece of equipment you are likely to use in advance. Since Ms. Smith's meal requires whipping cream for the shortcake just before serving, scout out the mixer, and determine whether it works. If not, make a note to bring a hand-held model. Will you need to bring the bowl to whip the cream in, too? If you anticipate your needs in advance, you'll know what to bring later or what changes have to be made in the menu.

As you tour the kitchen take note of the space available to you as well as any special things to be used. Once you get the job you'll need to ask the client to leave you clear counters and to reserve some shelves in the refrigerator for your use. Also, anything special that she wants you to use will need to be available and ready when you arrive. Washing baking pans, or scrubbing a coffeepot in the rush of the big event is a big waste of your time.

If the party space is not the client's home, it is particularly important to find out what sort of kitchen facilities are available. You may find a gorgeous professional kitchen or you may find nothing. If there is no kitchen space, you will have to plan on dishes that can be prepared completely in advance and anticipate renting hot plates and possibly other large pieces of equipment. Make notes of needed equipment as you explore.

Paul Neuman and Stacy Bogdonoff once catered a birthday cocktail party for about 150 people from a fairly unusual kitchen. The kitchen of the large apartment was directly in the line of guest traffic and it was decided it would be too confusing to use it. The caterers and client chose instead to use an upstairs bedroom that was convenient to both the stairs and a bathroom. Needless to say, the food had to be planned thoroughly so that there was a minimum of preparation at the site. All hot foods had to arrive close to the party time in insulated carriers or in heated containers. In instances such as this, the most that can be done by way of preparation is the final arranging and garnishing of plates and platters. The party was a great success; one of the guests commented that having a kitchen upstairs was "such a wonderful idea."

On an even grander scale, Remember Basil's Liberty Weekend parties for the New York *Times*, took place on a boat in New York harbor. First they took a boatload of about three hundred people out for breakfast and lunch, then they came back and took another three hundred or so people out for cocktails. There was no way to dash out to the corner for an extra head of lettuce or run back for a whisk or serving platter. Everything had to be prepared in advance and every eventuality considered. "Mary Kadet, our party coordinator, figured the logistics, and she set it up like a military operation," says Donald Beckwith. The operation included having back-up refrigerated trucks and an ice truck stationed at strategic locations along the route from the kitchens to the boat in case there was a traffic snarl or other hold-up that might throw off the schedule.

As you check out the premises, assess the arrangement of the site in general. Where is the best place for the bar? How will waiters move from the kitchen and through the crowd? Are there spots where people are likely to congregate and cause congestion? Should furniture be moved? Where will people be putting their coats, and will someone need to coordinate it?

Discuss the traffic patterns and placement of food tables with the client, and offer suggestions where appropriate. In Jane Smith's case the logistics are fairly simple. The bar, since it will be required to serve only a dozen people, can be placed in the hallway to the dining room. And since the dinner will be seated, there is no need for an intense study of the traffic flow.

However, what if it were a large party of, say, seventy-five people? Joe Sorencino very neatly solved the problem of placing food tables and the bar when catering the wedding reception of a couple in their apartment. A bedroom and an office were logical locations for the buffet setups, but finding space for the bar required a little creativity. The solution offered itself when Joe spotted an immense old console television in a corner of the living room. It measured almost 5 feet in length, was 2 feet deep and almost 3 feet high. Draped with a large tablecloth, it made a perfect bar.

As these stories suggest, almost any difficulty can be overcome—but only with proper advance planning.

What Else Will You Need?

Jane Smith plans to use her own dishes, serving platters, and bowls. Indeed, she looks at the party as an opportunity to use her beautiful and rarely-seen formal china. Ask to see the serving ware and a sample or two of the china, noting which ones will be most useful for the dishes you plan to prepare. Make notes of what the client wants you to use and of what you will need to provide. Be sure that there are enough plates, utensils, and glasses.

Simply designed plain white china is useful for the pieces that you provide, for it is more likely to harmonize with a client's own patterns. Your taste may not be the same, but it is unseemly and unprofessional to make a point of it. If you feel you must, tactfully steer a client away from using a pattern that would fight with the look of a particular dish. However, it is ultimately the client's wishes that must prevail, and while it sounds like a sentimental cliché, you are being hired to make him or her happy.

You may find yourself in the position of decorating advisor, having to choose among a selection of serving bowls, platters, and place settings. Here you really have a chance to work with the client to design the look of the table and meal. This can be part of the fun of catering if the two of you are getting on well and you enjoy planning table arrangements—after all, catering is about entertaining and atmosphere, and visual concerns can be as important as good food.

Many people don't realize that linens, flowers, and decorations should be used as complements to the food as much as serving bowls, utensils, and place settings. The client may well consider this area completely separate from your functions, which is a welcome relief to some caterers. However, even if you are not responsible for what the client uses, try to find out what's planned for the table and keep it in mind when you plan the food presentation.

Some caterers provide their own decorations as part of their presentation. Neuman and Bogdonoff display their collection of unusual antique kitchen tools next to their platters of food as their signature. They also make beautiful displays of leaves and herbs on the table around their platters. If you plan on using decorations of your own be sure to discuss it with the client first. She may have the table arrangements all planned, or be intending to use delicate crystal candlesticks that fight with your treenware bowl filled with miniature fruits and vegetables. Leave your wooden bowl at home, or arrange to display it elsewhere, perhaps by the bar, or on a side table.

Jane Smith's party is a seated dinner, but at one point she considered having about twenty-five people, which would have required a buffet table. It is particularly important to know the layout of a buffet table, because it can affect how you serve the food and what you present it on. Suzy Barnes, a Maryland caterer, tells the story of a time when she didn't think to ask about the decorations for a buffet table, assuming that most of its space would be hers to use. She was more than a little shocked when she arrived and discovered a breathtakingly beautiful—and huge—arrangement of exotic flowers. She found herself quickly refiguring the placement of every dish and finally had to resort to a small card table hastily set up in another part of the room to handle the overflow.

Such misunderstandings are easily avoided if you find out what the customer plans to use. Occasionally, you may be able to anticipate trouble and avoid it early: if necessary, suggest that the freesias Jane Smith is considering are too fragrant and will fight with the aroma of the food. If tables are to be set for a seated dinner, suggest that the decorations not be too high, or diners will be craning around the flowers to speak with one another.

Some people expect the caterer to provide everything in the way of table decorations. Make sure you know what the client expects, and unless you love to arrange flowers and are sure you have the time, be prepared to work with a professional flower arranger or florist. Angelique Graziano tells of arriving bearing food for a wedding reception in a couple's home. She was providing the food and service. The couple were handling everything else, but at least one thing had been left undone in the haste of getting the wedding together; there was only one miserable and garish bouquet. Taking pity on the couple, she quickly sent out for reinforcements, much to their relief. Acts of emergency charity notwithstanding, providing flowers is an extra service that should be planned in advance with the client.

Rentals. In discussing the party arrangements determine whether any party equipment will need to be rented. Everything from forks to nickelodeon machines can be hired. If the party will be too large to be handled by the hostess's stock and the style of the party suggests that real glasses, plates, and cutlery are appropriate, it makes sense to discuss the prospect of renting. Elegant food amid stylish surroundings tends to lose appeal when served on paper plates and eaten with plastic cutlery, while with picnic food it doesn't much matter, so long as the disposable goods are stylish.

Jane Smith has almost everything required in the way of

china, linens, and crystal, but, surprisingly, she doesn't have enough chairs. She asks what you can suggest to avoid the untidy look of mixing and matching from all over the house. You suggest renting them. You then offer to handle it, as this is one of the services you are equipped to provide. She says, "Great, one less thing to worry about." You make a note of it.

Determining the Staffing. From the first conversation, you should have a general sense of the party to be given and the kind of help, if any, that will be needed. Now is the time to discuss it fully. You should be able to provide waiters, waitresses, and bartenders, but be prepared in case the client wants to use her own.

Clients often don't realize how many people are really needed to make a party work. It is usually obvious when waiters, waitresses, and bartenders are needed, but determining how many are required is a little more complicated. As discussed in chapter 5, one of the rules of thumb for staffing is one waiter or waitress for every ten people. This assures that there will be a constant flow of food and attentive service. Figure at least one person working in the kitchen for every twenty-five guests. One bartender will probably be enough for the average party of fifty to seventy-five people. Often a client will assume that for less formal parties a bartender will not be needed, that a man (sexist, but there it is), be it husband or friend, will be glad to do it. Make sure that the client understands that serving drinks can be a full-time job requiring careful attention.

Ms. Smith's party will require two people to serve, including drinks, and you in the kitchen. For a party of twelve you might get away with doubling the kitchen person as a server.

WRAPPING IT UP

You and Ms. Smith have established the basis for a good working relationship in your interview and have reached an understanding on you catering the party. You have discussed the food and your prices, the table, kitchen, and house arrangement, and extra service. You will have taken notes on all of the topics covered. Before the meeting ends and you go home to plan, mention that you will write up your understanding along with your final quotation either in the form of a contract or a letter of understanding (see chapter 3). If Ms. Smith balks at this, assure her that this is intended to protect both of you from misunderstandings and is not binding until signed. Also make arrangements to get back in touch regarding pending bits of business, such as the chair rental, and your final quotation.

Now, it's time to celebrate; you have just conducted a successful interview and landed a job.

DETERMINING THE FINAL MENU AND PRICE

Once you've conducted a successful interview, it's time to get down to the business of seriously planning the party. It is at this stage that a few hours of work can save headaches at every stage of the event. Sean Driscoll echoes the sentiments of all caterers when he says "You can't ever do enough preproduction work."

With that somewhat daunting thought in mind, what do you really need to plan for at this point? You will want to check prices and food availability, arrange for rentals, flowers or decorations, and hire help. Follow up on all the notes you took. Foremost among the key steps is establishing your final quotation, because it confirms that you will be doing the party.

Sitting down to prepare the final menu and plans for a client signals the beginning of the real business of catering a party. It is at this point that you incorporate any final changes or substitutions. Such changes can be based on a number of things, from problematical on-site kitchen facilities to the client's last-minute special request for a dish.

PREMISES CHECKLIST

Kitchen Arrangement

Are there ample work surfaces?

Is the kitchen large enough for two or more people to work in? If not, is there another space where someone can work?

Is there a stove; does it work and how big is it?

Is there a refrigerator; is it standard-sized or will you need to bring extra coolers?

Is there a sink?

Is there a microwave or convection oven for heating?

Are there other small appliances such as a mixer, food processor, or blender and do they work?

Will small utensils such as spoons, knives, a can opener, a bottle opener be available?

Will dishtowels, pot holders, paper towels and other small kitchen items be furnished, or will you need to bring them?

Will you need to rent equipment such as a portable oven, large pots, a small refrigerator?

Party Ware and Decorations

Will you need to bring equipment, such as platters, serving bowls, a punch bowl, a champagne fountain with you; will you need to rent?

Does the client have serving dishes to use?

What dishes will you need to provide?

Will glasses, silverware, dinnerware, tablecloths need to be rented? Will you be responsible for arranging for such rentals?

Does the client want you to be responsible for flowers or other decorations?

Beverage and Bar Arrangements

What will be served and when? (e.g., full range of cock-
tails before dinner, red wine with dinner, champagne
with dessert or white wine before dinner, red with
dinner or a champagne toast only with a wedding cake)
Who will be responsible for beverages?
Will you need to hire a bartender?
Is there an established place for a bar?
Who will be responsible for buying the liquor?
Will the client be responsible for all setups?
Is the client well equipped, or will you bring extra equip-
ment?

Logistics of the Party Space

What will the traffic pattern be?
Will furniture need to be moved?
Will you be responsible for moving the furniture? (If so,
you will need to plan for the extra time involved.)
Where will tables be set up?
Will there be easy access to the kitchen?
Will you need to hire someone to tend to the coats and
rent a coatrack?

Determining Your Food Price

When you prepared your initial menu for the client, you
probably were aware of at least the general range of prices
for the foods you suggested. Perhaps you even costed it out
carefully. But since your conversation with Jane Smith the
menu has changed a little, and you aren't sure of the cost of
some ingredients. After all, foods that are a bargain one
week may not be the next, so check the current costs and
availability of the specific foods needed for the meal—in
the case of Jane Smith's party, the prices of the lamb, straw-

berries, peas, and fiddleheads are subject to change. Check also on the availability of the fiddleheads and peas. Produce, meats, fish, and seafood are particularly susceptible to sudden and drastic market changes.

The suppliers you use or would like to use are the best sources of information. Call and ask which ingredients might be subject to short-term changes and if they are likely to be available at a good price at the time of the party. If necessary, place an order to reserve them.

Sometimes market vagaries can work to your advantage, too. If, by chance, you should find that asparagus are likely to be a particularly good buy at the time of the party and you had planned broccoli, suggest the change when you confirm the menu with the client.

You may find after your final figuring that you cannot provide the meal you agreed on at the price you initially quoted and still make a profit. This is embarrassing, and your first temptation may be to stick to the price and write off the lack of profit (or the loss) as one of the costs of starting a business.

Don't. Rather than resigning yourself to a money-losing meal, go back to your menu and look for possible substitutes. Consider using a cheaper meat, or a less expensive vegetable that would allow you to keep the price. Then, create an alternative menu to present to the client when you call to confirm. Unless you were way off in your original calculations, you probably won't need it. Besides there are economies that can be made in other areas, which we will get to shortly.

Once you know what your food costs will be, determine your food prices using the methods described in chapter 2. Basically, you will want to consider the cost of the food, the cost of labor and overhead, your profit needs, and the budget of the client. Also to be included in the overall price will be the additional costs of rentals (in this case the chairs), decorations (in this case none), and service (two people).

Final Extras

Any extra services you provide, other than the rentals, decorations, musicians, and staff should be added into your final price. Such extras would include bar setups, such as mixers, ice, lemons and limes, for which you can charge a per-person setup fee or a total reflecting primarily the cost of the ingredients. Other extras might include use of your own special serving dishes, platters and plates, which wear out and get broken. You may also include use of your own goods as part of your overhead.

If you were providing delivery service only, you might want to consider a delivery charge. People who live in cities without the use of a car often build taxi fares into their costs, which can add up to a considerable sum.

Check through your lists to make sure that everything you can foresee is covered. Then do your calculations and juggling to reach your final price.

The final price, the one you quote to the client in the confirming telephone call, really is your final price (unless an unavoidable change must be made at the last minute, which you discuss with your client). It takes into account the food, service staff, rentals, and any extras such as flowers, decorations, rental of a site, and music. As Sean Driscoll says, "What a host or hostess does not want to have is a bill sent to them that was not discussed prior to the party." Therefore, you have to include the costs of everything when you make your final price.

As mentioned in chapter 3, you can add all your costs together and divide by the number of people attending the party and charge a per-head cost or you can break the per-head food cost out and list the extra costs separately.

The Confirming Telephone Call

When you have answered as many of the outstanding questions from your meeting as possible, gathered information about rentals and decorations (if necessary), and made your final price, call the client to confirm. Run down the list of items that you agreed on during your visit, adjusting as needed. Confirm the menu or make substitutions as discussed above. Explain any rental costs and arrangements, what you and your staff will expect to do, and when you will appear on the day of the party.

As an example, when you call Jane Smith back you confirm the menu as discussed at your interview. Your calculations were on the mark and the client has not changed her mind on the menu.

You will also discuss the dozen gold chairs you have ordered, which will arrive the day before the party. We'll say you have already established an account with a rental company and they would prefer to bill through you. You explain that the rental bill will be handled by you and included on your bill. If Ms. Smith demurs on this point, offer to have the bill sent directly to her. You then explain all of the fees to be incurred, including the deposit if you require one, and any policies of yours, such as who gets the leftovers.

Most caterers feel that food prepared for a client is theirs, and that leftovers are for the client to keep, unless there is a particularly large quantity. As Stacy Bogdonoff says, "Basically any food that is sent usually belongs to the client. However, I will sometimes say to them 'I will serve enough smoked salmon for your party, but I'm bringing an extra side. It doesn't belong to you, but when the cocktail hour is over everyone will have had as much as they want and I will bring back what's left."

You then confirm the time you and your staff will arrive. Ms. Smith has a meeting on the date of the party, and during the conversation it becomes apparent that she would like you there a little ahead of time to make sure everything is set up properly, as she may not have time to do it all herself. Fine, you agree to appear two hours before the party. You also confirm the number of people you will be bringing and what their basic duties will be (setting up for the party, partially preparing the food on site, serving the food, and cleaning up the kitchen).

The other detail you must be sure to cover is the date when you must know the final count of guests, if the party is large. The client must understand, as well, that the price you quote is based on the final number as you know it. If it changes, so will the final price. Some clients, when they get nervous about money, will begin cutting the number of guests. This can happen all the way up to the day before a party—if you let it. They often don't realize that the more they cut the less they save, as the per-head cost must rise. Your actual food costs will drop, but your labor costs will not. It is imperative that you make this clear.

One last detail regarding dates should be checked. Confirm the date and day of the party. It's awfully easy to miss by a day. Donald Beckwith remembers the party for a neighborhood law firm their first year. They were to arrive on Saturday at four o'clock to set up and the guests were due at six o'clock. At three on Friday afternoon Donald asked Dounia to check the schedule. Of course, the party was for Friday. "We called up the hosts and told them we'd had a fire in the kitchen and that we would be a little late," remembers Beckwith. "We worked like fury—luckily we had begun to prepare a few things in advance—and arrived forty-five minutes before the guests. It was a very nice party."

Once you've finished with your side of the conversation, Ms. Smith will say, "Fine, the food sounds great, the price is fine, I want you to handle everything and all I want to know is that you will be here and make a beautiful party for me. When can I send a check?"

Jane Smith is ideal, but what if the client doesn't like your final price, or has changed his or her mind about the food or the service, or something else? If the response indicates that the final presentation presents a problem, talk it through.

Most often problems arise from a final price quotation. If

it's just that your price is too high, then offer any menu substitutions you may have prepared, having anticipated such a problem. Don't offer the changes first, as you shouldn't have to compromise your meal unnecessarily.

Another possibility is that when you call with your final quotation and rental costs the client may gulp hugely and balk at the costs of renting equipment. Always the professional, you explain that there are certain economies that can be made if really necessary. "But first," you say, "consider the cost of having someone to wash up all the dishes and the costs of laundering linen." Someone hired to wash the dishes as they are used and reused will run about $10 per hour.

If the client is still upset by the cost of renting you can suggest such economies as using high-quality paper napkins instead of linen. You can change the menu to cut down on the number of utensils used by serving foods that require only forks. You may also suggest using a lesser grade of rental equipment or that the client provide some of the equipment, if, for instance, she has an inventory of plates, linen, or serving bowls and platters.

Whatever compromises you reach, make sure you both understand your final agreement in full. Also, check to make sure all of the details are straight. Stacy Bogdonoff is still a little embarrassed about the time she forgot to check on a detail of a birthday party. The celebration was for a distinguished elderly doctor. The family had requested his name on a traditional cake. On the night of the party Stacy opened the box and discovered the message "Happy Birthday, Butch." The birthday celebrant's name was Chuck. Somehow, she had mistaken the name. Luckily, she didn't panic but flicked off "Butch," smoothed the icing as best she could, and took a few small flowers from a table arrangement and draped them over the missing name. No one seemed to notice.

Once you've hashed out all the details and reached an agreement, it's time to explain the letter or contract detailing your understanding that will be following immediately. You can then cordially sign off and continue planning the party. "All" you need to do is prepare the contract or letter, order food and rentals as needed, arrange for help, and prepare a work plan. Then you can forget about the party until a week before the event.

10

Doing the Job

For most people, actually doing a job is the heart of catering. It's your opportunity to show your stuff and to make an event memorable for your client and the guests. It's a chance to plant the seeds for more business. But, as usual, a bit of planning stands between you and the exodus of serving platters from kitchen to dining room.

PLANNING YOUR WORK TIME

Some people can rely on keeping detailed tasks straight in their heads, but for most mortals this can be risky. For the majority of caterers, a well-prepared plan serves as an outline to the steps of the party, from the early moments of casual preparation to the action of the event itself. The plan should be detailed enough to clue you and your staff to every job to be done, but not so detailed that a person reading will get bogged down in minutiae.

A basic work plan lists the duties to be done and the time allotted to do them. It usually begins about a week before a party, as starting the tasks much earlier will stretch out the job unnecessarily, and the food will no longer be fresh. The days immediately before a party are usually filled with last-minute ordering and checking of the arrangements, confirming the party and the number of guests. You will place any rental orders and buy or order the food. With the party a day or two away the work plans will be filled with food preparation duties.

The following menu and work plan for Ms. Smith's spring dinner shows how they might look.

In Part Four, you will find complete recipes for this menu.

SPRING DINNER FOR TWELVE

CHEDDAR AND CHIVE STRAWS

FIDDLEHEAD SOUP

ROAST LEG OF LAMB WITH LEMON AND HERBS

FRESH PEAS WITH MINT

RED POTATOES BAKED WITH CREAM

BOSTON AND RADICCHIO SALAD

WITH VINAIGRETTE DRESSING

FRENCH BREAD AND SWEET BUTTER

STRAWBERRY SHORTCAKE

COFFEE

FOOD NEEDED

FRESH VEGETABLES, FRUIT, HERBS

Fiddleheads (2 pounds)
Peas (4 pounds in shell)
Red Potatoes (4 pounds)
Onions (4)
Garlic (in two dishes) (1 head)
Boston lettuce (3 heads)

Radicchio (2 heads)
Strawberries (3 quarts)
Lemons (in 3 dishes) (1 dozen)
Mint (1 small bunch)
Rosemary (1 bunch)
Marjoram (1 bunch)
Chives (1 bunch)

DAIRY
Vermont cheddar cheese (4
  ounces)
Butter (1 pound)
Light cream (1 quart)
Heavy cream (1 quart)
Yogurt (1 cup)
Milk (2 dishes) (1 quart)

MEAT
2 5- to 6-pound lamb legs

STAPLES
Chicken broth (64 ounces)
Dijon mustard (1/4 cup)

Balsamic vinegar (3/4 cup)
Salt and pepper
Flour (in two dishes) (4 cups)
Baking powder
Sugar (11/2 cups)
Confectioners' sugar,
  optional

MISCELLANEOUS
Puff pastry (1 pound)
Dry white wine (1 bottle)
Coffee

EQUIPMENT NEEDED

2 large saucepans (soup,
  peas)
2 roasting pans with racks
2 oval baking dishes
  (potatoes)
Large bowl for mixing salad
2 baking sheets for shortcakes

2 bowls for preparing
  strawberries
1 bowl for whipping cream
Electric mixer for whipping
  cream
Carving knife and fork
Ladle

FOOD PREPARATION WORK PLAN

Date of Party: Saturday, April 14 at 6:30 P.M.

ONE WEEK AHEAD

Confirm party and number of guests with Ms. Smith.
Order lamb from butcher.
Order fiddleheads from greengrocer or wholesaler.
Confirm kitchen help and service people.

THE DAY BEFORE

Shop for staples, meat, and dairy goods.

Prepare cheese straws (about 1 hour); refrigerate.

Prepare shortcake mix up to point of adding milk (about 40 minutes); refrigerate.

Prepare salad dressing (15 minutes).

THE DAY OF THE PARTY

Shop for vegetables and fruits or take delivery.

IN THE KITCHEN

Wash salad greens and herbs (20 minutes); store in damp towel in plastic bag in refrigerator.

Prepare soup (about 1 hour); chill.

Prepare lamb for cooking (30 minutes); refrigerate until two hours before leaving. Two hours before leaving, put lamb on to cook rare.

Prepare potato dish and cook for 30 minutes (1 hour). Cool and cover.

Shell peas (about 30 minutes).

Prepare strawberries; refrigerate.

AT THE SITE

Warm cheese straws.

Finish cooking potatoes.

Heat soup.

Heat lamb.

Assemble salad greens.

Cook peas; garnish with fresh mint leaves.

Garnish soup before serving.

Add milk to shortcake mix. Roll out and bake in 450 degree oven.

Combine strawberries.

Whip cream.

Make coffee.

Assemble shortcakes.

Working plans should also be created for any kitchen and serving help you hire. It may sound like overprogramming to do so, but jotting down even the simple tasks you want someone else to do will save you having to remember to tell them and, as soon as things get busy, your attention will be needed on many fronts. If you make simple lists of what you need done, from chopping the onions to washing the greens someone else can take care of them without interrupting to ask what they should be doing next. Such lists can also serve as reminders to you as the day wears on.

Make notes of the special duties you want the service help to perform as well. If platters will need to be refilled, who do you want to be responsible? Someone will need to keep glasses, napkins, and cocktail skewers cleared, and ashtrays emptied. Although Ms. Smith's party is fairly straightforward, and requires only one or two people to help serve and no extra person in the kitchen, the following service plan is an example of how one might look if you were busy, say, working on two parties at once.

SERVICE WORK PLAN FOR MS. SMITH'S PARTY, APRIL 14

Kitchen helper to arrive at my house, April 14, at 2 P.M.

WHAT'S NEEDED

Onions chopped for soup.

Wash salad greens and herbs; wrap in damp toweling.

Slice potatoes, cover with water, and refrigerate. Shell peas, cover, and refrigerate.

Hull strawberries and slice half of them. Place whole strawberries in a separate bowl. Cover and refrigerate.

Help pack up food.

Server to arrive at Ms. Smith's house, April 14, at 4:30 P.M.

WHAT'S NEEDED BEFORE PARTY

Set up bar for party, move furniture as needed.
Set dinner tables with linen, silver, crystal, flowers, place cards.

WHAT'S NEEDED DURING PARTY

Circulate with trays of cheese straws.
Refill cocktails as needed; empty ashtrays when filled.

ORDER OF DINNER SERVICE

First course: Soup
Main course (to be plated in the kitchen): Lamb, peas, potatoes
Salad course (to be plated in the kitchen)
Dessert: Strawberry shortcake (plated in the kitchen); extra cream passed separately
Cream and sugar placed on table before coffee served with dessert

AFTER DINNER

Clear table.
Help clean up and pack up.

Shopping and Equipment Lists

Along with work plans you will need shopping and equipment lists. A discussion of shopping methods and lists takes place in chapter 7. The lists included here are for the Smith party and are included as part of the packet of material you create for each job. A week before the party you take out all your lists and begin to work through them.

PREPARING THE FOOD

At long last, it's time to cook for Jane Smith and her guests. You have planned, shopped, and ordered. The menu is set, the guest list final (after an interim increase to fourteen, the count remains at twelve), the rental company has confirmed your order, the food has arrived, the serving staff is booked. You know how the food will be presented.

A week in advance of the party, get out your work plans and recipes and check through everything one last time. Now is the time to add any forgotten or changed ingredients and to make sure that you have allowed yourself enough time in your calculations to complete each task. Post your work plans near the work spaces for everyone's easy reference. That way, anybody can step in if needed to help.

Setting Up Your Batterie de Cuisine. Your life is about to change. When you cook on a tight schedule there is no room for hunting, or substituting at the last moment: there's no holding the meal up.

One of the secrets to efficient cooking is having everything you need at hand. Every piece of equipment needed should be ready to use, and every ingredient should be measured before the cooking begins. Few of us do it consistently because we can usually get away without being properly organized, and if something goes awry, we can usually take the pan off the heat to hunt for the colander or the spice we need. It only takes a couple of minutes, and then we're back on track. And besides, so what if dinner is a few minutes late?

It is not the same when you go pro. Paying customers are a lot less forgiving than friends and family, but luckily, your plans and recipes will give you a frame within which to work.

Of course, no matter how well you have planned, occasionally things will happen that are out of your control. As Sally Godfrey says, "One out of ten times something is bound to go wrong." That's exactly why you have to work methodically and check details thoroughly, in order to limit the possibility of things that can go wrong; otherwise, you run the risk of losing control.

It's still a good idea, however, to steel yourself just in

case you face trouble, for even the best-laid plans can sometimes go awry. June Jenkins recently did a summer baby shower that featured a selection of cold buffet food, including fried chicken, cole slaw, and one hot dish: creamed corn. She had scraped the kernels from two dozen ears of corn and assembled everything needed to complete the dish. She also had assembled the ingredients for the dessert, which included a caramel rum sauce. She gave the creamed corn recipe to a very capable cook from her Tex-Mex restaurant, Juanita's. When she returned she found the corn smothered in caramel sauce, beautifully garnished and ready for the table. She had forgotten that the cook didn't read English. "He was mortified when he discovered it wasn't what I wanted."

Keeping a Tasteful Watch. If you've prepared yourself thoroughly for this party, you may find at first that the volume of food is overwhelming. But as the number of tasks dwindle, the cooking, while a lot of work, will become fun again, just like cooking always has been. That's good. Keep in your mind the notion that this is cooking like all other cooking, and you may find it easier to keep in control. You must also never lose sight of the fact that food, in the end, is a matter of taste, as well as production.

As you go along, some things will require more adjustment than you expected. Despite what the recipe says, perhaps the fiddlehead soup needs a little more seasoning, or the peas aren't quite as sweet as they should be and need a pinch of sugar. Some of the strawberries need a little zing and so you add a tablespoon of orange juice. Everything else seems to go as planned, and by four o'clock you are through with your home preparations.

GATHERING AND GOING

"The biggest headache is the schlepping," according to Stacy Bogdonoff. "The loading, the traffic on the road, and the unloading all have to be planned for and everyone has trouble getting the food to a party at some time or another."

Sally Godfrey told me a story about a near disaster resulting from improper loading. It was a day with two weddings on opposite sides of Narragansett Bay. "I arrived at one, none too early, with no main course and no flatware. My husband was manning the other wedding, and he had it all. I figured out what must have happened and sent people over to him and went ahead and just set the tables with everything else. No one ever noticed."

Dounia Rathbone and Donald Beckwith experienced problems the first time they ever did two parties in a single day. One was for a company, the other for the opening of a dentist's new office. "When we finished with the first party we had little time to get to the next one," Donald remembers. "It was Christmas, and the traffic was impossible. I think I almost had a stroke as the cab inched through traffic. I think the dentist did, too, waiting for us. We got there fifteen minutes before the guests arrived, and it was fine."

Possibly the most disheartening story comes from Neuman and Bogdonoff. They tell one about a cake and an icy day. The crew was transporting the food to a party, and the centerpiece of the meal was a very special chocolate cake (ordered for a real chocolate hound), made with an especially rich batter and extraordinary icing, laced with rum. The top was decorated with beautiful chocolate roses. Needless to say, the cake fell victim to a fall on the ice—it flew from its carrier's hands. Paul and Stacy tried to figure out how, like Humpty Dumpty, it could be put back together again, but the cake was hopelessly crushed. They rushed out and bought two chocolate cakes from a nearby baker.

As these stories suggest, transporting food is a tricky business. You need to plan carefully, pack well, and hope that luck is on your side.

Packing it Up

Preparing a Pack List. Most caterers agree that a good packing list is crucial to a smooth-running party. You cannot afford to leave something out and risk being stranded. With all the lists you've prepared so far, getting your packing right will be simple.

First, take your menu and make a separate list of each dish. Next to each listing note what's needed. For Jane Smith's party, for instance, you will need the lamb itself in a roasting pan for reheating, a pair of spatulas to handle it, a carving knife and fork, extra lemon and herbs for garnishing, and a serving platter. For every dish, you will need to take the food itself, including all ingredients not yet added, equipment needed to cook and handle, garnishes, and serving equipment. Each dish of a meal should be considered and planned in this way, from last-minute preparation to serving.

Your basic pack list for Jane Smith's party might look like this:

Cheese straws in metal tin
Package of doilies to line tray
Soup in large covered container
Garnishes: fiddleheads for soup, mint for peas, herbs for lamb
Lamb in roasting pans (placed inside cardboard boxes), covered
Potatoes in baking pans (placed inside cardboard boxes), covered
Peas in covered bowl
Salad greens in plastic bags
Salad dressing in covered jar
Shortcake mix in covered bowl
Strawberries in covered bowls
Cream
Sugar
Coffee

EQUIPMENT

Saucepan for peas
Bowl for whipping cream
Ladle
4 serving spoons (soup, peas, potatoes, strawberries, and
     whipped cream)
Carving knife and fork
2 metal spatulas for transferring meat
Salad servers
1 rubber spatula for whipping cream
Electric mixer for whipping cream

In addition to the food and its equipment, you will need to take a few basic kitchen goods along, which can be kept in a separate box or basket. These should include:

BASIC KITCHENWARE

Pot holders	Dish towels
Paper towels	Aluminum foil
Plastic wrap	2 sponges
Garbage bags	Rubber spatula
1 large sharp knife	1 sharp paring knife
Several large spoons	Can opener
Disposable containers	

EMERGENCY BARWARE

Bottle/can opener	Jigger
Corkscrew	Small knife
Lemons, limes	Worcestershire sauce
Hot sauce	

Once you know everything you need to take, pack it carefully. The box the lamb rides in should fit tightly around the pan to keep it from moving. Make sure the salad greens can't be crushed. The bowls containing the soup, peas, and strawberries should be tightly covered. Also, try to pack logically. The things you will need first should be easy to get to. Once you're packed, check everything one last time and tick it off.

PARTY, PARTY, PARTY

You packed the food carefully, and the fiddlehead soup didn't slosh all over the car. The traffic wasn't too bad, and the rain wasn't too hard. You're backstage and the curtain is about to rise. By this time, everything is so well planned that all you have to do is quickly rehearse the party with your staff, set up the tables, finish the food, and serve it.

Swinging into Action. Once you've unloaded (no small task, particularly if it's a twenty-story apartment building), you can set about completing the tasks for the party.

First, review everything that needs to be done with your staff, and post any service work plans (see page 170), detailing the serving of cocktails, the cheese straws, and the courses of the dinner. Discuss how you will set up the bar in the hallway, and how to set the tables with Ms. Smith's linens, china, and silverware. You just realize that you forgot to ask where the coats will go, and ask Ms. Smith.

You also ask Ms. Smith at what times she would like the courses served. Since the party will be moving on to a fundraising event, the cocktail hour will be fairly short and the guests won't linger too long over the courses.

Next, take out your work plans for preparing the food. Divide tasks, and after unpacking your food and equipment, begin preparing the food. The more systematically you can set up the preparation area, the more efficiently you will be able to work. Try to get as much done as possible before guests arrive, for once the party starts you will be consumed with the mechanics of serving.

Before the guests arrive, try to cadge a quiet moment or two to catch your breath and review with the staff the order of events. The moment the doorbell rings the show is on and you must be confident and in full charge.

"You can never show your emotions." says Sean Driscoll.

"The caterer cannot let the client know that the soup congealed, or whatever. Somehow you have to work it out." Nine times out of ten, everything will work so smoothly you won't even need to worry about the soup. All you will have to do is concentrate on keeping the glasses replenished, getting the food out, and making sure everyone is happy.

Keeping It Flowing

Generally speaking, you will be spending more of your time in the kitchen attending to the food than out on the floor. But both kitchen and serving area need your attention.

Once a party gets underway, it will assume its own cadence and the elements will fall into place, barring disasters. You do need to be keeping a watchful eye at all times, particularly when working with others, though. As June Jenkins points out, "You have to be careful of details and the way everything is put together. You can't have someone reheating the beautifully cooked cassoulet who's going to ruin it for you by letting it dry out in the oven." Again, anyone who works for you has to be able to follow instructions.

Saving the Meal When the Flow Stops. Sometimes, no matter what you do, something disastrous will happen, but you cannot ever let on that this upsets you. Instead, you must call upon your composure and pretend that nothing has happened. For instance, what if a dish of the potatoes slips when going into the oven and falls on the floor? Luckily, Ms. Smith has a bag of potatoes, and you brought some extra butter and cream, so you can begin that dish again. But what if it had just come out of the oven? Scoop up what didn't hit the floor and adjust the portions.

"How do you make it look as though nothing is wrong when the kitchen is falling apart?," asks Fanny Farkas. "The waiter walks out with a calm face and you keep your cool in the kitchen, even though you're sweating," she replies. Perhaps you can stall the guests with another glass of wine, or you pass the bread again, or they just wait. Often they don't even notice, particularly if the party is going well. In other words, you just plod on through until it's over.

At other times you have to call on your quick-witted resources. Everybody has had disasters at one time or another and everybody has emerged triumphant. For Fanny Farkas such quick thinking is exemplified by one occasion. At one, Fanny and Arlene Cotler were doing a raw oyster bar. As they started opening the oysters, bought from their usual fine purveyor, they noticed that something was wrong with the texture. They weren't spoiled, but they were mealy. Clearly, they couldn't be served, but it was too late to send them back. It was a Saturday afternoon and it was snowing when they started trying to find a neighborhood fish store. The closest they found was ten blocks away, but luckily, the owner sold them his last oysters. They had to buy them retail, but that was better than scrapping the dish.

Cleaning Up and Heading Home

The party has gone smoothly, and Ms. Smith seems pleased. This is not surprising for as Ray Bonifer says, "In nearly every case people are there to have fun." You find yourself moving along with the flow of the party. The guests are gathering to leave for the fund-raiser. Now it's time to clean up and leave.

Cleaning up is easier if you do it as you go along. Your serving people will have bused ashtrays and glasses all evening long. They also will have cleared stray empty plates and removed the dishes after each dinner course (except dessert at a formal seated dinner, which is left until the guests leave the room). As the dishes have arrived back in the kitchen, you have rinsed them for later washing. Had this been a large party, the pantry person, who has been helping with the food, would have rinsed them and loaded them back into the rental cartons. You have also been washing up pots and pans in spare moments.

Any extra food is either left for the client or packed up to go home, as agreed in advance.

Once washed, equipment and utensils must be sorted between Ms. Smith's and yours. Hers are then either put away or stacked neatly, as she prefers. Your stuff is packed back into the boxes and either packed back in the car, or moved out ready for taxi loading.

As soon as the party has wound down, the kitchen is clear, and you're all packed, you pay the staff. Then you say goodbye to Ms. Smith (in this case with a note, since she is at the fund-raiser), collecting any tips for the staff, and leave, exhausted, no doubt, but triumphant.

You've just completed your first job, and the client was pleased. It was a job well done.

Afternotes. Your evening was a success, but the job's not over. The next day, prepare your bill, then sit down and assess your profitability, as discussed in chapter 2. Then start jotting down thoughts about the party, noting what went particularly well and what you would do differently next time. Keep these references for the next party, which, given the success of last night's venture and the excellent word-of-mouth advertising Ms. Smith and her friends will be giving you, is just around the corner.

PART FOUR

A Sampling of Parties: Menus and Recipes

BUSINESS BREAKFAST FOR 8

FRESH FRUIT JUICE OR SPICED TOMATO JUICE
EGGS DIJON
FRIED GRITS AND HAM
BUTTERED FRENCH BREAD TOAST
SLICED ORANGES AND GRAPEFRUIT WITH RASPBERRY SAUCE

EGGS DIJON

This is a classic Louisiana breakfast dish. Serves 8.

Butter for greasing
  ramekins
16 eggs
1½ cups sour cream
½ cup chopped fresh dill
  or parsley
½ cup grated Gruyère
  cheese

3 tablespoons dry white
  wine
Salt and pepper to taste
¼ cup buttered bread
  crumbs
Sprigs of dill or parsley to
  garnish

Preheat the oven to 350 degrees. Butter 8 ramekins.

Break two eggs into each ramekin. Combine the sour cream, dill or parsley, Gruyère, and white wine. Pour this sauce over the eggs. Sprinkle with salt and pepper to taste and cover with the bread crumbs.

Place the ramekins in a baking pan and pour an inch of water around the cups. Place in the preheated oven and bake 15 minutes for fairly soft eggs, 20 minutes for firmer ones. Garnish with sprigs of dill or parsley and serve immediately.

FRIED GRITS AND HAM

Many people think of grits as strictly Southern food. I like to think of grits as an American form of polenta. This dish is both subtle and satisfying. The grits can be prepared up to two days ahead, if kept covered and refrigerated. Serves 8.

3 cups water   1/2 cup flour
1/2 teaspoon salt   1/4 teaspoon pepper
1 cup grits   2 eggs, lightly beaten
6 ounces country ham,   1/2 cup vegetable oil
  prosciutto, or other   6 tablespoons butter
  ham, finely chopped

Bring the water and half of the salt to a boil and stir in the grits. Cover and return to a boil. Lower the heat and simmer for about 10 minutes, until thickened.

Pour half the grits into a rectangular baking dish. Sprinkle with the finely chopped ham or prosciutto and cover with the remaining grits. Cover and refrigerate for several hours, or overnight.

Mix the flour with the pepper and remaining salt. Lightly beat the eggs.

Slice the cold grits and ham into either 8 or 16 pieces. Dip each slice into flour, then in the eggs, and back into the flour.

Heat the oil and butter in a large skillet and when hot, cook the grits, a few pieces at a time, browning well on each side. Add more oil and butter to the pan as necessary.

Drain on paper towels and serve hot. These may be made up to two hours in advance and warmed before serving.

SLICED ORANGES AND GRAPEFRUIT WITH RASPBERRY SAUCE

Serves 8.

6 oranges
1 grapefruit
1/3 cup superfine sugar

10-ounce package frozen
raspberries or 1 quart
fresh raspberries

Peel the oranges and divide the pulp into sections. Work over a bowl to catch the juices. Peel and section the grapefruit in the same manner.

Combine the fruit juice with the sugar and raspberries and let sit for a few minutes to mingle. Purée in a food processor or blender. Strain the seeds if you wish.

Pour a few tablespoons of the sauce on individual dessert plates or bowls. Arrange the fruit sections in a fan shape on the plates or bowls, on top of the sauce.

Substitutions may be made in the Business Breakfast. The following is one possible alternative.

FRESH FRUIT JUICE or SPICED TOMATO JUICE
SORREL AND PROSCIUTTO FLAN, p. 186
CORN STICKS, p. 187, or BUTTERMILK SCONES, p. 229
FRESH STRAWBERRIES

SIMPLE LUNCH FOR 10

SORREL AND PROSCIUTTO FLAN
CORN STICKS
SLICED TOMATOES AND BASIL WITH BALSAMIC VINAIGRETTE
MIXED BERRIES WITH CARAMEL SAUCE

SORREL AND PROSCIUTTO FLAN

Serves 10.

Butter for greasing baking pan
4 tablespoons unsalted butter
1 onion, finely chopped
1 small clove garlic, minced
8 cups (about 2 pounds) sorrel leaves, rinsed, dried, and trimmed
4 ounces prosciutto, coarsely chopped

2 cups grated Gruyère cheese
12 eggs
1/2 cup chopped fresh parsley
2 cups milk
2 cups heavy cream
1/4 teaspoon freshly grated nutmeg
Salt and freshly ground pepper to taste

Preheat the oven to 350 degrees. Grease a 9 x 13-inch baking pan.

Heat the butter in a large skillet and add the onion and garlic. Sauté until translucent, stirring frequently, about 10 minutes. Add the sorrel leaves, cover, and steam for about 10 minutes, until completely wilted. Stir occasionally, if necessary. Remove the pan from the heat.

Spoon the vegetable mixture over the bottom of the prepared pan. Layer the prosciutto over the sorrel mixture. Sprinkle the cheese over the prosciutto.

Beat the eggs lightly. Stir in the parsley and then the milk and cream. Finally, stir in the nutmeg and salt and pepper to taste. Pour over the sorrel, prosciutto, and cheese.

Bake the flan in the preheated oven for about an hour, until a knife inserted in the center comes out clean, and the top is golden brown. Serve warm.

VARIATIONS:

• To make a spinach flan, substitute spinach for the sorrel.

• You can also substitute country ham or any other ham, for the prosciutto.

• Parmesan cheese may be used in place of the Gruyère if you wish.

CORN STICKS

Makes about 2½ dozen corn sticks.

Vegetable shortening for greasing pans	1 teaspoon salt
1¼ cups flour	2¾ cups yellow cornmeal
¼ cup sugar	2 eggs, lightly beaten
2 tablespoons baking powder	4 tablespoons melted butter or vegetable oil
	2 cups milk

Preheat the oven to 425 degrees. Lightly grease 5 corn stick pans with vegetable shortening (5 6-stick pans). Place in the heating oven, while you make the batter.

Sift together the flour, sugar, baking powder, and salt. Stir in the cornmeal.

Combine the eggs, butter or vegetable oil, and milk. Add this mixture to the dry ingredients and stir quickly, just enough to incorporate the ingredients. Do not overmix.

The mixture should fall in clumps from the spoon, not in a stream like a cake batter.

Fill the sizzling pans two thirds full. Bake in the preheated oven for 15 to 20 minutes.

SLICED TOMATOES AND BASIL WITH BALSAMIC VINAIGRETTE

Serves 10.

3 pounds ripe tomatoes
1 cup Balsamic Vinaigrette Dressing (recipe follows)
1 bunch bush basil, washed and separated into sprigs, or regular basil, washed and shredded

Blanch the tomatoes briefly in boiling water to loosen the skins. Slip the skins from the tomatoes; core and slice. Arrange in a serving bowl or on individual salad plates. Dress with the vinaigrette and garnish with small sprigs of bush basil or toss with shredded basil.

BALSAMIC VINAIGRETTE DRESSING

Makes 2 cups.

1 cup extra virgin olive oil
¾ cup balsamic vinegar
¼ cup Dijon mustard, grainy or smooth

1 large clove garlic, finely chopped, optional
Salt and freshly ground pepper to taste

Combine all of the ingredients in a jar with a tight-fitting lid. Shake vigorously to form an emulsion. Season to taste. Store, refrigerated, for up to a week.

VARIATIONS:

• For a lighter vinaigrette, substitute any good red wine or white wine vinegar for the balsamic vinegar and increase the proportion of olive oil to vinegar to as much as 2/3 olive oil, 1/3 vinegar.

• To make a blue cheese vinaigrette, substitute up to 1/2 cup finely crumbled blue cheese for the mustard. Freshly grated Parmesan cheese is also a good addition to a basic vinaigrette.

• Chopped fresh herbs such as basil, tarragon, marjoram, and oregano make delicious additions to a vinaigrette dressing.

MIXED BERRIES WITH CARAMEL SAUCE

This is the kind of simple dessert that can be made with almost any berry or fruit that is in season. Serves 10.

2 quarts strawberries, hulled
1 quart blueberries
1 cup sugar
1 cup water
Fresh mint leaves to garnish

Toss the berries in a large serving bowl or in individual bowls. Cover and refrigerate for up to two hours before serving.

To make the sauce, combine the sugar and 1/2 cup of the water in a heavy saucepan over moderately high heat. Heat, stirring occasionally, until the sugar dissolves. Cook the syrup, swirling and stirring constantly, until the mixture turns light brown in color, about 5 minutes. Watch the syrup carefully, as the sugar can darken rapidly. Remove the mixture from the heat and cool. It will harden.

Add the remaining water to the mixture and return the pan to the heat. Cook over low heat, stirring, until the caramel dissolves. Serve warm or cooled. This can be kept for several weeks covered and refrigerated.

Drizzle about a quarter to a half of the sauce over the

fruit, and serve the remainder separately. Garnish the fruit with mint leaves, if desired.

VARIATIONS: In summer use peaches or nectarines. In autumn, use pears or plums. In winter, use grapefruit or kiwi.

Substitutions may be made in the Simple Lunch. The following slightly more elaborate menu is just one possible alternative.

CHEDDAR AND CHIVE STRAWS, p. 244
SMOKED TURKEY SALAD ON ENDIVE TIPS, p. 221
CORN STICKS
TOSSED GREENS WITH BLUE CHEESE VINAIGRETTE, p. 279
STRAWBERRY SHORTCAKE, p. 249, or
GINGER PEAR TART, p. 264

BRUNCH BUFFET FOR 24
FROM CULINARY CENTER OF
NEW YORK

CHEESE TRUFFLES
SPICY CRACKED GREEN OLIVES
KALAMATA OLIVES WITH LEMON ANISETTE
OIL-CURED OLIVES WITH GARLIC AND HERBS
LAYERED PASTA FRITTATA
BROCCOLI AND ROASTED PEPPERS
WITH GARLIC-SCENTED OIL
CHOCOLATE RUM CAKE

CHEESE TRUFFLES

Makes about 4 dozen.

12 ounces Brie or
Bonchampi, trimmed of
rind, softened
8 tablespoons unsalted
butter, softened
4 ounces cream cheese,
softened

2 tablespoons cognac
4 drops hot pepper sauce
Salt and freshly ground
white pepper to taste
5 ounces dense
pumpernickel bread,
cubed

Combine the Brie or Bonchampi, butter, cream cheese, cognac, hot pepper sauce, and salt and pepper to taste and beat until smooth. Chill the mixture overnight. This can be refrigerated up to three days in advance of a party.

Process the bread cubes in a food processor to make fine crumbs. Roll the cheese mixture into balls about 1-inch in diameter. Roll the balls in the crumbs to coat completely. Cover and refrigerate for up to a day before serving.

Bring the truffles to room temperature 15 minutes before serving. To serve, place the truffles in paper candy cups and arrange on a platter. As an alternative, fold a napkin decoratively and place on the platter. Arrange the truffles in a pyramid in the center of the napkin.

SPICY CRACKED GREEN OLIVES

The first of a trio of flavored olives, which together or singly make a nice presentation. Each takes only about 5 minutes to prepare. Makes 1 pound.

1 pound cracked green olives, drained
2 tablespoons olive oil
1 to 2 teaspoons dried red pepper flakes

Combine the olives, olive oil, and pepper flakes in a jar with a tight-fitting lid. Shake well. Leave the olives to marinate at room temperature for 2 days, shaking the jar once daily.

KALAMATA OLIVES WITH LEMON ANISETTE

Makes 1 pound.

1 pound Greek Kalamata   2 tablespoons anisette
  olives, drained   1 large lemon
2 tablespoons olive oil

Place the olives in a jar. Add the oil and anisette. Cut the rind from the lemon into 1-inch-wide strips, using a serrated knife. Cut each peel lengthwise into 2 spirals. Add to the olives. Squeeze in the juice from the lemon. Cover the jar tightly and shake well. Leave the olives to marinate at room temperature for 3 days, shaking the jar once daily.

OIL-CURED OLIVES WITH GARLIC AND HERBS

Makes 1 pound.

1 pound oil-cured black or
    Greek olives, drained
2 tablespoons olive oil
2 tablespoons finely
    chopped fresh herbs

such as oregano, thyme,
    basil and/or rosemary,
    or 2 teaspoons dried
3 cloves garlic, slightly
    crushed

Combine the olives, olive oil, herbs, and garlic in a jar with a tight-fitting lid and shake well. Leave the olives to marinate at room temperature for 2 days, shaking the jar once daily. Remove the garlic cloves before serving.

LAYERED PASTA FRITTATA

Makes 3; each serves 8.

1½ pounds spaghetti
6 tablespoons unsalted
    butter, softened
½ cup olive oil
1½ cups finely chopped
    onion
3 32 to 35-ounce cans
    peeled Italian plum
    tomatoes, chopped and
    drained at least 1 hour
1 pound mozzarella
    cheese, cut into ⅜-inch
    cubes

1½ cups freshly grated
    Parmesan cheese
Salt and freshly ground
    pepper
3 tablespoons olive oil
1½ cups pine nuts
1½ cups loosely packed
    fresh basil, chopped
15 eggs
12 tablespoons finely
    chopped fresh Italian
    parsley
¾ cup clarified butter

Cook the spaghetti al dente in a large pot of rapidly boiling salted water, about 8 minutes. Drain the pasta and toss in a large bowl with the 6 tablespoons butter. Cool.

This can be prepared up to 3 days in advance and kept refrigerated. Bring to room temperature before using.

Heat the 1/2 cup of olive oil in a large, heavy skillet over moderate heat. Add the onion and cook until tender and golden, stirring occasionally, about 10 minutes. Increase the heat to moderately high and add the tomatoes. Cook the mixture until thick, stirring frequently, 10 to 15 minutes. Transfer the mixture to a large bowl and cool to room temperature.

Stir the mozzarella and 3/4 cup of the Parmesan cheese into the tomato mixture. Season to taste with salt and pepper. This, too, can be prepared up to 3 days in advance and kept refrigerated. Bring to room temperature before using.

Heat the 3 tablespoons of olive oil in a medium-sized heavy skillet over moderate heat. Add the pine nuts and sauté until lightly browned, about 5 minutes. Remove with a slotted spoon and drain on paper towels. Stir the pine nuts and chopped basil into the tomato and cheese mixture.

Preheat the broiler. To make 1 frittata, beat 5 of the eggs in a large bowl. Stir in 1/3 of the pasta, 1/4 cup Parmesan cheese and 2 tablespoons finely chopped parsley. Season to taste with salt and pepper. Heat 1/4 cup of the clarified butter in a heavy 12-inch skillet over high heat. Spread half of the pasta-egg mixture evenly in the pan and cook for 1 minute, shaking the pan to prevent sticking. Reduce the heat to moderate. Spread 1/3 of the tomato-cheese mixture over the egg and pasta, leaving a 1/2-inch border. Top with the remaining pasta-egg mixture, spreading to the edges of the pan. Cook until the mixture is almost set and the bottom is golden brown, about 3 minutes.

Transfer the pan to the broiler and broil 2 inches from the heat, until the top is softly set and just golden brown, about a minute. Do not let it overcook. Sprinkle 2 tablespoons of the finely chopped parsley over the top. Cut into 8 wedges. Repeat the procedure with the remaining ingredients to make 2 more frittatas. Serve immediately, or leave to cool and serve at room temperature. Do not refrigerate, however.

BROCCOLI AND ROASTED PEPPERS WITH GARLIC-SCENTED OIL

Serves 24.

4 large, red bell peppers
10 pounds broccoli (5 to 6 heads), trimmed, separated into spears and peeled, if tough

5 cloves garlic
1 cup olive oil
1 dried red chili pepper
Salt to taste

Char the peppers under the broiler or over a flame, turning to blacken the skins evenly. Put the peppers in a paper bag to steam for 10 minutes. Peel and halve the peppers, discarding the seeds. Dice into ¼-inch cubes.

Soak the broccoli in lightly salted cold water for 10 minutes. Drain well. Blanch the broccoli in batches in a large amount of rapidly boiling water until the tip of a sharp knife pierces the stalks easily, 5 to 7 minutes. Plunge the broccoli into cold water to stop its cooking. Drain well and pat dry.

Crush the garlic and discard the skins. Heat the oil, garlic, and chili pepper in a heavy medium-sized skillet over high heat until bubbles appear around the garlic. Reduce the heat to moderate and cook until the garlic and chili are light brown in color, turning constantly. Discard the garlic and chili and strain the oil if necessary. Cool the oil slightly and season with salt to taste. This can be made a day in advance and reheated before combining with the vegetables.

When ready to serve, brush the broccoli and red peppers generously with the oil. Arrange the broccoli spears stem down in a large bowl and garnish with the red peppers.

CHOCOLATE RUM CAKE

Serves 12. (To serve 24, make 2 cakes.)

CHOCOLATE GÉNOISE:
Butter and flour for
  preparing jelly roll pan
1/2 cup sifted flour
1/2 cup unsweetened cocoa
  powder, preferably
  Dutch process
6 eggs, at room
  temperature
1 cup superfine sugar
1 teaspoon vanilla extract
1/2 cup clarified butter,
  cooled to lukewarm

RUM SYRUP (enough for 2
cakes):
1/2 cup water
1/4 cup sugar
1/4 cup dark rum

CHOCOLATE RUM
  BUTTERCREAM:
12 ounces unsalted butter,

cut into 1/4-inch pieces,
  softened
6 ounces semisweet
  chocolate, coarsely
  chopped
2 ounces unsweetened
  chocolate, coarsely
  chopped
3/4 cup water
3 tablespoons dark rum
1 tablespoon instant
  espresso powder
3 egg yolks, at room
  temperature
1 1/4 cups sugar
1/4 teaspoon cream of
  tartar

2 cups almonds, toasted
  and coarsely chopped
12 chocolate coffee beans

Preheat the oven to 350 degrees. The oven rack should be positioned in the center. Grease a 10 1/2 × 15 1/2-inch jelly roll pan. Line with parchment paper and lightly grease and flour the paper.

To make the génoise, sift together the flour and the cocoa powder. Whisk the eggs and sugar in a double boiler over a pan of simmering water, until the mixture feels warm to the touch, 3 to 4 minutes. Remove the pan from the heat and beat with an electric mixer at high speed until the mixture is cool and tripled in volume. The mixture should form slowly dissolving ribbons when the beaters are lifted from the bowl. Fold the flour mixture into the egg mixture in thirds.

Stir the vanilla into the lukewarm clarified butter, mixing well. Fold this into the batter. Pour the mixture into the prepared pan. Bake for 25 to 30 minutes, or until the cake feels springy to the touch. Remove the cake from the pan carefully and transfer to a rack to cool completely.

To make the syrup, combine the water and sugar in a small heavy saucepan placed over low heat. Heat until the sugar dissolves, swirling the pan occasionally. Increase the heat and bring to a boil. Cool the syrup completely. Stir in the rum. This may be made well ahead, up to several weeks, and kept refrigerated.

To make the buttercream frosting, beat the softened butter until light and fluffy.

Combine the semisweet and unsweetened chocolates, 1/4 cup of the water, the rum and the espresso powder in a small heavy saucepan over low heat. Heat, stirring constantly, until the chocolate melts. Remove the mixture from the heat and cool.

Beat the egg yolks until slightly thickened. Combine the sugar, cream of tartar, and remaining 1/2 cup water in a small heavy saucepan and cook over low heat until the sugar dissolves, swirling the pan occasionally. Increase the heat and bring the mixture to a boil. Cook, at a boil, until the syrup registers 225 degrees on a candy thermometer. Add the syrup to the yolks in a slow steady stream, beating constantly at low speed. Continue beating until the mixture is thick and cool. Beat in the butter a little at a time, incorporating each addition completely before adding the next. Beat in the chocolate mixture. Refrigerate until spreadable.

To assemble the cake, cut a 5 × 10-inch piece of cardboard. Cover it with foil. Cut the cake into three 5 × 10-inch layers. Place 1 layer on the cardboard. Pierce the cake with a fork and brush generously with the rum syrup.

Spread 1/4 of the buttercream over the cake. Top with the
second layer, pierce again, and brush with rum syrup.
Spread with 1/4 of the buttercream. Repeat the procedure
with the third layer, spreading the buttercream over the top
and sides of the cake. Spoon the remaining buttercream
into a pastry bag fitted with a star tip and pipe 12 rosettes
down the center of the cake, spacing them evenly. Set the
cake on a rack over a baking sheet. Gently pat the coarsely
chopped almonds onto the sides of the cake. Top each
rosette with a coffee bean. Refrigerate the cake overnight.
Let stand at room temperature at least 30 minutes before
serving.

CULINARY CENTER'S
ITALIAN-INSPIRED BUFFET
FOR 24

PÂTÉ EGGS
RICE AND HAM CROQUETTES
SEAFOOD SALAD WITH SUMMER VEGETABLES IN TONNATO
SAUCE
BEEF CARPACCIO
PEPPER AND CHEESE BISCUIT FINGERS
GREEN, WHITE, AND RED SALAD
FLOATING "CAKE" WITH FRESH BERRIES AND RASPBERRY
SAUCE

PÂTÉ EGGS

Makes about 5½ dozen.

5 tablespoons unsalted butter, softened	Freshly ground pepper to taste
5 tablespoons chicken fat, at room temperature	½ cup chicken broth, preferably homemade
⅔ cup chopped onion	3 tablespoons cognac
1 large clove garlic, finely chopped	2 hard-cooked eggs, coarsely chopped
1 pound chicken livers, trimmed and patted dry	1 cup unsalted pistachios, finely chopped
¾ teaspoon salt	Shredded lettuce to garnish
½ teaspoon dried thyme, crumbled	

Melt 2 tablespoons of the butter with 2 tablespoons of
the chicken fat in a large heavy skillet over moderately low
heat. Add the onion and cook until tender and golden,

stirring occasionally, about 15 minutes. Stir in the garlic. Increase the heat and add the chicken livers. Cook, stirring, for 2 minutes. Stir in the salt, thyme, and pepper to taste. Blend in the broth and cook until the livers are medium-rare, 4 to 5 minutes.

Transfer the livers to a bowl with a slotted spoon. Boil the cooking liquid rapidly to reduce to about 5 tablespoons. Stir in the cognac and pour the liquid over the livers. Let the mixture cool to room temperature.

Purée the livers and their liquid in a food processor. Add the hard-cooked eggs, the remaining butter and chicken fat and blend until smooth, scraping down the sides of the bowl, about 45 seconds. Adjust the seasoning as needed. Turn the pâté into a bowl. Refrigerate at least 4 hours and up to 2 days.

Spread the pistachios in a shallow pan. Roll the pâté into ¾-inch balls. Coat each ball completely in the pistachios, pressing into an egg shape. Place the eggs on a baking sheet; cover and refrigerate for up to 2 hours before using.

Mound the lettuce on a round tray to form a nest. Arrange the eggs on the lettuce.

RICE AND HAM CROQUETTES

Makes about 5 dozen.

BÉCHAMEL SAUCE
3 tablespoons unsalted butter
3 tablespoons flour
¾ cup half-and-half
¼ cup heavy cream
¼ teaspoon salt
⅛ teaspoon freshly ground white pepper
Pinch of ground red pepper

CROQUETTES
Butter for greasing baking sheet
1 tablespoon unsalted butter
¾ cup finely chopped mushrooms
2 teaspoons fresh lemon juice
2 tablespoons dry sherry

6 ounces mild ham, diced into 1/4-inch cubes

3/4 cup cooked long-grain rice

1 egg yolk, at room temperature

1/2 cup dry bread crumbs

Salt and freshly ground pepper to taste

Freshly grated nutmeg to taste

Hot pepper sauce to taste

1/4 cup snipped fresh chives

2 1/2 cups dry bread crumbs

3 eggs, lightly beaten

Peanut oil or corn oil for deep frying

To make the béchamel sauce, melt the butter in a heavy saucepan over moderately low heat. Add the flour and stir for 3 minutes. Remove from the heat and stir in the half-and-half. Increase the heat and bring to a boil, stirring constantly. Stir in the heavy cream and the salt, pepper, and red pepper to taste. Cook, stirring until very thick, about 1 minute. Cool.

To make the croquettes, grease a baking sheet. Melt the tablespoon of butter in a heavy saucepan over moderate heat. Add the mushrooms and lemon juice and cook until the mushrooms begin to brown, about 5 minutes. Add the sherry and cook until the liquid evaporates. Stir in the ham and the rice, then the béchamel sauce. Remove the mixture from the heat and mix in the egg yolk. Stir in 1/2 cup of the bread crumbs. Season to taste with salt, freshly ground pepper, freshly ground nutmeg, and a few drops of hot pepper sauce.

Spread the mixture evenly on the prepared baking sheet. Cover with plastic wrap and refrigerate for at least 6 hours, and up to 2 days.

Sprinkle the chives over the croquette mixture. Shape the mixture into balls about 1 inch in diameter. Roll each ball in the remaining bread crumbs, then dip in the lightly beaten eggs, coating completely. Dip in the egg again and reroll in the crumbs. Return the balls to the baking sheet. Chill at least 20 minutes, or overnight.

When ready to cook, heat about 2 inches of oil in a deep fryer or skillet to 375 degrees. Fry the croquettes, a few at a time, until golden brown, about 2½ minutes. Drain on paper towels. Keep warm up to 20 minutes before serving. Arrange the croquettes on a platter before serving. Serve warm.

SEAFOOD SALAD WITH SUMMER VEGETABLES IN TONNATO SAUCE

Serves 24.

COURT BOUILLON
4 cups water
1 cup dry white wine
1 carrot, cut into 1-inch pieces
2 slices onion
3 sprigs parsley
1 bay leaf
1 teaspoon salt
½ teaspoon peppercorns

3 pounds whole bay scallops or sea scallops, sliced ¼-inch thick
3 pounds large unpeeled shrimp

3 carrots, peeled
3 celery stalks, peeled

2 medium-size zucchini, halved lengthwise and seeded
2 medium-size yellow summer squash, halved lengthwise

Tonnato Sauce (recipe follows)
Fresh lemon juice
Salt and freshly ground pepper

For garnish
8 scallions, thinly sliced
Romaine lettuce leaves
Lemon wedges, optional
½ cup finely chopped fresh parsley, optional

Combine the ingredients for the court bouillon in a large saucepan and bring to a boil. Reduce the heat and simmer for 20 minutes. Strain the liquid into another large saucepan.

Bring the court bouillon to a boil and add the scallops. Remove from the heat and let stand until the scallops just turn opaque, about 2 minutes. Remove the scallops with a slotted spoon. Return the court bouillon to the heat and bring to a boil. Add the shrimp, remove from the heat again and let stand until the shrimp just turn pink, about 3 minutes. Drain and cool. Peel and devein the shrimp. The shrimp and scallops can be prepared up to a day ahead, if kept covered, separately, and refrigerated.

Cut the carrots, celery, zucchini, and summer squash into 3/8-inch cubes.

Drain the scallops and shrimp of any juices. Combine with the diced vegetables in a large bowl. Fold in half of the Tonnato Sauce. Season with lemon juice and salt and pepper to taste. Chill the salad for at least 3 hours before serving.

Fold the scallions into the salad. Line a large shallow bowl with the romaine lettuce and mound the salad in the center. Garnish with the lemon wedges and parsley, if desired. The composed salad can be prepared and refrigerated up to an hour before serving. Pass the remaining sauce separately.

TONNATO SAUCE

Makes about 1 quart.

6 egg yolks, at room temperature
3/4 cup fresh lemon juice
1 1/2 cups olive oil
3 3 1/2-ounce cans Italian tuna in olive oil, undrained

9 tablespoons heavy cream
8 anchovies, rinsed and cut into 1/4-inch pieces
7 tablespoons capers, rinsed and drained

Combine the yolks and lemon juice in a blender or food processor and blend or process briefly. Turn the machine on and add the oil in a very thin stream and blend until creamy. Add the tuna, cream, and anchovies and blend or process until smooth. Transfer the mixture to a bowl. Stir in the capers. Refrigerate overnight to allow the flavors to develop.

BEEF CARPACCIO

Classically prepared with raw beef, this dish can also be made using smoked beef or turkey. Serves 24.

3½ pounds top round,
  well trimmed
¼ cup fresh lemon juice
2 egg yolks, at room
  temperature
2 tablespoons freshly
  grated Parmesan cheese
2 anchovy fillets, minced
2 cloves garlic, finely
  chopped

1 teaspoon Dijon mustard
Freshly ground pepper
1 cup olive oil
6 to 8 sun-dried tomatoes
  packed in oil, well
  drained and cut into 48
  2 × ¼-inch strips

Place the meat in the freezer for about 20 minutes to make it easy to slice. Slice the meat into 48 paper-thin pieces. If necessary, place each piece between 2 sheets of wax paper and pound with a skillet to make it very thin and even. Alternatively, a friendly butcher might be persuaded to slice it for you. Cover and set aside while you make the carpaccio dressing.

Combine the lemon juice, egg yolks, Parmesan cheese, anchovy fillets, garlic, Dijon mustard, and freshly ground pepper to taste in a food processor and blend until smooth, about 15 seconds. Turn the machine on and pour ¾ cup of the olive oil in a very thin stream into the mixture and process until thick and creamy. Refrigerate for up to a day before using.

Spread 1 teaspoon of the dressing evenly over each slice of beef. Roll up jelly-roll fashion starting at one short end.

Brush lightly with the remaining olive oil. Arrange the rolls on a serving platter. Garnish each roll with a strip of sun-dried tomato.

PEPPER AND CHEESE BISCUIT FINGERS

Makes about 2 dozen.

⅔ cup freshly grated Parmesan cheese

1 teaspoon medium-grind cracked pepper

2 cups flour

1 tablespoon baking powder

½ teaspoon salt

½ teaspoon baking soda

3 tablespoons unsalted butter, chilled and cut into ½-inch slices

1 cup buttermilk

2 tablespoons unsalted butter, melted

Preheat the oven to 450 degrees. Line a baking sheet with baking parchment, or use a non-stick sheet.

Combine the cheese and cracked pepper in a food processor.

Sift in the flour, baking powder, salt, and baking soda. Mix to blend, using the pulse button, or stir everything together in a mixing bowl. Cut in the chilled butter, until the mixture resembles coarse meal. Pour the buttermilk into the mixture, with the machine running, and blend until the dough just begins to gather together. Do not let the mixture form a ball. If not using a processor, add the buttermilk and stir quickly to incorporate the ingredients lightly.

Flour your hands and gather the dough into a ball. Knead on a lightly floured surface until just smooth, about 10 times. Roll the dough out with a lightly floured rolling pin into a rectangle about 9 × 12 inches. Cut into 1½ × 3-inch fingers, using a sharp knife. Gather together the scraps, reroll and cut into more fingers.

Arrange the biscuit fingers on the prepared baking sheet or nonstick baking sheet, spacing an inch apart. Brush the tops with the melted butter. Bake in the preheated oven for about 10 minutes, until golden brown.

GREEN, WHITE, AND RED SALAD

Serves 24.

¾ cup tarragon vinegar
¼ cup fresh tarragon leaves, or 4 teaspoons dried, crumbled
2 small egg yolks
4 teaspoons Dijon mustard
1 large clove garlic, finely chopped
6 drops hot pepper sauce
1 cup olive oil
1 cup vegetable oil

Salt and freshly ground pepper to taste
6 to 8 bunches watercress, stems removed
12 Belgian endive, trimmed, leaves separated and cut into julienne strips
1 pound radicchio, cored and leaves separated

Blend together the vinegar, tarragon, egg yolks, mustard, garlic, and hot pepper sauce. Slowly beat in the oils. Add salt and pepper to taste. Let the dressing stand at room temperature for several hours to allow the flavors to develop.

To serve, arrange the watercress leaves on the left side of a rimmed rectangular serving platter. Place the endive in the center and the radicchio at the right to resemble the Italian flag. Shake or blend the dressing again and dress the salad.

FLOATING "CAKE" WITH FRESH BERRIES AND RASPBERRY SAUCE

Make two cakes to serve 24. Prepare each meringue separately. There is enough caramel sauce for two cakes. Makes 12 servings.

MERINGUE
Butter for greasing bundt pan and parchment paper; superfine sugar for sprinkling in pan
8 egg whites, at room temperature
¼ teaspoon cream of tartar
⅛ teaspoon salt
1 cup superfine sugar
¼ teaspoon almond extract

CARAMEL SAUCE
2 tablespoons hot water
2 tablespoons light corn syrup
½ cup superfine sugar

Fresh raspberries and/or strawberries
Raspberry Sauce (recipe follows)

Preheat the oven to 350 degrees. Move the rack to the center of the oven. Generously grease a 12-cup bundt pan (non-stick, if possible) with butter and sprinkle with superfine sugar, tapping out any excess. Cut parchment to fit the top of the pan; grease the paper with butter.

Beat the egg whites with the cream of tartar and salt to form soft peaks. Add the cup of superfine sugar, 1 tablespoon at a time, beating until the whites are stiff and glossy. Stir in the almond extract. Gently spoon the meringue into the prepared pan, smoothing the surface to release any air pockets. Cover the top with the parchment, buttered side down.

Place the pan in a deep roasting pan. Pour boiling water into the roasting pan to reach halfway up the sides of the bundt pan. Bake until the meringue rises about 1 inch above the edge of the pan and is lightly colored, about 30 minutes. Transfer the bundt pan to a rack and cool completely. This can be prepared up to 2 days ahead, if kept covered with plastic and refrigerated.

Remove the parchment from the top. Dip the pan into warm water for several seconds to loosen the meringue and then invert onto a serving platter. Blot any syrup on the meringue or the platter.

To make the caramel sauce, combine the water and corn syrup in a small saucepan. Add the sugar and cook over low heat, swirling occasionally, until the sugar dissolves. Increase the heat and boil until the mixture is light brown in color. Cool until slightly thickened. This can be made up to an hour ahead. Drizzle the caramel over the meringue.

Just before serving, fill the center of the meringue with berries. Spoon some Raspberry Sauce around the meringue. Serve the remaining sauce and berries separately.

RASPBERRY SAUCE

Makes about 2½ cups.

2 10-ounce packages frozen raspberries, thawed or 2 pints raspberries sprinkled lightly with sugar, bruised, and left to soften for about an hour
¼ cup superfine sugar
2 tablespoons framboise

Purée all the ingredients in a food processor. Strain in a small bowl, cover, and refrigerate for up to 2 days before serving.

SUMMER PICNIC FOR 20

HERB-STUFFED EGGS
CHICKEN, ARTICHOKE, AND FENNEL IN PITA
MARINATED VEGETABLE STRIPS
MINIATURE CHEESECAKES
FRESH FRUIT

HERB-STUFFED EGGS

Stuffed eggs are forever popular and, the basic egg being of a rather bland nature, infinitely variable. The following includes a recipe for a basic, but slightly spruced-up deviled egg and variations for expanding the repertoire of the basic preparation. Makes 48, serving 20.

2 dozen large eggs
1/2 cup mayonnaise, preferably homemade (see p. 211)
1/2 cup plain yogurt or sour cream
Up to 1/2 cup finely chopped basil, dill, tarragon, marjoram, or parsley, or a combination of herbs

2 tablespoons Dijon mustard
1 tablespoon grainy Dijon mustard
About 1 tablespoon white wine or lemon juice
Salt and freshly ground pepper to taste

Place the eggs in a large saucepan or two medium-sized ones. Cover with cold water and heat to a boil. Reduce the heat and simmer the eggs for 10 minutes. Drain and run cold water over the eggs for about 10 minutes, until they are cool enough to handle.

Shell the eggs, slice in half, and place the yolks in a large bowl. Break up the egg yolks with a fork or in a food processor, pulsing a few times. Stir in the mayonnaise, yogurt or sour cream, half of the herbs, mustards, white wine or lemon juice, and salt and freshly ground pepper to taste. Stuff the eggs and sprinkle with the remaining herbs. If not using immediately, cover the eggs and the mixture tightly and store in the refrigerator until ready to use.

VARIATIONS:

• Caviar: Omit the mustard and herbs and top each stuffed egg with 1/4 teaspoon caviar, or to taste.

• Smoked fish: Stir 1/2 cup finely chopped smoked trout or salmon into the basic mixture, omitting the herbs.

• Chutney: Place a small dollop (1/4 teaspoon) chutney on top of basic deviled eggs, omitting the herbs.

CHICKEN, ARTICHOKE, AND FENNEL IN PITA

This basic salad can be served cold or at room temperature, stuffed into pita or kaiser rolls or served on a bed of greens. Serves 20.

4 pounds chicken breasts	quartered, or 3 10-ounce
2 cloves garlic, peeled and	packages frozen
halved	1 large fennel bulb
2 tablespoons vegetable oil	1 medium-size onion
Salt and freshly ground	2 cups Basic Mayonnaise
pepper to taste	(recipe follows)
1/2 cup balsamic vinegar	1 head Boston or romaine
1/4 cup fruity olive oil	lettuce
1/2 cup grainy mustard	1 head radicchio or red
2 pounds fresh miniature	cabbage
artichoke hearts	

Preheat the oven to 350 degrees.

Rub the chicken breasts with the garlic cloves, vegetable oil, and salt and pepper to taste. Roast in the preheated oven for about 45 minutes. Cool and refrigerate until ready to use, up to a day in advance. When ready to use, remove the chicken meat from the bone and cut into chunks.

Combine ¼ cup of the balsamic vinegar with the olive oil, ¼ cup of the mustard, and salt and pepper to taste.

Place the artichoke hearts in a saucepan and add about 2 inches of water. Cover the pan, bring to a boil, and cook for 10 to 15 minutes, if fresh, 5 to 7 minutes, if frozen. Drain well and place in a bowl. Pour the mustard vinaigrette over the artichokes, making sure to coat them well. Leave to marinate while you prepare the rest of the salad.

Chop finely the fennel and the onion. Combine with the chicken meat and half of the artichoke hearts in a large bowl. Combine the mayonnaise with the remaining vinegar, mustard, and salt and pepper to taste. Toss the mixture with the chicken, fennel, and artichoke hearts. The salad may be kept tightly covered and refrigerated for up to 8 hours.

When ready to serve, slice the pita pockets. Separate the lettuce leaves and shred the radicchio or red cabbage. Stuff a lettuce leaf in each pocket and line with the shredded radicchio or cabbage. Stuff the salad into the pocket, on top of the lettuce. Garnish each sandwich with a piece of the remaining artichoke hearts.

BASIC MAYONNAISE

Makes about 2 cups.

3 egg yolks	Salt and pepper to taste
3 tablespoons lemon juice, or herb vinegar	1½ cups olive oil or vegetable oil
1 tablespoon Dijon, grainy, or other wine mustard	

Combine the egg yolks, lemon juice or vinegar, mustard, and salt and pepper to taste in the bowl of a food processor. Pulse once or twice to combine the ingredients. Turn the motor on and begin adding the oil very slowly in a very thin stream. After about half of the oil has been added you can pour it a little more quickly. Taste the mayonnaise and adjust the seasoning if necessary.

To keep the mayonnaise for up to five days, transfer it to a jar with a tight-fitting lid and refrigerate.

VARIATIONS:

• Mustard mayonnaise: stir 1/4 to 1/3 cup Dijon or grainy mustard into the basic mayonnaise.

• Horseradish mayonnaise: stir 3 tablespoons prepared horseradish into the basic mayonnaise.

• Herb mayonnaise: combine 2 cups fresh watercress, 1/4 cup loosely packed parsley, and 1 tablespoon fresh tarragon leaves in a food processor. Process to chop finely. Stir the mixture into the basic mayonnaise.

Tomato herb mayonnaise: stir 1 tablespoon tomato paste and 1/3 cup finely chopped fresh basil or marjoram into the basic mayonnaise.

MARINATED VEGETABLE STRIPS
Serves 20.

2 pounds carrots	Vinaigrette Dressing (see
2 yellow peppers	p. 188)
2 red peppers	2 pounds green beans
2 bunches scallions	

Wash the carrots; peel if necessary, and cut into strips about 1/4-inch thick × 2 inches. Seed the peppers and cut into strips about the same size. Chop the scallions finely. Combine the vegetables in a large bowl and dress with vinaigrette dressing to taste.

Top and tail the beans. Blanch for about 7 minutes in boiling water. Add to the vegetable mixture while still warm and toss to mix. Cover the vegetables, refrigerate, and leave to marinate for at least 6 hours. Drain before serving.

MINIATURE CHEESECAKES

Makes 4 dozen.

24 ounces cream cheese,
  softened
5 eggs, at room
  temperature
1 cup sugar
2½ teaspoons vanilla
  extract

TOPPING
1 cup sour cream, at room
  temperature
2 tablespoons sugar
2 teaspoons vanilla extract
Strawberries or blueberries
  to garnish, optional

Preheat the oven to 350 degrees. Line miniature muffin cups with papers.

Cream the cheese until light. Blend in the eggs one at a time. Beat in the sugar and vanilla, mixing until smooth.

Fill the lined muffin cups to ⅛ inch from the rim. Bake for 20 to 25 minutes. The cakes should look well set and may have a hint of brown on top. Remove the cakes from the oven and let cool 5 minutes.

While the cakes bake, make the topping by combining the sour cream, sugar, and vanilla. Spread the mixture on the slightly cooled cakes and return them to the oven for an additional 5 minutes. Cool on racks, and refrigerate until ready to serve.

Garnish the cakes with strawberries or blueberries, if you wish.

Substitutions may be made in the Picnic. The following is one alternative.

CAVIAR-STUFFED EGGS
SMOKED TURKEY SALAD ON ENDIVE TIPS, p. 221
MARINATED VEGETABLE STRIPS
MONTEREY BLACKOUTS, p. 231
SKEWERED STRAWBERRIES AND CRÈME FRAÎCHE, p. 221

AFTERNOON WEDDING RECEPTION FOR 75

HUMMUS BI TAHINI WITH CRISP PITA CHIPS
OYSTER PUFFS
SHRIMP AND GINGER ON CUCUMBER
SPINACH AND PHYLLO KISSES
PROSCIUTTO-WRAPPED ASPARAGUS SPEARS
SLICED SAUSAGE WITH HONEY MUSTARD
SMOKED TURKEY SALAD ON ENDIVE TIPS
SKEWERED STRAWBERRIES AND CRÈME FRAÎCHE
WEDDING CAKE

Most of the recipes for this menu are given in quantities to serve 25. They can all be easily tripled to serve 75.

HUMMUS BI TAHINI WITH CRISP PITA CHIPS

The combination of chick-peas and sesame seed paste is a time-honored Middle Eastern specialty. However, hummus has become a basic American party dish, suitable as a dip for the traditional torn pita and as a dip and stuffing for vegetables. Makes about 4 cups, serving 25.

HUMMUS
4 cloves garlic
2 cans chick-peas
½ cup tahini
¼ cup water
¼ cup olive oil
¼ cup fresh lemon juice,
  or to taste

1 teaspoon ground cumin
Salt and pepper to taste

CRISP PITA CHIPS
2 pounds pita bread
½ cup olive oil

Chop the garlic finely in a food processor using the steel blade. Add the chick-peas and tahini and process briefly. Add the water, olive oil, lemon juice, cumin, and salt and pepper to taste. Process until smooth. May be made a day ahead. Cover and refrigerate. Serve with the crisp pita chips.

To make the pita chips, preheat the oven to 300 degrees. Slice the pita rounds in half, and cut each half into triangles. Brush the triangles lightly with the olive oil, place on a baking sheet and toast in the preheated oven for about 30 minutes, or until the bread is crisp. Serve warm or cooled. These will keep for about 2 weeks if kept in a tightly covered container.

Note: Tahini is found in specialty shops as well as in Middle Eastern grocery stores. If you can't find it, you can make it by grinding 3/4 cup sesame seeds in a blender, adding 1/4 cup water and 2 tablespoons vegetable oil and blending again until smooth.

OYSTER PUFFS

Makes about 50, serving 25.

Choux Paste (recipe
  follows)
Oyster-mushroom filling:
2 tablespoons butter
1 small onion, finely
  chopped
1/4 pound mushrooms,
  finely chopped

Salt and pepper
8 ounces cream cheese,
  softened
1 can smoked oysters,
  drained and chopped
2 teaspoons lemon juice

Prepare miniature choux puffs, as directed below.

To make the filling, melt the butter in a skillet. Add the onion and sauté for about 5 minutes, until the onions begin to look transparent. Add the mushrooms and cook, stirring, occasionally, for an additional 10 minutes, until most of the mushroom liquid has evaporated. Season the mixture to taste with salt and pepper and set aside to cool.

Beat the cream cheese until light and almost fluffy. Stir in the mushroom mixture, the chopped oysters, and the lemon juice. Fill the choux puffs with the mixture, using a pastry bag or small spoon.

CHOUX PASTE

Choux paste is one of the most versatile of basic preparations, since it can be used to make puffs for hors d'oeuvre, main courses, and desserts. Makes about 4 dozen miniature puffs or éclairs.

Butter for greasing baking sheets	8 tablespoons butter
	1/4 teaspoon salt
1 cup water or half milk, half water	1 cup sifted flour
	4 eggs

Preheat the oven to 400 degrees. Lightly grease two or three baking sheets.

Combine the water, butter, and salt in a saucepan. Heat to a boil, stirring briefly to combine the ingredients. Remove the mixture from the heat and add the flour all at once. Stir vigorously with a wooden spoon until the mixture leaves the sides of the pan and clings to the spoon. Set the pan aside to cool for two or three minutes.

Add the eggs, one at a time, beating well after each addition. The mixture should be smooth and glossy before adding the next egg. This step may be done in a food processor, but while doing it by hand takes arm power, it saves a step as well as a pot.

Drop the mixture by rounded teaspoons, or pipe with a pastry bag, onto the prepared sheets. Leave about 2 inches between puffs to allow for expansion.

Bake the choux for 10 minutes. Reduce the heat to 350

degrees and bake for an additional 15 minutes, until the puffs are golden brown and feel rigid to the touch.

Turn off the oven. Slit the puffs in the side or bottom to allow steam to escape and return to the oven for about 30 minutes to dry out. This step is not absolutely necessary, but it will make the puffs drier. Or pull out the insides if they are moist and discard.

Note: Choux paste may be made a day in advance and refrigerated. When ready to refrigerate, brush the top with melted butter before covering. To use, place the mixture in a heavy saucepan and warm over a low flame until just tepid, stirring constantly. Choux paste that has been made in advance may not puff as high as freshly made, making it most suitable for small appetizer fillings.

Cooked shells also freeze well, allowing you to make several batches at a time. Place cooled shells into plastic bags or boxes and freeze. When ready to use, preheat the oven to 425 degrees. Place the shells on a baking sheet and heat for 3 to 4 minutes. Fill as for any puffs.

Fillings for choux puffs: pâté, salmon mousse, Roquefort and cognac, soft goat cheese, herbed cream cheese.

SHRIMP AND GINGER ON CUCUMBER

Makes about 50, serving 25.

1½ pounds medium-size
  shrimp
4 English cucumbers
¼ cup mayonnaise,

preferably homemade
  (see p. 211)
½ cup pickled ginger

Fill a steamer with an inch of water. Place the shrimp in the basket and steam for about 3 minutes, until the shrimp just turn pink. Remove and let cool. Peel the shrimp and slice in half lengthwise. Remove the sandy vein.

Score the cucumbers with a zester or fork. Slice into ¼-inch pieces, slightly on the diagonal. Spread a tiny dab of mayonnaise on each cucumber slice, then fit with a piece of pickled ginger, trimming to fit if necessary. Top with a shrimp half.

Place the canapés on serving platters and garnish with herbs or leaves.

SPINACH AND PHYLLO KISSES

These pastries can be kept refrigerated for up to a day before cooking. Makes 60, serving 25.

Spinach Filling:
10 ounces frozen chopped spinach, defrosted
2 tablespoons butter
1 tablespoon olive oil
1/2 cup finely chopped onion
1 clove garlic, finely chopped
1/2 cup ricotta cheese
1/3 cup feta cheese, finely crumbled
1/4 teaspoon freshly ground nutmeg
Salt and freshly ground pepper to taste

4 sheets phyllo dough
8 tablespoons butter, melted

Drain and then squeeze the spinach dry of as much water as possible.

Melt the 2 tablespoons butter and olive oil in a skillet. Add the onion and garlic and cook over moderately low heat, stirring occasionally, until the onions are tender, about 15 minutes. Stir in the spinach and cook for an additional 10 to 15 minutes, until all liquid has evaporated.

Combine the ricotta cheese, feta cheese, nutmeg, and salt and freshly ground pepper to taste. Stir in the spinach mixture.

Preheat the oven to 350 degrees.

Place 1 phyllo sheet on a work surface and brush quickly with melted butter. Cover the first sheet with a second and brush it with butter. Keep the remaining phyllo dough covered with a damp towel.

Cut the buttered dough into 30 squares. Place a little bit of the spinach filling in the center of each square, and working quickly, gather the corners of the dough and twist over the filling to form a kiss. Place on a baking sheet.

Repeat the procedure for the remaining dough and filling.

Bake the pastries in the preheated oven for about 10 minutes, until the phyllo is golden brown. Serve immediately.

PROSCIUTTO-WRAPPED ASPARAGUS SPEARS

Makes 50 pieces.

50 asparagus spears
1/2 pound prosciutto

Wash and trim the asparagus spears as necessary. Snap the stalks where tender. Fill a steamer with an inch of water and bring to a boil. Add the asparagus and cook for about 3 minutes, or until just tender. Plunge the asparagus in cold water to stop their cooking; drain and dry.

Cut the prosciutto into 50 strips and wrap a strip around each asparagus spear. Arrange on serving platters, cover, and refrigerate until 30 minutes before serving. These may be made several hours ahead.

SLICED SAUSAGE WITH HONEY MUSTARD

Makes about 50, serving 25.

2 pounds smoked sausage, such as kielbasa
Vegetable oil
2 cups grainy Dijon mustard
1 cup smooth Dijon mustard

½ cup honey
2 tablespoons orange liqueur
2 loaves ficelle (very thin French bread), sliced
1 bunch fresh sage leaves, for garnish

Slice the sausage diagonally into ¼-inch-thick ovals.

Heat a few tablespoons of the oil in a large skillet. Add sausage slices to fit the pan in one layer and cook over moderate heat, until browned on each side. Drain the sausage on paper towels. Add more sausage to the pan, and more oil as necessary, and brown on both sides. Drain and repeat the procedure until all the sausage is cooked. Place the sausage in a roasting pan for reheating. The browned sausage can be covered and refrigerated for up to a day before serving.

When ready to assemble, reheat the sausage in a 300 degree oven for about 15 minutes.

Combine the mustards, honey, and orange liqueur. Spread the bread with a very thin layer of the mustard. Place a piece of sausage on each piece of bread and top with another tiny bit of mustard. Garnish each with a small slice of sage leaf before serving. Garnish the serving plates with sage leaves.

SMOKED TURKEY SALAD ON
ENDIVE TIPS

Serves 25.

2 pounds smoked turkey
   breast, julienned
1/2 pound prosciutto, or
   other cured ham,
   coarsely chopped
1/4 pound Gruyère or
   Jarlsberg cheese,
   julienned
1 cup finely chopped
   celery

1 1/2 cups Herb Mayonnaise
   (see pp. 211–12)
1 tablespoon green
   peppercorns, optional
1 pound Belgian endive,
   separated into leaves
Fresh herbs for garnish

Combine the turkey, prosciutto, cheese, and celery in a
bowl. Fold in the mayonnaise and the green peppercorns.
This salad can be made up to 3 hours ahead and kept
refrigerated.

Place a teaspoonful of the salad on the tips of the endive
leaves. Arrange on serving platters and garnish with fresh
herbs before serving.

SKEWERED STRAWBERRIES
AND CRÈME FRAÎCHE

Serves 25.

2 vanilla beans
2 cups superfine sugar
75 strawberries

1 bunch fresh mint leaves
1 package bamboo skewers
2 cups crème fraîche

Combine the vanilla beans and superfine sugar in a jar
with a lid, shake, and set aside for at least a day.

Rinse, drain, hull, and dry the strawberries.

To assemble the skewers, separate the mint leaves. Thread a mint leaf on each skewer, followed by three strawberries, ending with a mint leaf. Sprinkle with the vanilla sugar and serve, accompanied by bowls of crème fraîche and garnished with more mint leaves, if desired.

Many substitutions may be made in the Wedding Reception. The following are two possible alternatives.

ALTERNATIVE 1:

BASKET OF FRESH ASPARAGUS
WITH SESAME-CHIVE SAUCE, p. 252
BAKED CLAMS WITH CORIANDER BUTTER, p. 266
SMOKED SALMON WITH BROWN BREAD AND BUTTER, p. 276
SHRIMP AND GINGER ON CUCUMBER
SPINACH AND PHYLLO KISSES
FRESH FIGS WRAPPED WITH WESTPHALIAN HAM, p. 253
ROASTED BEEF TENDERLOIN, p. 277
SKEWERED STRAWBERRIES AND CRÈME FRAÎCHE
WEDDING CAKE

ALTERNATIVE 2:

MARINATED OLIVES, p. 192
PUFF PASTRY FILLED WITH HERBED CHEESE
AND PESTO, p. 235
PÂTÉ EGGS, p. 199
PHYLLO CUPS WITH GUACAMOLE, p. 254
PROSCIUTTO-WRAPPED ASPARAGUS SPEARS
SMOKED TURKEY SALAD ON ENDIVE TIPS
COUNTRY HAM WITH HOT LITTLE BISCUITS, p. 240
SKEWERED STRAWBERRIES AND CRÈME FRAÎCHE
WEDDING CAKE

GALLIMAUFREY'S AFTER-SKI
REFRESHMENTS FOR 10

TWEED CAKE
LINZERTORTE
HOT COCOA
MULLED APPLE CIDER

TWEED CAKE

Serves 10.

CAKE
Butter and flour for
preparing cake pans
8 tablespoons butter or
margarine
1 cup sugar
2 cups cake flour
1 tablespoon baking
powder
Scant 1/8 teaspoon salt
1 cup milk
1 teaspoon vanilla extract
3 ounces frozen bitter
chocolate
3 egg whites

FROSTING
12 tablespoons butter,
softened
3 egg yolks
2 1/4 cups sifted
confectioners' sugar

CHOCOLATE SHADOW
1 cup chocolate chips (or 6
ounces semisweet
chocolate)
2 tablespoons water

To make the cake, preheat the oven to 350 degrees.
Grease and flour 2 9-inch round cake pans.

Beat together the butter and 1/2 cup of the sugar until
creamy. Sift together the flour, baking powder, and salt.

Combine the milk and vanilla. Add the flour mixture and

milk mixture alternately to the creamed butter and sugar, beginning and ending with the flour. Beat in each addition until smooth.

Finely grate the chocolate. This can be done in a food processor, but its texture is best if done by hand on a grater, which is why you want the chocolate icy cold. Blend the chocolate into the batter.

Beat the egg whites until foamy. Add the remaining sugar a tablespoon at a time, beating constantly, until the whites are stiff and glossy, forming a meringue. Fold into the batter gently.

Fill the prepared pans with the batter and bake for 20 to 25 minutes. Cool slightly before turning out onto racks to cool thoroughly.

Note: Despite the baking powder and meringue, this is not a high-rising cake.

To make the frosting, combine the softened butter, egg yolks, and sifted confectioners' sugar and beat until smooth. Fill and frost the cake. Refrigerate to chill.

To make the shadow, melt the chocolate chips or chocolate in a heavy saucepan over very low heat. Add the water and stir until smooth. Pour over the top of the chilled cake and let it drip down the sides a bit.

One last note: Don't try this cake in any other but 9-inch pans, as it is fussy. However, the eating more than makes up for its idiosyncrasies.

LINZERTORTE

With a mug full of hot something, this is almost worth a northern winter's gray days, says Sally Godfrey. Serves 10.

2 cups flour	8 ounces unblanched
1 tablespoon cinnamon	almonds, finely ground
1/2 teaspoon ground cloves	1 1/2 teaspoons grated
8 ounces butter	lemon rind
1 cup sugar	1 cup raspberry or apricot
2 egg yolks	preserves

Preheat the oven to 350 degrees. Combine the flour, cinnamon, and ground cloves.

Cream the butter and sugar well. Add the egg yolks, almonds, lemon rind, and the flour mixture and mix thoroughly. Pat about two thirds of the dough into the bottom and up the sides of a 10-inch tart pan. Spread the preserves over the whole surface.

Roll the remaining dough out and cut into strips to make a lattice top. This is the only difficult part of the recipe. If you prefer a less frustrating and just as attractive top, roll out the dough and cut into shapes with cookie cutters. Decorate the torte with the shapes.

Bake the torte in the preheated oven for 30 to 40 minutes, until the crust is brown and crisp.

MULLED APPLE CIDER

Serves 10.

1 gallon apple cider
About 48 whole cloves
4 teaspoons whole allspice
4 sticks cinnamon, broken
   into pieces

¾ cup sugar
1 cup orange juice
½ cup lemon juice

Combine all of the ingredients in a stockpot, over moderate heat. Simmer for 10 to 20 minutes, and serve hot.

The mulled cider will keep for at least a week or two refrigerated, and, in fact, gets better with age.

SWEET SATISFACTION'S
AFTERNOON TEA FOR 12

POPPY SEED RING CAKE
ORANGE MARMALADE RAISIN MUFFINS
BUTTERMILK SCONES
WALNUT AND CINNAMON SCONES
MONTEREY BLACKOUTS
CURRANT SHORTBREAD
TEA

POPPY SEED RING CAKE

Makes 8 to 10 slices.

1/4 cup poppy seeds	3/4 cup vegetable oil
5 ounces evaporated milk	1/2 teaspoon vanilla extract
Butter for greasing ring mold	1 1/2 cups sifted flour
2 eggs	1 tablespoon baking powder
1/2 cup sugar	1/2 teaspoon salt

Soak the poppy seeds in the milk overnight.

Preheat the oven to 350 degrees. Grease well a 4-cup ring mold.

Beat the eggs and sugar until thick and pale, using a food processor or mixer. Stir in the oil, vanilla, and poppy seed mixture.

Sift together the flour, baking powder, and salt. Blend into the poppy mixture, stirring until thoroughly incorporated.

Pour the batter into the prepared mold. Place in the preheated oven and bake for 45 minutes, or until a cake tester inserted in the center comes out clean. Let the cake cool slightly before turning out onto a rack to cool completely.

ORANGE MARMALADE RAISIN MUFFINS

Original American teatime baked goods, combined with a truly British concoction—marmalade—muffins are an essential companion to tea. Makes 12 muffins.

Butter for greasing muffin cups
1 2/3 cups flour
1/4 cup sugar
1 1/2 teaspoons baking powder
1/4 teaspoon salt
1/8 teaspoon ground cloves
4 tablespoons unsalted butter

1/3 cup raisins
1 tablespoon grated orange rind
1/3 cup good quality orange marmalade
1/4 cup milk
1 egg, beaten

Preheat the oven to 350 degrees. Grease 12 muffin cups well.

Sift together the flour, sugar, baking powder, salt, and cloves in a large mixing bowl. Cut in the butter with a pastry blender or two knives. Toss in the raisins and orange rind.

Combine the marmalade, milk, and egg, and mix well. Add this to the flour mixture, stirring just until incorporated. Spoon the batter into the muffin cups, filling three-quarters full.

Bake in the preheated oven for 20 minutes, or until golden brown and a cake tester inserted in the center comes out clean. Cool slightly before serving with butter.

BUTTERMILK SCONES

The two scone recipes here should be served with a selection of butter, jam, honey, and clotted or whipped cream. These buttermilk scones are light and flaky. Makes 12 small round scones or 8 larger triangular ones.

Butter for greasing baking sheet
2 cups flour
2 tablespoons baking powder
1/4 cup sugar

1/2 teaspoon salt
8 tablespoons unsalted butter, chilled
2 eggs
2/3 cup buttermilk, plus 2 tablespoons for glaze

Preheat the oven to 400 degrees. Grease a baking sheet.

Sift together the flour, baking powder, sugar, and salt. Cut in the butter, using a pastry blender or two knives, until the mixture resembles coarse meal.

Beat together the eggs and the 2/3 cup buttermilk.

Make a well in the center of the dry ingredients and pour in the egg-milk mixture. Stir the mixture with a fork to incorporate the wet with the dry, and mix until a sticky ball forms.

Roll out the dough on a lightly floured work surface into a flat 3/4-inch-thick round. Cut out scones with a 2-inch cookie cutter, rerolling any leftover scraps. Alternatively, leave the dough whole and score into 8 triangles.

Place the dough on the greased baking sheet and brush with the remaining buttermilk. Bake in the preheated oven for 15 to 20 minutes, or until golden brown. If making the scored scones, check after 20 minutes and cook an extra 5 minutes or so, if necessary. Serve warm with butter or clotted cream and jam.

WALNUT AND CINNAMON SCONES

These scones are dense and hearty. Makes 12 to 15 scones.

Butter for greasing baking
sheet
2 cups flour
2 teaspoons baking
powder
1 teaspoon ground
cinnamon
1/2 teaspoon baking soda
1/2 teaspoon salt
8 tablespoons unsalted
butter, chilled

1/2 cup finely chopped
walnuts
2 eggs, beaten
2/3 cup milk
1/2 cup honey
1 egg beaten with 1
tablespoon milk for egg
wash

Preheat the oven to 425 degrees. Lightly grease a baking
sheet.

Sift together the flour, baking powder, cinnamon, baking
soda, and salt. Cut in the butter with a pastry blender or
two knives until the mixture resembles coarse meal. Stir in
the nuts.

Combine the eggs, milk, and honey in a food processor
or blender, and process well. Make a well in the center of
the dry ingredients, and pour in the liquid mixture. Stir
with a fork until the ingredients are just incorporated and a
ball forms.

Working quickly, and handling the dough lightly, shape
the dough into small 2-inch rounds, about 3/4-inch thick.
Place the rounds on the greased baking sheet and brush the
tops with the egg wash. Bake in the preheated oven for 10
minutes, or until the bottoms are golden brown.

MONTEREY BLACKOUTS

Makes 2 dozen.

CRUST

1 cup flour
1/4 cup unsweetened cocoa
  powder
2 tablespoons sugar
Scant 1/8 teaspoon salt
8 tablespoons cold butter,
  cut into small pieces
1/4 cup prepared espresso
  coffee, chilled

FILLING

1 cup (6 ounces)
  semisweet chocolate
  chips, melted

1/4 cup sugar
1 tablespoon butter,
  melted
1 1/2 teaspoons milk
1 1/2 teaspoons coffee
  liqueur
1 1/2 teaspoons vanilla
  extract
1 egg at room temperature
1/4 cup finely chopped
  toasted walnuts or other
  nuts

To make the crust, sift together the flour, cocoa, sugar, and salt into the bowl of a food processor or large mixing bowl. Cut in the butter until the mixture resembles coarse meal. Gradually add the coffee, mixing just until incorporated. Turn the dough out of the bowl and pat into a log. Wrap in wax paper or plastic wrap and refrigerate at least 3 hours or overnight.

Cut the dough into 2 equal pieces. Working with one piece at a time (keeping the remainder refrigerated), roll the dough into a thin circle, approximately 14 inches in diameter and 1/8-inch thick. Cut the dough into rounds with a 3-inch cookie cutter or inverted glass. Gently mold the dough into miniature muffin pans. Repeat with the remaining dough. Chill.

Preheat the oven to 375 degrees.

To make the filling, combine the melted chocolate,

sugar, melted butter, milk, coffee liqueur, and vanilla in a food processor or medium-sized mixing bowl. Process or mix to blend well. Add the egg and process or beat until smooth. Fold in the walnuts.

Place a rounded teaspoon of filling into each muffin cup. Bake the tartlets for 20 to 25 minutes, or until a cake tester inserted in the middle comes out clean. Cool in the pans for 15 to 20 minutes before transferring to wire racks to cool completely.

CURRANT SHORTBREAD

Because no tea is complete without shortbread, try these with the interesting twist of currants. Makes 8 or 16 shortbread wedges.

1/2 cup currants	3/4 cup rice flour
1/3 cup fresh lemon juice	1/2 cup confectioners'
8 ounces unsalted butter,	sugar
softened	1/4 teaspoon salt
3/4 cup flour	

Soak the currants in the lemon juice for 1 hour. Drain thoroughly, pat dry with paper towels, and set aside.

Preheat the oven to 325 degrees.

Cream the butter until smooth in a food processor or with a mixer.

Sift together the flour, rice flour, confectioners' sugar, and salt. Blend in the butter until thoroughly incorporated. Stir in the currants.

Press the mixture evenly into a shallow 8-inch round cake pan. Smooth the dough over the currants, so that none are exposed on top. Score with a knife into 8 wedges; prick all over with a fork.

Bake in the preheated oven for 20 to 30 minutes, or until

the shortbread is very lightly golden. Cut into wedges while hot (if desired, cut carefully into small wedges). Leave in the pan to cool completely. These cookies will keep several days if kept tightly covered.

COCKTAIL PARTY FOR 50

CUCUMBERS WITH TARAMASALATA
PUFF PASTRY FILLED WITH HERBED CHEESE AND PESTO
MONTRACHET IN PHYLLO
NEW POTATOES STUFFED WITH CAVIAR
CHICKEN SATAY WITH PEANUT SAUCE
COUNTRY HAM WITH HOT LITTLE BISCUITS
BLACK-BOTTOM NUT TARTLETS

CUCUMBERS WITH TARAMASALATA

Makes about 50, serving 25.

4 English cucumbers
2 cups Taramasalata (recipe follows)
Fresh coriander to garnish

Cut the cucumbers into rounds about 3/4-inch thick. Scoop out a portion of the seeds with a small melon baller. Discard the pulp. Fill the cucumber rounds with taramasalata and garnish with a small sprig of fresh coriander. Fresh cucumbers should be served within an hour of preparing.

TARAMASALATA

Makes about 2 cups.

2 slices firm white bread
2 cloves garlic
2/3 cup olive oil

2/3 cup tarama (mullet roe)
1/4 cup fresh lemon juice

Soak the bread in water until well softened, about 10 minutes, then drain and squeeze out the water.

Chop the garlic finely in the food processor. Add the soaked bread, olive oil, tarama, and lemon juice. Process until the mixture is smooth and thick. Thin with a little water or lemon juice, if necessary.

Note: Taramasalata can be served as a dip with pita triangles, water crackers, raw vegetables, or stuffed into endive leaves, cherry tomatoes, mushroom caps, or baby pattypan squash caps.

PUFF PASTRY FILLED WITH HERBED CHEESE AND PESTO

Makes about 100, serving 50.

2 pounds frozen puff pastry, thawed
8 ounces soft herbed cheese
1 cup Pesto Sauce (recipe follows)

Preheat the oven to 500 degrees.

Roll the pastry out according to the package directions. Cut into 1-inch circles, place on ungreased baking sheets and bake in the preheated oven for five minutes. Lower the temperature to 375 degrees and bake for an additional 10 minutes, or until puffed and golden in color. Cool the pastry on racks.

Slit the cooled pastries and fill half of them with a teaspoon of the herbed cheese, and the other half with a teaspoon of pesto.

Note: If you can't find herbed cheese, stir 2 tablespoons chopped fresh marjoram and 2 tablespoons chopped fresh thyme and 1 clove very finely chopped garlic or 1 teaspoon very finely chopped scallion into softened cream cheese.

PESTO SAUCE

Makes about 1 1/2 cups.

2 ounces Parmesan cheese
1/4 cup pecans
2 cloves garlic
4 cups fresh basil leaves

1/4 cup best-quality olive
oil
1/4 teaspoon salt

Finely grate the cheese in a food processor. There will be about 1/2 cup. Transfer to a small bowl. Add the pecans and garlic to the food processor, and process for a few seconds. Transfer the mixture to another small bowl. Add the basil leaves to the food processor and chop finely. Add the pecans and garlic to the mixture, process very briefly, and then add the cheese. Pour in the olive oil and the salt and process briefly. The mixture should be a thick paste. If it's too thick, thin with olive oil to taste. Taste and adjust the seasoning with more cheese or salt.

Note: This pesto sauce can be served on pasta as a side dish or luncheon main course, or as a dip for vegetables, crackers, or bread, or stuffing for tomatoes or tea sandwiches.

MONTRACHET IN PHYLLO

Serves 25.

Butter for greasing baking
sheet
12 sheets phyllo dough
1/2 pound unsalted butter,
melted

1 1/2 cups herbed bread
crumbs
3 Montrachet logs

Preheat the oven to 350 degrees. Grease a baking sheet. Place a sheet of phyllo dough on the baking sheet, brush with butter, and add another sheet: butter and add another. Repeat the procedure with a total of 4 of the sheets, making sure to keep the unused sheets covered with a damp towel. Moisten the bread crumbs with about 1/2 cup of the butter. Cover each log with bread crumbs, pressing them in well. Place a log on one edge of the buttered phyllo. Fold the ends in and roll up. Repeat the procedure with the remaining phyllo dough and cheese.

Bake the phyllo-wrapped Montrachet in the preheated oven for 20 to 30 minutes, until the pastry is golden in color. Remove and let cool for at least 30 minutes before serving. This can be made up to 3 hours ahead.

NEW POTATOES STUFFED WITH CAVIAR

Makes 50, serving 25.

50 very small new potatoes (about 2½ pounds, depending on size)
1/2 teaspoon salt
1/4 cup vegetable oil, approximately

1 cup sour cream
Salt and pepper to taste
4 ounces caviar—black, red, or golden

Wash the potatoes and place in a large saucepan. Cover with water, add the salt and bring to a boil. Cook until the potatoes are tender, about 20 minutes. Drain and cool.

Cut a small slice off the bottom of each potato so that it will stand up. Scoop out about half of the flesh from each potato—a melon baller is useful for this task. Place the potato pulp in a bowl and mash with a fork. Rub the potato skins with the oil. If you wish, you may cover and refrigerate the potatoes for up to 2 days.

Combine the mashed potatoes and the sour cream. Season with salt and pepper. Fill the potato skins with the mixture and place a small amount of caviar atop each one.

VARIATIONS:

• To make cheese-filled potatoes substitute grated Parmesan, cheddar, or jalapeño cheese, or finely crumbled blue, soft goat cheese, or herb cheese for the sour cream and caviar. Stir up to 1/4 cup milk into the potato mixture, if necessary, to make it a spreading consistency. Warm the filled potatoes in a 350 degree oven for 5 to 10 minutes. Serve warm or cold.

• To make ham or bacon-filled potatoes, stir 1/4 pound finely chopped smoked ham or crisp, crumbled bacon into the mashed potatoes.

CHICKEN SATAY WITH PEANUT SAUCE

Makes about 75 skewers, serving 50.

5 pounds boneless chicken breasts, cut into 1/2-inch-wide strips
1/2 cup sesame oil
1/2 cup vegetable oil
1 cup dry sherry
3/4 cup soy sauce
2 tablespoons finely chopped garlic
2 tablespoons finely chopped fresh ginger
1/2 teaspoon salt
1/2 teaspoon pepper

SAUCE
1/4 cup vegetable oil
2 tablespoons sesame oil
2 teaspoons hot oil, optional
1 bunch scallions, finely chopped

1/3 cup finely chopped garlic
1 small onion, finely chopped
2 tablespoons finely chopped fresh ginger
3 tablespoons red wine vinegar
3 tablespoons sugar
1 1/2 cups peanut butter
1 cup hot water
1/3 cup soy sauce
3 tablespoons fresh lime juice
1 tablespoon ground coriander
1 1/2 teaspoons black pepper
Small bamboo skewers
1 bunch fresh coriander for garnish

Place the chicken in a large bowl. Combine the sesame oil, vegetable oil, sherry, soy sauce, garlic, ginger, and salt and pepper in a jar with a tight-fitting lid. Shake the mixture vigorously and pour over the chicken. Cover, refrigerate, and marinate for up to 12 hours, turning occasionally.

To make the sauce, heat the vegetable oil, sesame oil, and optional hot oil in a large saucepan. Add the scallions, garlic, onion, and ginger and cook gently for about 5 minutes, over moderate heat, until the scallions are translucent. Add the vinegar and sugar and cook, stirring constantly, until the sauce caramelizes, about 3 minutes. Remove from the heat and stir in the peanut butter, hot water, soy sauce, lime juice, coriander, and pepper. Cover and refrigerate until 1 hour before serving.

An hour before cooking, soak the bamboo skewers in water.

When ready to cook, thread the marinated chicken onto the soaked skewers and place on racks in baking pans.

Preheat the oven to 375 degrees. Bake the chicken for about 10 minutes. Serve the chicken immediately, accompanied by bowls of the peanut sauce, garnished with the fresh coriander.

Note: You may substitute shrimp, chicken, beef, or lamb for the chicken.

COUNTRY HAM WITH HOT LITTLE BISCUITS

Country ham is something of a nuisance to prepare, since it needs to be soaked for at least a day in advance of its long cooking. However, few people make it themselves and it is perfect special party food when sliced paper-thin and served with hot biscuits or little rolls and mustard. Serves 50.

16-pound country or   ¼ cup Dijon mustard
  Smithfield ham   ¼ cup apple juice or
Cloves   water
1 cup dark brown sugar

Place the ham in a large roaster and cover with water. Leave to soak for at least a whole day, preferably 36 hours. Scrub the ham well with a brush to remove any mold on the skin (this is normal). Discard the water. Return the ham to the roaster and place on a burner. Add water to cover.

Bring the water to a boil, lower the heat and simmer for 20 minutes per pound, about 3½ hours.

Preheat the oven to 425 degrees.

Drain the ham. When cool enough to handle, skin the ham. Trim the fat, leaving about ½ inch. Score the fat into a diamond pattern and place a clove in the point of each diamond. Combine the brown sugar and mustard and pat over the ham evenly. Brush with the apple juice or water and bake for about 20 minutes, just long enough to glaze. Baste occasionally with the apple juice or water.

Let the meat rest for about 15 minutes before carving. It can be served warm or cold. Slice the ham across the grain into paper-thin slices; this is essential. Serve with hot little biscuits (recipe follows) or miniature rolls.

HOT LITTLE BISCUITS

Makes about 100.

4 cups sifted flour
2 tablespoons baking
   powder
½ teaspoon salt

8 tablespoons chilled
   butter, cut into pieces
1½ cups heavy cream

Preheat the oven to 450 degrees.

Combine the flour, baking powder, and salt. Cut in the butter, either in the food processor or by hand, until the mixture resembles coarse crumbs. Add the cream all at once and stir quickly to combine.

Turn the dough onto a floured board, and knead gently and briefly. The longer you handle the dough, the tougher the biscuits. Divide the dough in quarters and roll out each quarter about ¼ to ⅜-inch thick. Cut with a small cutter into 1-inch biscuits. Place on ungreased baking sheets and bake for 8 to 10 minutes, or until golden brown on top.

Split and serve immediately. These taste best when freshly made, however, they can be made up to 2 hours in advance and warmed before serving.

BLACK-BOTTOM NUT TARTLETS

Makes about 25 1½-inch pastries.

PASTRY
2 cups flour
½ teaspoon salt
8 tablespoons unsalted butter, chilled, cut into pieces
6 tablespoons vegetable shortening, chilled, cut into pieces
5 to 6 tablespoons cold water, or as needed

FILLING
½ cup semisweet chocolate chips

3 eggs
1 cup dark brown sugar
¾ cup light corn syrup
4 tablespoons butter, melted
½ teaspoon salt
1½ cups chopped pecans or walnuts
½ teaspoon vanilla extract
Grated rind of 1 lemon
1 cup whipped cream, crème fraîche, or sour cream to garnish, optional

To make the crust, combine the flour and salt in a food processor or bowl. Add the butter and shortening and process with the pulse button of the processor, or cut in with a pastry blender or fork until the mixture resembles coarse meal. If using a food processor, transfer the dough to a bowl. Sprinkle the mixture with the water and stir to combine quickly, just until the mixture holds together. Form the dough into two balls, flatten each slightly, wrap in plastic wrap, and chill for at least an hour. This can be made up to two days in advance and kept refrigerated, or made up to two weeks in advance and kept frozen.

When ready to bake, preheat the oven to 400 degrees. Roll out the dough very thinly on a floured surface. Cut into 2½-inch rounds using a biscuit cutter or juice glass. Line miniature muffin cups with the pastry. Drop a couple of chocolate chips in the bottom of each lined cup.

To make the filling, beat the eggs until light. Add the brown sugar, corn syrup, butter, and salt and beat well. Stir in the chopped nuts, vanilla extract, and grated lemon rind. Spoon the mixture into the prepared tins.

Bake for 10 minutes, then lower the heat to 350 degrees and bake an additional 20 minutes, or until the tartlets are puffed and the crust is golden in color. Remove from the oven and cool on wire racks (the filling will settle).

Serve the tartlets garnished with whipped cream, crème fraîche, or sour cream, if desired.

Many substitutions may be made in the Cocktail Party menu. The following are two possible alternatives.

ALTERNATIVE 1:

OYSTER PUFFS, p. 215
HERB-STUFFED EGGS, p. 209
HERBED BRIE EN CROUTE, p. 252
NEW POTATOES STUFFED WITH CAVIAR
CHICKEN SATAY WITH PEANUT SAUCE
COUNTRY HAM WITH HOT LITTLE BISCUITS
STRAWBERRY SHORTCAKE, p. 249

ALTERNATIVE 2:

MARINATED OLIVES, p. 192
CHEESE TRUFFLES, p. 191
PESTO-STUFFED TOMATOES, p. 235
BEEF CARPACCIO, p. 204
CHICKEN SATAY WITH PEANUT SAUCE
SLICED SAUSAGE WITH HONEY MUSTARD, p. 220
SKEWERED STRAWBERRIES AND CRÈME FRAÎCHE, p. 221

SPRING DINNER FOR 12

CHEDDAR AND CHIVE STRAWS
FIDDLEHEAD SOUP
ROAST LEG OF LAMB WITH LEMON AND HERBS
FRESH PEAS WITH MINT
RED POTATOES BAKED WITH CREAM
BOSTON AND RADICCHIO SALAD
WITH VINAIGRETTE DRESSING
FRENCH BREAD AND SWEET BUTTER
STRAWBERRY SHORTCAKE

CHEDDAR AND CHIVE STRAWS

Makes about 4 dozen.

1/2 cup grated Vermont cheddar cheese
2 tablespoons finely snipped fresh chives
1 pound fresh or frozen puff pastry, thawed

Preheat the oven to 350 degrees.
Combine the cheese and snipped chives.
Roll out the dough into a 20 × 24-inch rectangle. Sprinkle a third of the cheese mixture over the dough. Press the cheese mixture into the dough with the rolling pin. Fold the dough and roll out into a 20 × 24-inch rectangle. Sprinkle with a third of the cheese and roll again. Repeat the procedure with the remaining third of the cheese mixture.
Cut the dough into strips 1/4 to 1/3-inch wide. Twist the strips into even corkscrews and place closely together on ungreased cookie sheets. The edges of the strips should touch lightly, to keep them from unfurling. Bake the straws in the preheated oven for 15 to 20 minutes.

Cut the straws into thirds immediately after removing from the oven. Transfer to racks to cool. Store in an airtight container or in the refrigerator until ready to serve. Serve warmed or cold. Cheese straws will stay fresh for up to a week.

Note: You may leave out the chives, if you wish, or substitute fresh dill or coriander.

VARIATIONS:

Parmesan straws: substitute grated Parmesan or Asiago for the cheddar and 1 clove garlic, very finely chopped, for the chives.

Gruyère straws: substitute grated Gruyère for the cheddar and Dijon mustard for the chives.

FIDDLEHEAD SOUP

Fiddlehead ferns are a spring treat available for only a short time. Their taste is that of a mild green and they have a tender but slightly crunchy texture. Makes 12 servings.

2 pounds fiddleheads	2 cups dry white wine
(reserve 12 for garnish)	2 tablespoons lemon juice
2 onions	½ teaspoon freshly
6 tablespoons butter	ground nutmeg
8 cups chicken broth,	1 cup heavy cream
preferably homemade	1 cup yogurt

Rinse the fiddleheads thoroughly and pinch off the ends of the stems.

Peel and chop the onions. Heat the butter in a large saucepan or Dutch oven. Add the onions and sauté over low heat until tender, about 15 minutes. Reserve 12 of the fiddleheads for garnish and add the remaining ones to the onions. Sauté gently for about 10 minutes.

Stir the chicken broth and wine into the vegetables and simmer over low heat for 30 minutes. Cool the soup for about 10 minutes before adding the lemon juice and nutmeg. Stir in the cream and yogurt. Purée the soup in small batches in a food processor or blender.

Cool and chill the soup until ready to use. Steam the reserved fiddleheads. Heat the soup gently to warm. Garnish each portion with a fiddlehead.

ROAST LEG OF LAMB WITH LEMON AND HERBS

Serves 12.

6 cloves garlic
2 5 to 6 pound legs of lamb
2/3 cup fresh lemon juice
4 sprigs fresh rosemary or 1 tablespoon dried rosemary

1 tablespoon fresh marjoram or 1 teaspoon dried
2 teaspoons black pepper
1 teaspoon salt

Peel and slice the garlic into slivers. Pierce the lamb randomly with the tip of a sharp knife. Stuff the slivers into the slits. Rub the lemon juice over the lamb. Sprinkle with the rosemary, marjoram, pepper, and salt, pressing in the seasonings lightly. Place the lamb in a large roasting pan (or two) and set aside until ready to cook. If you plan to cook the lamb more than a couple of hours from this point, refrigerate the meat until about an hour before cooking.

Preheat the oven to 450 degrees. Place the lamb in the oven. Reduce the temperature to 350 degrees and cook for about 1 1/2 hours, or until a meat thermometer registers medium-rare or to taste. Let the meat rest for about 15 minutes before carving.

If the lamb will be finished off at the party site, cook the meat to 1 to 1 1/4 hours, until a meat thermometer registers rare. Cool quickly and refrigerate until ready to heat. On site, cook the lamb in a 350 degree oven until a meat thermometer registers medium-rare, or to taste.

FRESH PEAS WITH MINT

Shelling fresh peas is labor intensive, indeed. However, for that very reason and the fact that nothing else tastes the same, they are considered a special treat. Serves 12.

6 cups fresh shelled peas (about 4 pounds in the shell)

1/2 teaspoon sugar, optional

1/4 cup fresh mint leaves, finely chopped

4 tablespoons butter, or to taste

Place the shelled peas in a large saucepan and add about 2 inches of water. Add the sugar only if the peas taste starchy. Bring the water to a boil, reduce the heat, and simmer the peas for about 20 minutes, or until tender. Drain and toss with the mint and the butter.

If you must cook them in advance, run the freshly cooked peas under cold water to stop their cooking. Drain and refrigerate until ready to serve. Place the peas in a basket over steaming water to warm. Toss with the mint and butter before serving.

VARIATION: Cook the peas with 2 cups peeled white pearl onions.

RED POTATOES BAKED WITH CREAM

Serves 12.

Butter for greasing baking
dishes
3 pounds red-skinned
potatoes
1 teaspoon salt
1 teaspoon freshly ground
pepper

8 tablespoons unsalted
butter, cut into pieces
1 cup light cream
1 cup milk

Preheat the oven to 350 degrees.
Generously butter two baking dishes.
Wash and slice the potatoes. Place a layer of potatoes in
each of the buttered baking dishes. Sprinkle with salt and
pepper and dot with butter. Add another layer of potatoes
and sprinkle with salt and pepper. Combine the cream and
milk and pour over the top.
Cover the dishes and bake in the preheated oven for 30
minutes. Uncover and bake an additional 30 minutes, until
the potatoes are tender and browned and the cream is
absorbed. Add more cream during cooking if the potatoes
begin to dry out.

BOSTON AND RADICCHIO SALAD
WITH VINAIGRETTE DRESSING

Serves 12.

3 heads Boston lettuce
1/2 pound radicchio
Balsamic Vinaigrette Dressing (see p. 188), to taste

Clean and dry the Boston lettuce. Separate the leaves,
roll in a damp towel, and keep refrigerated until ready to

serve. Tear or cut the lettuce into small pieces. Slice the radicchio into small pieces or cut into larger spears or separate and leave whole. Toss with Balsamic Vinaigrette Dressing to taste.

STRAWBERRY SHORTCAKE

Serves 12.

3 quarts strawberries
1½ cups sugar, or to taste
3 cups heavy cream
12 Shortcake Biscuits
  (recipe follows)

3 tablespoons butter, softened
Confectioners' sugar, optional

Rinse and hull the strawberries. Drain and pat dry. Slice any large berries, leave small ones whole. Divide the berries in half. Add the sugar to one half and bruise with a fork. Leave the berries for up to an hour, or refrigerate for several hours.

When ready to assemble, whip the cream until thickened, but not stiff. Bake the biscuits as directed or heat previously baked ones. Slit the biscuits and spread lightly with the softened butter.

Combine the crushed and non-crushed berries. Spoon berries and cream onto the bottom half of each shortcake. Replace the top half and spread with a little more cream and a strawberry or sprinkle with confectioners' sugar.

SHORTCAKE BISCUITS

Makes 12 3-inch biscuits.

4 cups flour
1/4 cup sugar
2 tablespoons baking
   powder

1/2 teaspoon salt
8 tablespoons butter, cut
   into pieces
1 1/2 cups milk

Preheat the oven to 450 degrees.

Sift together the flour, sugar, baking powder, and salt. Cut in the butter using a fork or pastry blender until the mixture resembles coarse meal. You may also do this in a food processor with a few pulses of the switch. Stir in the milk all at once, stirring only until the ingredients are moistened and the mixture forms a loose ball.

Roll the dough out on a floured board to about 1/2-inch-thick. Cut into 3-inch biscuits using a floured cutter.

Place the biscuits on baking sheets and bake for about 20 minutes, until risen and lightly browned.

Substitutions may be made in the Spring Dinner menu, naturally. The following is one possible alternative.

CHEESE PUFFS, p. 260
FIDDLEHEAD SOUP
VEAL ROAST WITH LEMON CAPER SAUCE, p. 255
ASPARAGUS WITH LEMON BUTTER, p. 278
NEW POTATOES WITH CRÈME FRAÎCHE AND CAVIAR, p. 268
ENDIVE SALAD WITH ROASTED PEPPERS IN RASPBERRY
VINAIGRETTE, p. 271
FRENCH BREAD AND SWEET BUTTER
STRAWBERRY CASSIS CAKE, p. 272

THE PANHANDLERS' SUMMER
BUFFET FOR 20

At the Bar
HERBED BRIE EN CROUTE
SALTED NUTS

Passed Hors d'Oeuvre
BASKET OF FRESH ASPARAGUS WITH SESAME-CHIVE SAUCE
FRESH FIGS WRAPPED WITH WESTPHALIAN HAM
PHYLLO CUPS WITH GUACAMOLE

Served Buffet Style
VEAL ROAST WITH LEMON CAPER SAUCE
GRILLED PRAWNS
WARM SESAME NOODLES
JICAMA, CARROT, AND SNOW PEA SALAD
WITH LIME VINAIGRETTE
ASSORTED BREADS
REINE DE SABA
GRAPEFRUIT CAMPARI SORBET
COFFEE

HERBED BRIE EN CROUTE

Serves 20 to 25.

1 pound brioche dough (made with about 2½ cups flour)
1 herbed Brie
1 egg yolk mixed with 2 tablespoons water

Preheat the oven to 375 degrees.

Roll the dough out to ¼-inch thick and wrap around the Brie. Brush with the egg wash. Cut out leaf shapes from any remaining dough and place on the top to decorate. Brush with the glaze again.

Place on a baking sheet and bake for 40 minutes, until golden brown in color.

Note: The Brie can be wrapped in dough and kept, covered and refrigerated, for up to 12 hours before cooking. It can also be frozen before baking.

BASKET OF FRESH ASPARAGUS
WITH SESAME-CHIVE SAUCE

Makes about 1½ cups.

60 asparagus stalks
2 egg yolks, at room temperature
1 tablespoon lemon juice
1 tablespoon tarragon vinegar
1½ teaspoons Dijon mustard
½ teaspoon finely chopped garlic

⅛ teaspoon salt
⅛ teaspoon white pepper
½ cup vegetable oil
½ cup olive oil
1 teaspoon hot sesame oil
3 tablespoons sour cream
2 tablespoons chopped fresh chives
1 tablespoon chopped fresh Italian parsley

Trim the asparagus and steam lightly. Cool and store, covered and refrigerated, for up to a day before serving. Arrange in a basket accompanied by a bowl of the sesame-chive sauce for dipping.

To make the sesame-chive sauce, place the egg yolks, lemon juice, vinegar, mustard, garlic, salt, and pepper in a blender or food processor and process until smooth. Add the vegetable oil and then the olive oil in a very thin steady stream. Blend until smooth. Add the sesame oil and blend again until smooth. Stir in the sour cream, chives, and parsley. Cover and refrigerate until ready to use—up to two days.

FRESH FIGS WRAPPED WITH WESTPHALIAN HAM

This hardly needs a recipe, it's so easy to do. Makes 40.

1/4 pound Westphalian or other ham, thinly sliced
40 small fresh figs

Slice the ham into forty strips. Wrap a strip of ham around each fig.

PHYLLO CUPS WITH GUACAMOLE

This recipe calls for a package of phyllo dough, a good deal of which will be left over. However, you can form the remaining dough into cups and freeze them for up to a month before using. Makes 40 pastries.

1 pound package phyllo
  dough, thawed, if frozen
Butter for greasing muffin
  cups
About 8 tablespoons
  butter, melted
½ red onion, finely
  chopped

2 chiles serranos, optional
2 sprigs fresh coriander
2 medium-ripe avocados
1 large tomato, seeded,
  coarsely chopped
1 teaspoon salt
¼ cup fresh lime juice
Fresh coriander to garnish

Preheat the oven to 375 degrees.

Cut the phyllo dough into 2-inch squares. Butter miniature muffin cups. Press a square of dough into each cup, and brush with melted butter; add another square and brush with butter; repeat with a third square. Bake the phyllo for 10 minutes. Cool the pastry and gently remove from the cups.

Finely chop the onion, chiles, and coriander in a food processor. Add the avocados and the tomato, and pulse a few times to incorporate, but do not overprocess. Chunks of avocado should remain visible. Stir in the salt and lime juice to taste.

When ready to serve, spoon 1 teaspoon of the guacamole into each cup and garnish with a sprig of coriander.

VEAL ROAST WITH LEMON CAPER SAUCE

Serves 20 to 25.

1 bunch Italian parsley
6 cloves garlic
8 ounces softened butter
Salt and white pepper to
    taste
2 boned shoulders of veal,
    each weighing 4 to 5
    pounds

LEMON CAPER SAUCE
2 eggs
2 egg yolks

2 tablespoons Dijon
    mustard
Grated zest of 4 lemons
Juice of 2 lemons
2 cups olive oil
3 tablespoons capers
2 teaspoons dried oregano
Salt and pepper to taste

10 slices prosciutto
8 ounces butter
1 1/2 cups dry white wine

Combine the parsley and garlic in a food processor and process briefly. Add the softened butter, salt and white pepper to taste, and process until smooth. Spread this mixture on the inside of each roast and roll and tie them. If you wish, ask the butcher to do this for you.

To make the Lemon Caper Sauce, combine the eggs, egg yolks, mustard, lemon zest, and lemon juice in a food processor and process briefly. Turn the machine on and add the oil in a very thin steady stream. Add the capers, oregano, salt and pepper to taste, and process for 10 seconds.

Place the veal in a shallow pan. Pour 1 cup of the sauce over each roast. Lay the prosciutto slices around the roast, over the sauce. Place half of the butter on top of each roast to melt as it cooks.

Roast the veal for 2 1/2 hours, basting with the white wine

and pan juices. Slice and serve with the remaining Lemon Caper Sauce. This dish is equally delicious served at room temperature.

GRILLED PRAWNS

Serves 20.

40 jumbo shrimp, peeled and deveined, but with tails left on

3 red onions, peeled and cut into 2-inch wedges

3 red peppers, seeded and cut into 2-inch wedges

3 yellow peppers, seeded and cut into 2-inch wedges

2 bunches fresh marjoram, chopped

Kosher salt to taste

Freshly ground pepper to taste

1 cup olive oil

Lemon wedges as garnish

Thread the shrimp, onions, and peppers alternately onto 20 metal skewers. Place the skewers in a shallow dish, layering if necessary, and sprinkle with chopped marjoram, kosher salt, freshly ground pepper to taste, and olive oil. Cover, refrigerate, and leave to marinate for 6 hours.

Preheat the grill or broiler. Grill the shrimp, basting with the accumulated marinade, 3 to 4 minutes per side. Serve immediately with lemon wedges.

WARM SESAME NOODLES

Serves 20.

3/4 cup sesame oil

9 tablespoons soy sauce

2 tablespoons rice vinegar

1 teaspoon crushed hot red pepper

1/2 cup sesame paste

3 pounds angel hair pasta

1 bunch scallions, finely sliced

1 cucumber, peeled and julienned, for garnish

Combine the sesame oil, soy sauce, rice vinegar, crushed hot red pepper, and sesame paste in a food processor. Process until smooth.

Cook the pasta in a large quantity of boiling, salted water until al dente. Toss with the sesame sauce and scallions. Garnish with the julienned cucumber. Serve warm or at room temperature.

JICAMA, CARROT, AND SNOW PEA SALAD WITH LIME VINAIGRETTE

Serves 20 to 25.

LIME VINAIGRETTE
1/2 cup fresh lime juice
2 tablespoons honey
1 tablespoon tamari soy sauce
1 tablespoon honey mustard
1 tablespoon finely chopped fresh ginger

Grated rind of 3 limes
1 cup walnut oil

2 jicama
2 pounds carrots
2 pounds snow peas

Combine the lime juice, honey, tamari, honey mustard, chopped ginger, and the lime rind in a food processor. Process very briefly. Turn the machine on and add the oil, in a very slow stream. Cover the sauce and refrigerate, up to 2 days, until ready to serve.

Peel the jicama and cut into strips 2½ inches × ¼-inch thick. Peel the carrots and cut into strips also 2½ inches long by ¼-inch thick. String the snow peas.

Blanch the snow peas in boiling water for 20 seconds. Rinse under cold water and drain well. Toss together the snow peas, jicama, and carrots. Place in a large attractive bowl, or on a serving platter. Dress with the lime vinaigrette when ready to serve.

REINE DE SABA

Serves 20 to 25.

Butter for greasing loaf
   pan
9 ounces walnuts, finely
   chopped (about 2 cups)
1½ pounds bittersweet
   chocolate

12 ounces butter
½ cup sugar
8 egg yolks
1¼ cups egg whites
   (about 10 egg whites)

Grease a 14 × 4½-inch loaf pan with butter. Line with waxed paper and grease again. Press the walnuts into the bottom of the pan, reserving ¼ cup for the cake mixture.

Melt the chocolate and the butter in a double boiler over hot water. Remove from the heat and cool for 5 minutes. Stir in the sugar. Add the egg yolks, one at a time, stirring well after each addition. Stir in the reserved nuts.

Beat the egg whites until stiff, but not dry. Fold into the batter. Pour the batter into the prepared pan. Cover and refrigerate overnight.

Unmold the dessert onto a serving platter. Slice thinly, as this is very rich.

GRAPEFRUIT CAMPARI SORBET

Makes about 7 cups, serving 20 people.

2 cups water
1½ cups sugar
4 cups fresh grapefruit
   juice

½ cup fresh lemon juice
¼ cup Campari
Grated rind of 1 grapefruit

Combine the water and sugar in a saucepan and bring to a boil. Lower the heat and simmer for 5 minutes. Remove the syrup from the heat and pour into a bowl to cool. When cool, chill.

Add the grapefruit juice, lemon juice, Campari, and grated grapefruit rind to the chilled syrup. Pour into an ice cream freezer and freeze according to manufacturer's instructions.

TASTE OF AUTUMN DINNER
FOR 20

CHEESE PUFFS
VEAL STEW WITH WILD MUSHROOMS AND PEARL ONIONS
WILD AND WHITE RICE
SAUTÉED CABBAGE WITH PECANS
FRENCH BREAD WITH SWEET BUTTER
TOSSED GREENS WITH BALSAMIC VINAIGRETTE
ASSORTED CHEESES AND CRACKERS
GINGER PEAR TART

CHEESE PUFFS

Makes about 50 puffs.

Butter for greasing baking sheets
Choux Paste, see page 216
2 cups shredded cheddar or Parmesan cheese

Preheat the oven to 400 degrees.
Lightly grease two or three baking sheets.
Combine the choux paste and the cheese and pipe or spoon into small mounds, about 1 inch in diameter.
Bake in the preheated oven for about 20 minutes, until puffed and golden brown. Serve immediately, or cool, chill, and reheat before serving.

VEAL STEW WITH WILD MUSHROOMS AND PEARL ONIONS

Serves 20.

7 pounds stewing veal, cut into chunks
½ cup flour
½ cup olive oil
½ cup vegetable oil
10 cloves garlic, peeled
2 tablespoons fresh rosemary, chopped
1 tablespoon fresh oregano
5 cups chicken broth

2 cups white wine
3 pounds pearl onions
1 pound fresh wild mushrooms, or 4 ounces dried
4 tablespoons butter, softened
2 teaspoons salt, or to taste
2 teaspoons freshly ground pepper

Dredge the veal in the flour. Combine the oils and heat in two heavy skillets or Dutch ovens. Brown the meat, a few pieces at a time, on all sides, in the hot oil. Set the browned meat aside to make room for the next batch.

Add the garlic to the pans, and cook gently for about 10 minutes. Discard most of any extra oil, leaving a tablespoon or two at most. Return the meat to the pans with the garlic, add the rosemary and oregano, and stir to coat. Pour in the chicken broth and wine. Cover and simmer on top of the stove or in a 325 degree oven for an hour, stirring occasionally.

While the stew cooks, bring a pot of water to a boil. Add the onions and blanch for about 5 minutes. Drain and run the onions under cold water to stop their cooking. When cool enough to handle, peel the skins.

Rinse the wild mushrooms and pat dry with paper towels. Slice. If using dried mushrooms, soak in warm water for about 20 minutes before draining and slicing.

Transfer the meat to a bowl. Strain the sauce if you wish it perfectly smooth, and return it to the casserole. Bring the liquid to a boil, and cook rapidly until reduced by about half.

Combine the softened butter and 3 tablespoons of the flour (left over from dredging) into a paste. Ladle a little of the reduced sauce into the butter mixture and stir until smooth. Stir this mixture into the reduced sauce in the casseroles. Cook, stirring frequently, for about 10 minutes, until slightly thickened. Return the meat to the pans, add the onions, mushrooms, salt to taste, and pepper and continue cooking for about 15 minutes, stirring occasionally.

Serve immediately, or cool, and refrigerate for up to two days before reheating and serving.

WILD AND WHITE RICE

Serves 20.

6 cups water
1½ cups raw wild rice
4 cups chicken broth
8 tablespoons unsalted butter, or 1 stick cut into tablespoons
2 onions, finely chopped
2 cloves garlic, finely chopped

2 cups raw long grain white rice
1½ teaspoons salt, optional
The julienned rind of 1 lemon for garnish

Bring the water to a boil and add to the wild rice. Return to a boil, reduce the heat, and simmer for 40 to 50 minutes, or until tender.

Bring the chicken broth to a boil in a large saucepan.

Meanwhile, heat 4 tablespoons of the butter in a large saucepan. Add the onions and garlic and cook, stirring, for about 5 minutes, or until the vegetables turn translucent. Stir in the white rice and cook for about 2 minutes, stirring constantly. Add the boiling broth (and the salt, if the broth is unsalted), cover, and bring to a boil. Reduce the heat and simmer for 18 to 20 minutes, until all the rice is tender.

Combine the wild rice and the white rice while still hot. Stir in the remaining butter. Garnish with the lemon rind.

SAUTÉED CABBAGE WITH PECANS

Serves 20.

8 tablespoons butter
1/2 cup vegetable oil
4 pounds cabbage, shredded

3/4 cup finely chopped pecans
Salt and pepper to taste

Heat half of the butter and vegetable oil in a large skillet. Add half the cabbage, half the pecans, and salt and pepper to taste. Sauté, stirring frequently, until the cabbage is tender, about 10 to 15 minutes. Repeat the procedure with the remaining cabbage and pecans. Season with salt and pepper to taste.

VARIATIONS: Substitute blanched broccoli or Brussels sprouts for the cabbage.

TOSSED GREENS WITH BALSAMIC VINAIGRETTE

Serves 20.

2 heads romaine lettuce
1 head Boston lettuce
1 head chicory

1 bunch watercress
Balsamic Vinaigrette Dressing (see p. 188)

Wash and dry the lettuce, chicory, and watercress. This can be done a day or two ahead. Tear or cut into small pieces and place in a large salad bowl. Reserve several of the watercress stalks. Refrigerate for up to two hours before serving. When ready to serve, toss with the dressing and present either in a large salad bowl, or on individual salad plates. Garnish with sprigs of watercress.

ASSORTED CHEESES AND CRACKERS

There is no set rule about what cheeses should be served at the end of the meal. You don't need forty different cheeses, either, just enough of diversity to show a range. As a guide, consider serving a pungent cheese such as a Stilton or other blue cheese, a creamy mild cheese such as Explorateur or other triple cream cheese, and a hard moderately flavored cheese, such as a cheddar or Cheshire. A selection of simple crackers, including water biscuits and wholemeal biscuits, or more of the bread from the meal is all you need to complete the presentation.

GINGER PEAR TART

This recipe makes three tarts. Serves 20.

3 single-crust tart crusts (recipe follows)
4 pounds winter pears, peeled, seeded, and sliced

2½ to 3 cups sugar
1 cup chopped crystallized ginger (about 6 ounces)
⅔ cup flour

Preheat the oven to 450 degrees. Roll out the pie crusts, fit into pans, preferably fluted 9-inch tart pans, weight with beans or pie weights, and bake for 5 to 7 minutes. Remove the shells and cool briefly.

Reduce the oven heat to 350 degrees.

Combine the fruit, sugar, ginger, and flour. Spoon into the prepared pie shells and return to the oven for 40 to 50 minutes, until the pies are bubbling and lightly browned.

TART CRUST

Makes crust for 3 9-inch tarts.

4 1/2 cups flour	chilled and cut into
1/4 cup sugar	tablespoons
1/4 teaspoon salt	3 egg yolks
12 ounces unsalted butter,	3 tablespoons cold water

Combine the flour, sugar, and salt in a food processor. Process very briefly. Add the butter and pulse briefly, until the mixture resembles coarse meal. Beat the egg yolks slightly and mix in the water. Transfer the dough to a large bowl and stir the egg and water mixture in with a fork, mixing only until the pastry forms a ball. Divide the dough into three balls, flatten each slightly, wrap in plastic wrap, and refrigerate for at least an hour before using.

Note: This dough can be made in advance and kept frozen for up to a month before using.

Substitutions may be made in the Taste of Autumn Dinner. The following is one possible alternative menu.

CHEDDAR AND CHIVE STRAWS, p. 244

VEAL STEW WITH WILD MUSHROOMS AND PEARL ONIONS

ROASTED RED NEW POTATOES WITH ROSEMARY, p. 278

BAKED BRUSSELS SPROUTS WITH BACON, p. 270 or

BROCCOLI AND ROASTED PEPPERS

WITH GARLIC-SCENTED OIL, p. 195

FRENCH BREAD WITH SWEET BUTTER

ASSORTED CHEESES AND CRACKERS

LINZERTORTE, p. 225, or TWEED CAKE, p. 223

SPECIAL WINTER DINNER
FOR 10
FROM DAVID ZIFF COOKING

BAKED CLAMS WITH CORIANDER BUTTER
DEEP-FRIED OYSTERS WITH DILL-SHALLOT MAYONNAISE
NEW POTATOES WITH CRÈME FRAÎCHE AND CAVIAR
ROSEMARY LAMB CHOPS
CANDIED ORANGE SHELLS WITH CRANBERRIES AND GINGER
BAKED BRUSSELS SPROUTS WITH BACON
ENDIVE SALAD WITH ROASTED PEPPERS IN RASPBERRY
VINAIGRETTE
STRAWBERRY CASSIS CAKE
CHOCOLATE TRUFFLES

BAKED CLAMS WITH CORIANDER BUTTER

Serves 10.

20 littleneck clams
8 tablespoons butter,
  softened
¼ cup finely chopped
  fresh coriander

1 tablespoon minced or
  grated fresh ginger
3 tablespoons soy sauce

Preheat the oven to 450 degrees. Open the clams and place them, on the half shell, in a shallow baking pan.

Combine the butter, coriander, ginger, and soy sauce. Spoon a small amount of the mixture on each clam. Bake in the preheated oven for about 3 minutes. Serve immediately.

DEEP-FRIED OYSTERS WITH DILL-SHALLOT MAYONNAISE

Serves 10 to 15.

20 shucked oysters
2 eggs
1/2 cup heavy cream
1 cup flour
1 1/2 cups homemade bread
  crumbs

Salt, black pepper, and
  cayenne pepper to taste
Vegetable oil for frying

Drain the oysters on paper towels. Beat the eggs with the cream.

Dip each oyster first in the flour, shaking off any excess, then in the egg mixture, and finally in the bread crumbs to coat thoroughly. Season each oyster with salt, black pepper, and cayenne pepper to taste.

Heat about 2 inches of oil (enough to deep-fry the oysters) to 375 degrees in a wok, skillet, or deep fryer. Deep-fry the oysters until lightly browned, about 4 minutes. Drain on paper towels. Skewer the oysters with toothpicks and serve with Dill-Shallot Mayonnaise (recipe follows).

DILL-SHALLOT MAYONNAISE

Makes about 1 cup.

2 egg yolks
3/4 cup safflower oil
1 bunch dill, chopped

3 shallots, finely chopped
Salt and pepper to taste

Place the egg yolks in the bowl of the food processor. Turn the machine on and dribble the oil very slowly into the yolks. When about half the oil has been added, you may dribble a little faster. When all the oil has been added and the mixture is thick, add the dill and shallots. Season with salt and pepper to taste.

NEW POTATOES WITH CRÈME FRAÎCHE AND CAVIAR

Serves 10 as a first course.

3½ pounds new potatoes
8 tablespoons butter
Salt and pepper to taste
1¼ cups crème fraîche

5 ounces American sturgeon caviar or any black caviar

Preheat the oven to warm.

Cook the new potatoes in water until just tender, but still firm. Drain and dice them. Stir in the butter and salt and pepper to taste. Keep warm in the oven.

When ready to serve, place ½ cup of potatoes in the center of individual salad plates. Top with 2 tablespoons of crème fraîche and 1 tablespoon of caviar.

ROSEMARY LAMB CHOPS

Serves 10.

½ cup grated Gruyère
  cheese
¾ cup grated Parmesan
  cheese
2 cups fresh coarse bread
  crumbs
3 tablespoons dried
  rosemary

20 single-rib lamb chops
4 eggs, beaten with ¼ cup
  water
Safflower oil
2 tablespoons butter
Salt and pepper to taste

Combine the Gruyère and Parmesan cheeses. Combine the bread crumbs and rosemary. This may be done up to a day in advance.

Pound the meat with a meat pounder until half as thick as the original chop. Moisten with water and press each chop into the Gruyère and Parmesan mixture. Combine the eggs and water. Then dip each chop into the egg mixture and finally in the rosemary-flavored bread crumbs.

Fill a skillet with ½ inch of safflower oil. Add the butter and heat until very hot, but not smoking (about 365 degrees). Add the chops, a few at a time, and cook until crispy and brown, about 4 minutes per side. Drain on paper towels and keep warm while cooking the remaining chops.

CANDIED ORANGE SHELLS
WITH CRANBERRIES AND GINGER

Serves 10.

5 small navel oranges	12-ounce package fresh
4 cups water	cranberries
2 cups sugar	2 ounces candied ginger
	(about ⅓ cup),
CRANBERRY MIXTURE	julienned
1 cup water	
½ cup sugar	

Halve and hollow the oranges.

Combine the water and sugar in a heavy saucepan and bring to a boil. Cook until the sugar dissolves. Add the orange shells and poach gently for 10 minutes. Drain the oranges. When cool, fill with the cranberry mixture.

To make the cranberry mixture, combine the water and sugar in a heavy saucepan and bring to a boil, cooking until the sugar dissolves. Meanwhile, pick over the cranberries and add to the sugar mixture. Bring to a boil, reduce the heat, and simmer for 5 minutes. Remove from the heat and stir in the candied ginger. When cool, spoon into the orange shells.

BAKED BRUSSELS SPROUTS
WITH BACON

Serves 10.

Butter for greasing baking	1 cup grated Gruyère
dish	cheese
1½ pounds Brussels	1 cup heavy cream
sprouts	1 cup bread crumbs.
1 pound bacon	Salt and pepper to taste

Preheat the oven to 375 degrees. Butter a baking dish.

Trim the Brussels sprouts and blanch in boiling water for 7 minutes. Drain and chop coarsely.

Coarsely chop the bacon and sauté in a skillet until crisp. Drain the bacon and discard the fat.

Combine the chopped Brussels sprouts, cooked bacon, cheese, cream, and all but 3 tablespoons of the bread crumbs. Season with salt and pepper to taste. Turn the mixture into the buttered baking dish and sprinkle with the remaining bread crumbs. Bake in the preheated oven for 20 minutes, until the top is lightly browned.

ENDIVE SALAD WITH ROASTED PEPPERS IN RASPBERRY VINAIGRETTE

Serves 10.

1 red bell pepper
1 yellow bell pepper
1 tablespoon vegetable oil
10 endive

RASPBERRY VINAIGRETTE
¾ cup safflower oil
5 tablespoons raspberry
  vinegar
Salt and pepper to taste

Preheat the broiler. Rub the peppers with the oil. Place the peppers under the broiler and roast until the skins begin to blacken. Turn and repeat. Remove from the oven, let cool slightly, then peel, seed, and cut into julienne strips.

Separate the endive leaves. Slice each leaf in half lengthwise.

To make the vinaigrette, combine the safflower oil, raspberry vinegar, and salt and pepper to taste.

Combine the endive leaves and pepper strips, and toss with the raspberry vinaigrette before serving.

STRAWBERRY CASSIS CAKE

Serves 10 to 15.

GÉNOISE
Butter and flour for
 preparing springform
 pan
1 cup flour
1 teaspoon baking powder
12 tablespoons unsalted
 butter, softened
1 cup sugar
3 eggs

FILLING
1/2 cup cassis
3/4 cup orange juice
1/2 cup apricot glaze or
 apricot jam
3 cups heavy cream
1 teaspoon vanilla extract
1/3 cup sugar
25 ripe strawberries

Preheat the oven to 375 degrees. Butter and flour a
9-inch springform pan.

Combine the flour and baking powder.

Beat together the butter and sugar until smooth. Add the
eggs, one at a time, and beat until smooth after each addition. Stir in the flour mixture, and mix until smooth.

Pour into the prepared pan and bake in the preheated
oven for 40 minutes. Cool on a rack. When cool, slice the
cake into 2 layers.

To make the filling, combine the cassis and orange juice.
Prick the cake layers all over with a fork and sprinkle with
the mixture.

Heat the apricot glaze or jam until melted, and spread on
top of the cake layers.

Whip the cream until thickened. Add the vanilla and
sugar and whip until peaks form. Spread 1/3 of this mixture
over the bottom layer of the cake. Reserve the remainder as
icing.

Wash, hull, and slice the strawberries in half. Cover the
bottom layer of the cake with the berries and assemble the

cake with the remaining layer. The cake can be kept, refrigerated, for up to 5 days at this point. Spread the remaining whipped cream with a spatula over the cake.

CHOCOLATE TRUFFLES

Makes 25 truffles.

1 tablespoon instant espresso	10 tablespoons unsalted butter, chilled
1/4 cup boiling water	1/4 cup orange liqueur
9 ounces Belgian or other good quality semisweet chocolate	1/2 cup unsweetened cocoa powder

Combine the instant espresso and boiling water. Add the chocolate and melt gently in a double boiler over hot water. Beat with a hand-held electric mixer until perfectly creamy. Remove from the water bath and continue beating until cool.

Cut the butter into slices 1/3-inch thick. Beat the butter slowly into the chocolate until smooth. Add the orange liqueur, slowly, beating constantly. Chill the mixture for an hour, or until firm.

Roll teaspoons of the mixture into balls and coat with the unsweetened cocoa. Keep chilled until shortly before serving. Pass the truffles after dessert.

TRADITIONAL DINNER
BUFFET FOR 50

CRUDITÉS WITH HERB DIP
CRAB-STUFFED CHOUX PASTRY
SMOKED SALMON WITH BROWN BREAD AND BUTTER
ROASTED BEEF TENDERLOIN
ASPARAGUS WITH LEMON BUTTER
ROASTED RED NEW POTATOES WITH ROSEMARY
SOURDOUGH BREAD WITH SWEET BUTTER
TOSSED GREENS WITH BLUE CHEESE VINAIGRETTE
ASSORTED CHEESES AND CRACKERS
CHOCOLATE MOUSSE
COFFEE

CRUDITÉS WITH HERB DIP

The following vegetables and their quantities are approximations. Feel free to use any combination of vegetables and suit the quantities to your own tastes, or the tastes of a client. Serves 50.

1 small head broccoli
1 small head cauliflower
1 pound snow peas or
sweet pea pods
1 pound carrots
3 long English cucumbers

1 pound mushrooms
½ pound Belgian endive
2 pints cherry tomatoes
3 red peppers
Basic Herb Dip, doubled
(recipe follows)

Break the broccoli into florets and steam briefly, until barely tender. Plunge into cold water to stop their cooking. Drain and dry.

Break the cauliflower into florets. Top, tail, and string the snow peas or edible sweet pods. Peel and cut the carrots and cucumbers into fingers. Wipe the mushrooms with a damp towel and trim the ends. Separate the endive leaves. Rinse and dry the cherry tomatoes. Core, seed, and slice the peppers.

Arrange all the vegetables on serving platters and place a small bowl of the dip in the center.

BASIC HERB DIP

This is a versatile dip that can be used for vegetables and chips, and as a stuffing for vegetables, choux puffs, or tea sandwiches. Makes about 2½ cups.

6 ounces cream cheese, softened	fresh dill, basil, coriander, or parsley
1 cup mayonnaise, preferably homemade	2 tablespoons Dijon mustard
¼ cup dry white wine	Salt and freshly ground pepper to taste
¼ cup finely chopped	

Beat the cream cheese until quite soft. Beat in the mayonnaise, white wine, herbs, mustard, and salt and pepper to taste.

VARIATIONS:

• To make a cheese dip, stir ½ cup finely grated Parmesan or sharp cheddar into the dip.

• To make a cucumber dip, peel and finely chop the flesh of 1 cucumber and stir into the dip.

CRAB-STUFFED CHOUX PASTRY

Makes about 100 puffs, serving 50.

Choux pastry (see p. 216), doubled
1 pound cream cheese, softened
1 pound cooked shrimp, coarsely chopped
1/3 cup snipped fresh chives
2 tablespoons chopped fresh dill, or 1 teaspoon dried
1 tablespoon lemon juice

Make the choux puffs as described on page 216.

Beat the cream cheese until light and almost fluffy. Stir in the shrimp, chives, dill, and lemon juice. Spoon or pipe the mixture into the puffs. These can be made up to 30 minutes in advance.

Arrange the puffs on attractive serving plates and either pass or place on a buffet table.

VARIATIONS: Crab, lobster, or smoked or fresh salmon may be substituted for the shrimp.

SMOKED SALMON WITH BROWN BREAD AND BUTTER

Serves 50.

1 side smoked salmon
8 ounces unsalted butter
1/4 cup chopped fresh dill
2 loaves fresh whole-grain bread
Capers
Fresh dill sprigs for garnish

Slice the salmon across the grain into paper-thin slices, or have the fishmonger do it—by far the easiest method.

Cream the butter until light and stir in the chopped dill.

Cut the bread into very thin slices, and depending on the

size of the loaf, into halves or quarters. Spread the bread with the dill butter and cover each slice with a piece of salmon. Garnish with a few capers and a tiny sprig of dill, if desired. Place the canapés on serving trays and garnish with additional dill.

An alternative method of serving is to reassemble the salmon side and serve on a platter, garnish with the capers and dill, and serve the bread and butter or cream cheese separately.

VARIATION: Substitute cream cheese for the butter.

ROASTED BEEF TENDERLOIN

Serves 50.

8 tablespoons unsalted butter	1/2 cup coarsely ground black pepper
4 3½ to 4-pound beef tenderloins, trimmed and tied	Salt 16 bay leaves

Preheat the oven to 425 degrees.

Rub the butter over the meat. Sprinkle the meat with the pepper and salt to taste and press the pepper gently into the beef. Slip the bay leaves in under the strings. Place the meat in roasting pans, seam side down.

Roast the beef for 35 to 40 minutes for rare (130 degrees on a meat thermometer), 45 to 50 for medium-rare. Remove from the oven and let the meat rest for 15 minutes. Remove the strings before carving.

Reserve the pan juices to serve spooned over the meat.

ASPARAGUS WITH LEMON BUTTER
Serves 50.

3 cloves garlic, peeled
10 pounds asparagus,
    trimmed
1 pound unsalted butter

1 cup fresh lemon juice, or
    to taste
Salt

Fill a very large steamer, or two or three smaller ones with 1 to 2 inches of water. Add the garlic cloves and bring to a boil. Add the asparagus and cook until tender but still a little firm, anywhere from 5 to 10 minutes, depending on the size of the stalks. Or cook the asparagus in boiling water for 2 to 5 minutes, until just tender. If the asparagus will be kept before serving, plunge them into cold water to stop their cooking and to set the bright color. Drain, cool thoroughly, and refrigerate until almost ready to serve. When ready to serve, warm the asparagus briefly in a covered pan in a warm oven or in a steamer.

While the asparagus cook, melt the butter. Stir in the lemon juice and season with salt to taste.

Note: The asparagus can be cooked in small batches.

ROASTED RED NEW POTATOES WITH ROSEMARY
Serves 50.

15 pounds new red
    potatoes
1 cup butter
3/4 cup olive oil

Pan drippings from the
    beef tenderloin, optional
2 large bunches rosemary

Preheat the oven to 375 degrees.
Scrub the potatoes and place in large saucepans. Fill with

water and cook for 15 minutes. Drain and place in large roasting pans. Combine the butter and olive oil and pour over the potatoes, turning to coat the potatoes well. If you wish, pour a little of the pan drippings from the tenderloin over the potatoes. Place half the rosemary sprigs around the potatoes and place the pans in the preheated oven. Roast for 15 to 20 minutes, until tender, turning once or twice to coat the potatoes with the butter.

Transfer the potatoes to large serving bowls and garnish with the remaining rosemary sprigs.

TOSSED GREENS WITH BLUE CHEESE VINAIGRETTE

Serves 50.

2 heads romaine lettuce	½ pound radicchio
2 heads Boston lettuce	Blue Cheese Vinaigrette,
1 pound arugula	doubled (p. 189)

Wash the lettuce, arugula, and radicchio, and dry. Store, tightly covered, for up to a day before tearing or cutting into small pieces.

Combine the greens in a large serving bowl. When ready to serve, toss with the Blue Cheese Vinaigrette.

CHOCOLATE MOUSSE

Make this mousse at least a day in advance to allow the flavors to develop. Make the mousse twice to serve 50. Serves 25.

1½ pounds semisweet chocolate, coarsely chopped
½ pound unsweetened chocolate, coarsely chopped
2 cups heavy cream, chilled

12 eggs, at room temperature
1 cup sugar
¼ cup espresso coffee
¼ cup cognac
Fresh mint leaves or crystallized violets for garnishing

Combine the chocolate in the top of a double boiler over hot water, and melt, stirring frequently. Remove the pan from the heat and cool the mixture.

Whip the cream until stiff peaks form.

Separate the eggs. Beat together the egg yolks and the sugar until light and lemon-yellow in color. Stir in the coffee and the cognac. Beat the whites in a separate bowl until stiff peaks form. Fold the chocolate into the yolk mixture, then fold in the egg whites. Finally, fold in the whipped cream. Pour the mousse into glass serving bowls, or individual bowls. Cover and chill until half an hour to an hour before serving.

To serve, garnish the mousse with fresh mint leaves or crystallized violets.

Substitutions may be made in the Traditional Dinner Buffet for 50. The following is one alternative.

CHEESE TRUFFLES, p. 191
HUMMUS-STUFFED CHERRY TOMATOES, p. 214

SMOKED SALMON WITH BROWN BREAD AND BUTTER
ROASTED BEEF TENDERLOIN
FRESH PEAS WITH MINT, p. 247
WHITE AND WILD RICE, p. 262
FRENCH BREAD AND SWEET BUTTER
GREEN, WHITE, AND RED SALAD, p. 206
CHOCOLATE RUM CAKE, p. 196

MUSEUM BALL DINNER
FOR 1100
BY REMEMBER BASIL

SMOKED RAINBOW TROUT
BEEF FILET WITH GREEN PEPPERCORN SAUCE
YELLOW AND GREEN SQUASH, GREEN BEANS, AND RED
PEPPERS IN CHAMPAGNE VINAIGRETTE
RED NEW POTATO SALAD
FRENCH BREAD AND SWEET BUTTER
BLACK CURRANT MOUSSE
COFFEE, DECAFFEINATED COFFEE, TEA
WALNUT COOKIES

SMOKED RAINBOW TROUT

Serves 1100.

704 rainbow trout filets
(352 whole trout)
77 pounds Kirby
cucumbers
66 cups homemade
mayonnaise (recipe
follows)
88 cups heavy cream,
whipped
22 cups drained and
squeezed prepared white
horseradish

Salt and pepper to taste
154 heads red leaf lettuce
for garnish
30 pounds yellow or red
tomatoes for garnish
55 pounds Belgian endive
132 scallions, diagonally
sliced very very thinly
for garnish

Break the trout into pieces, about 1-inch long. Peel and
seed the cucumbers; slice diagonally into pieces 1/4-inch
thick. Combine the trout and cucumbers.

Combine the mayonnaise, whipped cream, horseradish, and salt and pepper to taste in a VERY large bowl or in several smaller ones.

Wash and dry the lettuce. Cut the tomatoes into fans.

When ready to serve, slice the endive horizontally ½ inch thick and add to the trout and cucumbers. Dress the mixture with the horseradish cream mayonnaise.

Line each of 1100 plates with a lettuce leaf. Place ¾ cup of the salad mixture on the lettuce. At 6 o'clock, place a fan of yellow or red tomato. Sprinkle 8 to 10 slices of scallion on top of the trout mixture and serve.

REMEMBER BASIL'S MAYONNAISE

This is good general-purpose mayonnaise and is also delicious used as a dip with crudités. To use with the Smoked Rainbow Trout, multiply the basic proportions of everything except the spiced salt, sugar, and mustard, by 20. Multiply the salt, sugar, and mustard by 10 and taste for seasoning. An easier method is to make 20 batches of the basic mayonnaise. To use with the Beef Tenderloin that follows, you will need almost 5 gallons, or 40 times the original recipe! Makes 3½ cups.

2 whole eggs
2 Spanish onions
1 tablespoon seasoned salt
  (your own or a
  commercial one)

2 to 3 cloves garlic
1½ teaspoons sugar
2 teaspoons dry mustard
2 to 3 cups vegetable oil
¼ cup lemon juice

Purée the eggs, onions, salt, garlic, sugar, and mustard in a blender. Very gradually, on high speed, add 1½ cups of the oil in a steady stream. When the oil is incorporated, add the lemon juice. Now add enough of the remaining oil so that the mixture is very thick and creamy.

BEEF FILET WITH GREEN PEPPERCORN SAUCE

Remember Basil often rubs a mixture of kosher salt, dried basil, marjoram, oregano, and oil over the trimmed filets and lets them marinate for at least 24 hours. Serves 1100.

380 pounds beef filet   3 to 4 cups green
22 bunches watercress   peppercorns (to taste)

GREEN PEPPERCORN SAUCE
8½ gallons (about 136
  cups) homemade
  mayonnaise

Preheat the ovens to 350 degrees. Roast the filets until they reach an internal temperature of 130 degrees for fairly rare beef. This takes 40 to 50 minutes, depending on how cold the meat is to start with. Cool and chill the meat. Slice about 1/4-inch thick and serve 4 slices per person. Garnish each serving with watercress sprigs.

Serve with Green Peppercorn Sauce which is made by mixing the mayonnaise mixed with the water-packed green peppercorns to taste.

YELLOW AND GREEN SQUASH, GREEN BEANS, AND RED PEPPERS IN CHAMPAGNE VINAIGRETTE

Serves 1100.

12 cups good white wine	40 cloves garlic
or champagne vinegar	160 pounds zucchini
43 to 45 cups vegetable oil	160 pounds yellow squash
Kosher salt, freshly ground	40 pounds red peppers
white pepper to taste	60 pounds green beans

Combine the wine or champagne vinegar, 37 cups of the vegetable oil, salt and freshly ground white pepper to taste, and the garlic. Leave for at least 48 hours so the garlic can infuse.

To prepare the zucchini and yellow squash, slice lengthwise and then, using a mandoline, slice horizontally on the diagonal, 1/4-inch thick. Blanch the squash in batches in unsalted boiling water for a few seconds. The easiest way is to lower them in colanders. Refresh well in cold water and dry.

To prepare the peppers, cut in half, remove the seeds and the stem. Then cut into julienne strips, by hand. Heat the remaining oil in several large skillets and sauté the peppers in batches, seasoning with salt and pepper to taste.

To prepare the beans, top and tail them. Slice diagonally about 1-inch long. Blanch the beans in batches in boiling water, seasoned with a little salt and baking soda if you wish, by lowering them in a colander. Refresh the beans under cold running water and drain. Change the water fairly often, as soon as it begins to get scummy.

When ready to serve, combine the vegetables and season with as much of the dressing (strained of garlic cloves) as the vegetables will absorb, and tastes good. Taste and season with salt and pepper to taste.

RED NEW POTATO SALAD

This salad can be made a day in advance of serving. Serves 1100.

350 pounds new red
potatoes
75 cups Italian Dressing
(recipe follows)
30 pounds red onion finely
chopped, by hand

20 cups hand-chopped
Italian parsley
Kosher salt and pepper to
taste

Cut the potatoes into quarters or sixths, depending on their size. Place in cold water while working and until ready to cook. Cook the potatoes in water, salted to taste, until tender, about 20 minutes. Drain.

While slightly warm, add the salad dressing, onions, and parsley and mix gently by hand. Season to taste with kosher salt and freshly ground pepper to taste. Serve at room temperature.

ITALIAN DRESSING

Makes 75 cups (roughly 4½ gallons).

7½ quarts chicken broth
10 cups olive oil
23 cups vegetable oil
12 cups champagne
vinegar

15 cloves garlic, crushed
Kosher salt and freshly
ground pepper to taste

Combine all of the ingredients and mix well.

BLACK CURRANT MOUSSE

Serves 1100.

44 33-ounce jars black
    currants
33 cups water, or enough
    to dissolve the sugar
33 pounds sugar
495 egg yolks
44 quarts heavy cream

5½ cups gelatin
14 cups lemon juice
36 quarts heavy cream,
    whipped, for garnish
Frosted Black Grapes
    (recipe follows) for
    garnish

First, go buy a trough!

Drain the jars of currants, reserving the juice. Purée the currants in a blender or food processor with a little juice in each batch.

Combine the water and sugar and heat to a boil. Cook until the mixture reaches the thread stage, 235 degrees.

Begin whisking the egg yolks at high speed in a stainless steel bowl. Slowly pour the syrup over the egg yolks and beat until very pale and thick.

Meanwhile, whip the 44 quarts of cream to form lightly firm peaks and chill. Dissolve the gelatin in the lemon juice in a double boiler or bain-marie over hot water. Stir in the black currant purée. Add the gelatin to the mousse on medium speed of the mixer, mixing in well. Pour the mixture into a large bowl and fold in the whipped cream. Pour the mousse into 110 10-cup glass bowls. These may be kept, covered and refrigerated, for several hours, or up to a day in advance.

Decorate the top of each bowl with the remaining whipped cream, and Frosted Black Grapes.

FROSTED BLACK GRAPES

41 pounds black grapes, cut into 300 clusters
4 egg whites
5 pounds granulated sugar

Wash the grapes and dry in front of a fan. Keep them at room temperature while you beat the egg whites until barely frothy. Coat each grape, using a small paint brush, with the egg white. Dust the grapes with granulated sugar, shaken through a strainer.

Lay the grapes on baking parchment, keeping the clusters separated, and let dry overnight.

We suggest arranging the frosted grape clusters around the bottom of the bowls of mousse as they sit on lavender napkins resting on silver trays.

WALNUT COOKIES

Serves 1100.

Butter for greasing baking sheets
4 pounds granulated sugar
2 pounds confectioners' sugar
9 1/2 pounds walnuts

9 1/2 pounds unsalted butter, softened
1/3 cup salt
3/4 cup vanilla extract
11 pounds flour

Preheat the oven to 350 degrees. Line baking sheets with baking parchment or wax paper or butter and flour the sheets. Combine half of the granulated sugar with the confectioners' sugar.

Toast the walnuts in the preheated oven for about 10 minutes. Remove from the oven, and let cool. Chop the nuts in a food processor. Cream the butter until fluffy. Add the remaining granulated sugar and salt, and cream until really fluffy.

Add the walnuts and vanilla extract, on the lowest speed of the mixer. Lastly, add the flour and barely mix to incorporate.

Form the dough into balls, a scant inch in diameter. Roll each ball in the sugar mixture and place on the prepared baking sheets. Bake for 12 to 15 minutes, until slightly browned on the outer edges. Transfer to racks to cool.

Pack the cooled cookies in layers separated by wax paper in a covered tin.

Index